THE BUSINESS CHEF

THE BUSINESS CHEF

Tom Miner

VNR VAN NOSTRAND REINHOLD
New York

Printed in the United States of America

Van Nostrand Reinhold
115 Fifth Avenue
New York, New York 10003

Van Nostrand Reinhold International Company Limited
11 New Fetter Lane
London EC4P 4EE, England

Van Nostrand Reinhold
480 La Trobe Street
Melbourne, Victoria 3000, Australia

Nelson Canada
1120 Birchmount Road
Scarborough, Ontario M1K 5G4, Canada

16   15   14   13   12   11   10   9   8   7   6   5   4   3   2   1

Library of Congress Cataloging-in-Publication Data

Miner, Tom, 1949-
    The business chef / Tom Miner.
        p.   cm.
    Includes index.
    ISBN 0-442-20763-8
    1. Food service management.   I. Title.
TX911.3.M27M55   1989
G42'.5 — dc19   89-5502
                                                            CIP

CONTENTS

PREFACE

The new sophistication in American dining habits has created a tremendous demand for innovative restaurants and qualified chefs. Taking advantage of diverse opportunities, chefs have used a combination of on-the-job experience, self-study and formal education to hone their talents. Locally and nationally prominent schools do a remarkable job of teaching cooking fundamentals, which is their primary goal, but the business aspects of chef management have been left largely to enterprise.

This book meets the informational needs of culinarians by showing how to make significant profits by merchandising creative, popular cuisine. It is designed as a handbook for established head chefs with specific business problems and for aggressive sous chefs who are trying to advance. Its principles of culinary business can be applied to any style or size of food service operation.

THE BUSINESS CHEF

PART 1

CREATIVITY, THE BUSINESS TOOL (HOW TO MAXIMIZE SALES)

Chapter 1

DEVELOPING CREATIVITY

Introduction

It's hard to imagine creativity as a deliberate act, something which can be planned and then executed with precision. Certainly in its finest moments it is pure art, eclectic and spontaneous. For a few geniuses, the process is a mystery attributed to talent. But for the most part, artists train and hone their skills for years before their art flows mysteriously to life. Chefs must do the same. Beginning with a basic talent, they constantly add to their repertoires until their dishes have a colorful flair. That the creations look appetizing and taste marvelous is a prerequisite for success—a foundation. Ordinary cooks can do that. Head chefs do more by adding the finishing touches and then merchandising the food to the public. With only a word or a phrase, they tantalize. When hungry customers' taste buds saturate upon first hearing the description of the food, that is a creative accomplishment par excellence.

Creativity in Business

Today's modern consumers dine out often as singles, pairs and family groups. That has led to a scramble for their patronage; competition is king. It is common to find a dining experience for five to fifteen dollars, including clowns serving cheeseburgers and video games between pizzas. Oddly, that's stiff competition for a classic French restaurant with a pris

3

fixe and a dress code. Merchandising has a strong influence on the eating patterns of Americans. On the outside is a veneer of sophisticated concern for cuisine, but under the surface the profit motive rages. Never underestimate the competition for customers. Use creative marketing techniques, if only to give culinary masterpieces a stage on which to appear. Assertive culinarians are accomplished in both fields; their skills are a marriage of creative cuisine and business sense. First, they develop the creative edge; then they translate it into added profits.

Dining Out

A chef visiting another restaurant is like a spy sneaking into enemy territory. There is much to be learned from successful competitors, especially when they are unaware. On the surface are the obvious touches— —the ambiance, the garnish, the prices, the menu's focus. Deeper within the target restaurant's workings are the clues to its more significant aspects, like the quality of the food being served and the business' profitability.

A customer's decision to eat in a specific restaurant is made because of some definite facts about it. Either it's the closest, the cheapest, the newest, or the coolest; has a fireplace; Mimi Sheraton gave it four stars; or friends keep saying it's fantastic—something. The larger the selection of restaurants in an area, the more impulsive that decision is. Listen to people when they're discussing food and restaurants. What interests them? Are they saying the same things that a chef would? Obviously not. Their interests are strictly personal and nonprofessional. Popularity is often a word-of-mouth phenomenon, but it is never fickle. Something concrete fills a restaurant night after night, generally aspects of value and quality which a particular house provides extremely well.

To discover these important aspects, listen carefully to comments about restaurants. This will enable you to follow the popular trends and to learn what customers feel is important. A chef's job begins at this very early stage, while customers are still deciding where to dine. The chef's influence must reach into the decision-making process; that takes inside information.

The regular customers at any restaurant will talk a lot about the popular places where they eat. Use this intelligence to define the competition. Direct competitors have definite similarities based on several characteristics: location, price, style of cuisine, dress code, service and reputation are the most significant. Every restaurant's characteristics differ, depending on what part of the country or city it's in. To extend their drawing power to the maximum, chefs must know what works and what doesn't. That means dining out, with the direct competitors as the hosts, especially the busiest and most successful competitors. The following is a good example of how a few evenings out can be turned into an incisive marketing survey and a creative boon.

Chef Blue runs the kitchen, doing all the purchasing and menu planning for *BILLY'S CAFE AMERICAIN.* The restaurant is reasonably priced, has no rating and serves an eclectic mix of cuisines, including regional, Nouvelle, Italian, French and Chinese dishes.

Chef Blue wants to increase sales by making his specials list more popular. Presently, Billy's has a turnover rate of one and a half, of which twelve to fifteen percent of the dinners are specials. The restaurant has some strong competition, which Chef Blue narrows down to three prime stores. The closest, *PASTA, PASTA...PASTA,* is on the next corner. It is the newest in the area and has been hurting his lunch and dinner business.

Chef Blue approached the restaurant with a list of basic questions or areas to be investigated, but absolutely no preconceived notion. His list included:

1. Outside impression.
    Is the menu and/or specials list outside?
    Cleanliness and general appearance.
2. Impression upon entering.
    Is the host on duty? Music? Cleanliness?
    The crowd—how busy, noisy or quiet?
        Families or singles.
    General ambiance.
    Is there a bar?
3. Is the service prompt and friendly?
4. The menu layout. Its lunch, dinner and brunch selections.
5. How do the prices compare?
6. Ask the waitress what she recommends.
7. Are the other customers happy?
8. The food: style, garnish, taste, plates, colors, herbs and spices.
9. Write down ideas. Steal a dish or two.
10. Ask for a copy of the menu.
11. Rate the food, service and dining experience on a scale of one to ten.

Chef Blue pretended to be talking to his wife while he recorded his findings on a cassette. Here are his notes: "Coming down the street about 7:00 P.M., I see a lot of windows. No specials listed outside, but a sandwich

board on the sidewalk has menus posted and hours listed. There is a large
"Open" sign. Looking inside, it's white. Looks busy. We go inside. There's a
sign asking us to wait to be seated, which we do. The host is pleasant; he
shows us to a table. The music is pop, loud and fast. The crowd is young
couples and a few children. The host returns with menus" (see Fig. 1-1).
"Water arrives right away, followed by a bread basket with a third of a loaf
of French bread and two pats of butter. The bread is unheated. They have a
bar way in the back, but it's only a service bar. The ceiling is low. The place
feels cozy, bright and clean. Our waitress arrives. She is very friendly and
dressed in an obviously regulation outfit: black pants, white shirt, black
tie, etc. We order two red wines which turn out to be a Burgundy, a good
pasta wine.

In two minutes the waitress is back, asking if we are ready to order. She
is friendly, but there is no dilly-dallying. We ask about specials. There are
none tonight. We order the smoked mozzarella appetizer to share, and my
wife orders spaghetti and meatballs, which comes in a marinara sauce.
The lunch and dinner menus are the same. Brunch too. What do you
recommend? I ask. The waitress talks on and on about what she likes (the
Two-Color Fettuccini with Seafood); what a lot of people like (the Tenderloin Tips, Mushrooms, and Spaghetti) and what sells the best (Penne,
Procuitto, Broccoli, Wine and Garlic). I order Green Fettuccini, Chicken
and Vegetables. The place is very busy; a line has started to form at the
host's station. Customers seem happy. Our appetizer arrives. No garnish, a
very plain presentation. It is served on a small round with a single leaf of
romaine under a liner—fresh, not brown. The olive oil and tomato are
nothing special. The smoked mozzarella is good, so overall the taste is
what we expected. No special effort was put into the plate, but the basic
design was solid. Our entrees arrive; the food is coming out perfectly for a
moderately paced meal. The pastas are hot. We are offered freshly ground
pepper, which we accept, and more wine, which we decline. The garnish
is chopped parsley sprinkled on top. The serving is ample. The green
fettuccini is dried rather than fresh. The chicken and vegetables have
been poached, not sauteed. The dish is in a cream sauce flavored with
prechopped garlic and dried basil or thyme, but very little of either. I add a
lot of parmesan, which is on every table, and proceed to eat almost
everything. My wife likes her dish but says it is nothing special. She
finishes abut half of it. "Too many meatballs," she says. But she does not
ask me to get it wrapped to go. I taste hers. It's spaghetti and meatballs,
but nothing unique. The busboy promptly clears the table. The waitress
offers a choice of desserts—cheesecake, tartufo, spumoni, bocconcini or
cherry almond bocco torte. Everything's three dollars. We say no and ask
for the bill. We pay the host twenty-three dollars and change and leave a

Pasta, Pasta . . . . . Pasta!

SOUPS

Minestrone	2.50
Soup du Jour	2.50
STARTERS HOUSE SALAD	2.25
Mellon & Procuitto	3.50
Stuffed Mushrooms Florentine	4.25
Smoked Mozzarella, Basil & Tomato	4.95

SALADS

Tricolor Fuscilli Primavera	6.95
Curry Chicken & Penne Two-Color Tortellini	7.95
Antipasto	7.95
Shrimp, Broccoli & Conchigle	8.95
Salad Sampler	9.95

Spaghetti Marinara   5.95
Spaghetti in Meat Sauce or Meat Balls   6.95
Fettucini & Vegetables Alfredo   6.95
Tortellini Carbonara (Meat or Cheese)   6.95
Linguini in Beefeater's Tomato Sauce   6.95
Spaghetti in Pink Clam Sauce   6.95
Penne, Procuitto, Broccoli, Wine & Garlic   6.95
Linguini or Fettucini Al Pesto   6.95
Pasta Primavera   6.95
Green Fettucini, Chicken & Vegetables   7.95
3 Nuts, Chicken & Linguini in Olive Oil & Garlic   7.95
Chicken & Tricolor Fuscilli in Basil Cream   7.95
Two-Color Fettucini with Seafood   8.95
Bay Scallops & Conchigle in Prociutto Carbonara   9.95
Tenderloin Tips, Mushrooms & Spaghetti   9.95
Smoked Salmon, Conchigle, Tomatoes & Cream   9.95

Figure 1-1. Pasta, Pasta ... Pasta! Menu.

tip. There is a line of four couples waiting to be seated. On a scale of one to ten, I give the place a six for food, eight for service, six for the dining experience and eight for accomplishing what they are trying to do."

What could Chef Blue possibly have learned from Pasta, Pasta...Pasta, an eating establishment which is a happy marriage between the pasta craze and the old "in and out," turnover method? Perhaps the most creative aspect was the eclectic nature of some of the dishes. This is nouveau American pasta, like their best-seller, Penne, Procuitto, Broccoli, Wine and Garlic. There is no visible bridge to the past of classic Italian pastas (at least far as the American eating public knows). The pasta craze is in full bloom, and there are no limits. Any ingredients a chef wishes to combine may now find a following. This understanding opens up an entire range of new dishes for Chef Blue, a complete genre of trendy specials.

As for the competitive aspects, Chef Blue should see a number of ways to directly challenge Pasta's stronghold. Their gimmick is dinner for less than ten dollars. Their weaknesses are that they don't include a house salad with the dinner and that all they serve are pastas. Their limited menu will ruin them if the pasta trend slumps, though that isn't likely. There seems to be an abundance of pasta eaters. Chef Blue can compete remarkably well by offering a lunch and dinner pasta special, something different every day. It must be fresh pasta, which is more flavorful than the dry variety. It must come with a house salad and never cost more than six dollars and ninety-five cents. There are literally thousands of pasta dishes which can be made for less than two dollars per plate. That's Chef Blue's creative challenge.

When a chef goes out for dinner, a part of that experience must be the intuitive gathering of information—the special garnishes, the unique tastes, the look and feel of the presentation and, of course, the competitive little business smarts which make a restaurant successful.

National Magazines

Perhaps the easiest way to receive ideas about dishes and trends is to have them delivered to the restaurant on the pages of magazines. Periodicals are a necessity for any chef, even those whose restaurants have formula menus and no specials to create, like some franchise operations. Trade publications can be business or cuisine oriented. An aggressive chef will read everything to gain the creative edge and to turn a competitive profit. The challenges are always the same: sharpen creativity to build sales volume and gain business acumen to enlarge the profit margin. Any smart careerist reads trade journals to learn the latest innovations in both areas. The following magazines are the best of their kind. Each is unique in format and style. No one magazine has it all, but perhaps that's good.

BON APPETIT — 5900 Wilshire Blvd., Los Angeles, CA 90036. Colorful, knowledgeable and well rounded, *Bon Appetit* offers the professional or home chef a superabundance of recipes every month. The photography is done with care to record style and flair. The articles may be of less relevance from a professional viewpoint, but they are generally pertinent to anyone with an interest in cuisine. For a quick reference on seasonal recipes, trendy recipes, and general information, *Bon Appetit* is one of the best.

COOK'S — 2710 North Avenue, Bridgeport, CT 06604. As its name implies, this magazine is directed to the professional. Virtually every type of information a chef needs is presented here: heavy equipment, kitchen supplies, special produce, seafood, restaurant recipes, information services, classified ads, book reviews, interviews with chefs, shopping guides, cooking lessons and featured articles. The photography is used to capture the uniqueness of each dish and as a training aid to show preparation techniques. *Cook's* is colorful, visually dynamic, informative and easy to read.

FOOD & WINE — 1120 Avenue of the Americas, New York, NY 10036. Here the emphasis is on food, with a few departments and articles on spirits. The approach is stylized and social, accenting when and how the food is eaten and by whom. This enhances the appeal of the recipes. A flip through the pages of *F&W* is a mouth-watering visual treat. Seasonal ingredients are used in trendy recipes which seem to come from the diners themselves rather than from the chefs. *F&W* is a highly inspirational source of menu and recipe sparkle.

GOURMET — 560 Lexington Avenue, New York, NY 10022. *Gourmet* is the premier restaurant review showcase, covering classic and trendy American, European and Asian success stories. Calling itself "The Magazine of Good Living," it portrays the gourmand as part chef, part traveler, part epicure and all class. It's size allows it to cover nearly all professional aspects with information services, seasonal and trendy recipes, cooking lessons from master chefs, cooking tips for difficult items, culinary school articles and sophisticated menus. It contains the largest number of recipes — over one hundred per month — including readers' favorites, classic fundamentals, featured hotel and master chef delicacies, and seasonal and au courant creations. *Gourmet* is required reading for any assertive chef.

MASTER CHEF—Suite 5121, 500 Fifth Avenue, New York, NY 10036. This is a specialized smaller journal which presents a unique view of American and European chefs preparing masterpieces in their own kitchens. The visual content is lively, showing the chef with customers and at work. Recipes and techniques are depicted explicitly through photography. Other features include biographies of and interviews with top chefs and a dining-out guide covering the United States and parts of Europe. *M.C.* is perhaps the only true trade journal for chefs.

RESTAURANT BUSINESS—633 Third Avenue, New York, NY 10017. *R.B.* supplies the information that all the other magazines miss—restaurant business trends and details. Here the emphasis is on corporate growth, dollar volume, markets, image building and industrywide concerns. Food trends are discussed in terms of national development. The articles are about real restaurants which are growing and successful. The facts are percentage oriented but easily understandable. *R.B.* also contains an extensive catalogue of kitchen equipment, services and goods available. Other features of *R.B.* are its recipes and menus by well-known chefs. This is the one magazine professional chefs need to develop their business acumen.

Regional Magazines

These magazines are as numerous as the states and cities which inspire them. Some, like *Country Cooking* (1700 Broadway, New York, NY 10019), have a national distribution and general format. They cover every aspect of cooking, kitchens and related subjects, this time from a down-home perspective. Others, like *Wine Country* (985 Lincoln, Benicia, CA 94501), include recipes as part of a regional celebration of life. Every city magazine has its restaurant reviews and recipes departments. These publications are unbeatable for their genuine regional flavor.

Cookbooks

Chefs who have learned the basics in restaurants rather than culinary school may have a different opinion about the usefulness of cookbooks than those who have been trained to learn from books. But as a key prerequisite to success in any field, a young executive on the rise must admit to the need for additional knowledge. Cookbooks play a multifaceted role in establishing the foundation and style of a career chef. They can supply accepted preparation procedures and cooking instruction for any area in which a chef needs to be more proficient.

Truly creative chefs are not bound by execution difficulties; they know that their reduction sauces, for example, work the first time and every time. The more diverse and proficient their skills, the more creative chefs are capable of being.

Approximately fifty thousand cookbooks are available. How does one choose the most helpful and necessary ones? A complete chef's library should include preparatory texts to cover the basics well, especially the following:

ESCOUFFIER LE GUIDE CULINARE, Van Nostrand Reinhold.

The grand master's classic continental approach to preparation techniques and over five thousand recipes.

LA TECHNIQUE, Pepin, New York Times Books.

A complete reference for preparation of vegetables, meats, fish, fowl, desserts and pastry. Over twenty-five hundred photographs make it extremely easy to use.

THE PROFESSIONAL CHEF, Folsom, Van Nostrand Reinhold.

From the Culinary Institute of America and the editors of *Institutions Magazine, T.P.C.* is primarily an excellent preparation reference. However, it also includes chapters on equipment, job responsibilities, sanitation, food costs and other career information.

Pocket dictionaries offer a quick reference for ingredients and spelling without the bulk of a large cookbook. These are especially handy in the kitchen when time is short and several specials need to be created. Dictionaries include the classics, which make a perfect counterbalance to the nouveau ideas found in magazines. The following offer a lot of inspiration at deadline time:

MARLING MENU MASTER

These tiny bilingual dictionaries are designed for travelers to Europe. The four books, one each for Italy, France, Germany and Spain, are organized like a menu in the categories of appetizers, soups, fish, and so on. Following the foreign term, a brief description explains the ingredients. Good for American continental chefs.

HERINGS DICTIONARY OF CLASSICAL & MODERN COOKERY, Vitue & Company.

An alphabetical list of every sauce known to the editors, who know the classics extremely well. The descriptions include ingredients and cooking methods. For chefs of classical and European restaurants, this reference is vital.

LA REPERTOIRE DE LA CUISINE, Barron's Educational Publishers. This dictionary contains sauces, dishes and other kitchen terms. It may be the most useful full-service dictionary for American chefs, as it tends to be more modern and less classical than the Herings dictionary.

Generally, cookbooks are fascinating, but in order to be worth buying for a professional kitchen, they must be specific — that is, they must fulfill immediate needs. What particular chefs deem necessary depends on their background and the demands of their restaurant's menus and specials. The following categories are the ones most likely to warrant the expense of a single reference cookbook: fish, meat, fowl, pastas, salads, sandwiches, egg dishes, appetizers, soups, vegetables and desserts. These basic cookbooks may offer only one or two recipes which will be considered creative enough to run as specials, but that isn't their primary value. Their purpose is to round out a chef's background, again to fill the resource pool from which creativity springs.

The only other types of cookbooks which a chef may find necessary are those which cover a specific trend. For example, Chef Blue's restaurant, Billy's Cafe Americain, prides itself on providing trendy American food. But when the Southwestern cuisine craze hits town, Chef Blue is caught unprepared. Suddenly, everyone is serving exotic salsas and enchiladas, but Blue doesn't know the difference between a tamale and a taco. He needs a cookbook which will fulfill several basic requirements. It must be colorful and visual in order to convey the look of the cuisine. The recipes must be clear, precise and professional, including explanations of equipment used and ingredients which are foreign. In fact, the ingredients of a trendy cuisine are often the cornerstone of the approach. There should be colorful diagrams and photographs of all ingredients. A history of the cuisine helps to convey a sense of how the food is served and eaten in its home area; this give clues to presentation. Mail order sources for hard-to-get ingredients are extremely helpful. There must be enough variety in the recipes presented to give Chef Blue a repertoire on which his own creativity can be based.

Cookbooks offer a fingertip resource but can only augment a chef's personal experience. A chef who creates dishes from books and nothing else is repetitious and without flair.

Travel

Although eating habits and restaurants have changed drastically in recent years, the food served in the United States tends to look and taste

American, even in restaurants featuring international or regional cuisine. It is impossible to duplicate the presentation and taste of a foreign locale. Everything is different by nature and society. The ingredients, both the way they are grown and their availability, are the main influences; another is the prep staff, who have a tradition of working in set ways. Plates, language, service and ambiance, all of which exist casually in the original, can be hollow reproductions, without flavor or style. That's why the most ordinary meal in France is a creative coup in Omaha.

Chefs working in an international or regional restaurant have quite a challenge. They must not only reproduce the taste and presentation of the food, but the ambiance must be so certainly Italian or Cajun, for example, that the meal becomes a dining experience. The special du jour of a continental-American restaurant, if it wishes to be international or regional, must capture the customer's imagination and taste buds in a little creative coup de cuisine. To achieve this level of mastery, a chef must travel. There is no substitute for the dining experience a chef gains in other cities and countries.

The following example from my own experience highlights another important benefit of travel.

The Magic Salade Nicoise

I turned out of my hotel room to join the Nicoise for a noon stroll along the Promenade, a French version of Atlantic City's boardwalk. The season didn't officially start until Bastille Day, July fourteenth, so only the locals and I were there to watch a few aficionados brave the cold sea. My plan was to spend the summer in Nice, luxuriating in the sun, working only enough to get by. Even though I had been a chef in New York and a cook in Paris, the restaurant business was beginning to bore me. I was anxious to try something exciting, like working the docks or crewing a yacht. I was out that Sunday to investigate the shoreline commerce.

It was suntan weather, so I stripped off my shirt and made an afternoon of it, walking past the end of the Promenade, by the airport, over the crossing of the Var River, into the village of Sainte Laurent du Var, a few miles west of Nice. By then it was early afternoon, and I had not eaten since breakfast. Turning away from the beach, I hiked up the hill, crossing the railroad tracks into the old town, a quiet hamlet of a few thousand people. The one busy street led to the town square, which was really just a wide spot in the road lined by several retail shops, including a cafe-restaurant. It looked deserted, a very bad sign, but I was famished, so I sat down on the terrace, thinking to order something simple and safe.

A Salade Nicoise and a small carafe of local rose, I requested in French. Then the waiter and I discussed the wine—not to decide which year

Pizza

SICILIENNE *14,50*
Tomate, anchois, câpres, olives
Tomato, anchovy, caper olives
NEPTUNE *18,50*
Tomate, thon
Tomato, tunny-fish
MARINARA *14,00*
Tomate, ail
Tomato, garlic
A L'OIGNON *14,00*
Tomate, oignons
Tomato, onion
MARGUERITE *16,00*
Tomate, mozzarella
Tomato, mozzarella cheese
NAPOLITAINE *16,50*
Tomate, mozzarella, anchois, câpres ,
Tomato, mozzarella cheese, anchovy, caper
ROMAINE *16,50*
Tomate, mozzarella, anchois
Tomato, mozzarella cheese, anchovy
PIZZA DU ROI *17,00*
Epaule, artichaut
Hans, artichoke
PIZZA A LA COQUE *16,50*
Tomate, mozzarella, œufs frais
Tomato, mozzarella cheese, fresh egg
PIZZA REGINA *18,00*
Tomate, épaule, champignons
Tomato, ham, mozzarella, mushroom
QUATRE-SAISONS *18,00*
Quatre goûts différents
Four different tastes
PIZZA PESCATORA *19,50*
Tomate, ail, moules, coques
Tomato, garlic, mussel, shell
PIZZA DU CHEF *19,00*
Merguez, œuf
PEPPA BELLA ....
JUVENTUS ....
Salami, artichaut, fromage
Salami, artichoke, cheese
TONINO *19,50*
Jambon, viande hachée, œuf, fromage
Ham, steak hashes, egg, cheese
SILVY ....
Aubergine, mozzarella, tomate, poivron
Egg-plant, mozzarella, tomatoes, poivron
VENEZIA *23,00*
Crevettes, moules, coquilles Saint-Jacques
Shrimp, mussels, Saint-Jacques shellfish
SUPER *24,00*
Tomate, fromage, artichaut, câpres, olives, anchois,
poivron, merguez, champignons
Tomatoes, cheese, artichoke, capers, prawns, anchovies,
sausage, mushrooms
SOUFFLE *18,00*
Epaule, mozzarella
Ham, mozzarella

Aubergines gratinées *21,00*

Poissons - Fish

CALAMARI FRITTI *23,00*
Fried calamari
CALAMARI ALLA NAPOLITAINE .....
Calamari with tomato sauce
SCAMPI FRITTI *27,00*
Fried scampi
MOULES FARCIES *21,00*
Mussels
FRITTO MISTO *26,00*
Mélange scampis-calamars
BROCHETTES DE GAMBAS ....
Skewer gambas
BROCHETTES DE COQUILLES
SAINT-JACQUES *29,00*
Skewer sellfish Saint-Jacques

Pâtes fraîches Maison

SPAGHETTI A L'AIL *14,00*
SPAGHETTI NAPOLITAINE *14,00*
Napolitaine
Tomato sauce
SPAGHETTI BOLOGNESE *15,00*
Bolognese
Meat sauce, carbonara, sea food
SPAGHETTI FRUITS DE MER *18,00*
SPAGHETTI CARBONERA *18,00*
RAVIOLI ALLA BOLOGNESE *18,00*
Meat with sauce, fresh, paste
TAGLIATELLE ALLA BOLOGNESE *18,00*
Fresh paste with egg and meat sauce
CANNELLONI GRATINE *18,00*
With meat sauce, cheese and upper crust
LASAGNE AL FORNO *18,00*
Pâtes fraîches aux œufs; sauce, viande, béchamelle
Fresh paste with egg, meat sauce with béchamelle
PASTA AL FORNO *18,00*
RAVIOLI CARBONARA ....
RAVIOLI ALLA RICOTTA ....
GNOCCHI DI PATETE ....
TORTELLINI BOLOGNESE *18,00*
TORTELLINI ALLA CREMA *18,00*
RAVIOLI CARBONARA ....
De viande
RIGATONI AL FORNO ....

Hors-d'œuvre

SAUMON FUME ....
SALADE ITALIENNE *17,50*
Italian salad
CŒURS DE PALMIERS *14,00*
SALADE DE TOMATES *9,50*
Tomato salad
TOMATES-ŒUF DUR *11,00*
Tomatoes and egg
POMMES A L'HUILE ....
Potatoes with oil
ANTIPASTO *19,00*
Charcuterie italienne et crudités
Italian pork buttcher and vegetables
TOMATE PALERMITAINE *14,00*
Tomate et thon
Tomato tunny fish
SALAMI *14,00*
COPPA *17,00*
MORTADELLA *14,00*
JAMBON D'ITALIE *25,00*
Raw ham from parma
TERRINE DE CAMPAGNE *10,00*
Pie of country
SALADE DE FRUITS DE MER ....

SERVICE 15% EN SUS

Figure 1-2. Cafe de la Mairie. Menu.

14

Omelettes

OMELETTE AUX OIGNONS	17.00
Omelet with onion	
OMELETTE JAMBON	17.00
Ham omelet	
OMELETTE CHAMPIGNONS	17.00
Omelet with mushrooms	
OMELETTE CREVETTES	20.00

Viandes - Meat

Garnies de frites ou salade ou spaghetti
ou riz
Chips or salad or spaghetti or rice

ESCALOPE ALLA PIZZAIOLA	28.00
Veal escalop pizzaiola	
ESCALOPE GRILLEE	26.00
Grill escalop	
ENTRECOTE BORDELAISE OU GRILLEE	29.00
Grill steak with shallots	
SCALOPINI ALLA MARSALA	28.00
Veal scalopini with marsala sauce	
ESCALOPE BOLOGNESE	31.00
ESCALOPE ALLA MILANESE	28.00
Escalop covered with bread crubs	
SALTIMBOCCA ROMANA	29.00
OSSO BUCO MILANESE	29.00
ESCALOPE A LA CREME	28.00
Veal fillet with cream	
ESCALOPE AU CITRON	28.00
Veal fillet with lemon	
COTE DE BŒUF GRILLEE	

Salades

SALADE MIXTE	9.50
SALADE VERTE	8.00
SALADE COMPOSEE	17.00
jambon, gruyère, riz, ananas, tomate et pomme à l'huile	

Fromages - Cheese

PROVOLONE	9.00
PROVOLA AFFUMICATA	9.00
GORGONZOLA	9.00
CAMEMBERT	7.50
MOZZARELLA	9.00
PECORINO	9.00

Fruits de Saison

ANANAS AU KIRSCH	10.00
Pine-apple with kirsch	
SALADE DE FRUITS MAISON	10.00
Fruit salad	
BANANE FLAMBEE	13.00

Gateaux - Pastry
Tartes

TARTE AUX AMANDES	10.00
TARTE AU CITRON	10.00
Tart with citron	
GATEAUX CHOCOLAT	10.00
Plain with chocolate	
CREME CARAMEL	10.00
Caramel cream	
MOUSSE AU CHOCOLAT	10.00
Chocolates mouss	

Spécialités Maison

TARTE A LA BANANE CHAUDE	
Banana tart	
TARTE AUX POMMES CHAUDES	
Warm apple tart	

Glaces - Ice Creame

COUPE ROMAINE	15.50
Gâteau au chocolat, glace, vanille, sauce chocolat, noisettes, chantilly	
Plain with chocolate, ice vanilla, chocolate sauce, nuts, chantilly	
SOUFFLE GLACE	8.00
Glace au Grand Marnier	
Ice-cream with Grand Marnier	
PARFUM DU JOUR	8.00
Noisette, vanille, chocolat, café, fraises	
Hazelnut, vanille, chocolate, coffee strawberry	
TRANCHE NAPOLITAINE	8.00
Chocolat, vanille, café	
Chocolate, vanille, coffee	
CHOCOLAT LIEGEOIS	11.00
Glace, chocolat, chantilly	
Ice coff.e with whipped cream	
CAFE LIEGEOIS	11.00
Café glacé, chantilly	
Ice coffee with whipped cream	
LIMONE FARCITO	11.00
Sorbet au citron	
Lemon sorbet	
ARANCIO FARCITO	11.00
Sorbet à l'orange	
Orange sorbet	
CASSATTA SICILIENNE	11.00
Glace aux fruits confits	
Ice-cream with sugared fruit	
PARFAIT AU CAFE	9.00
MYSTERE	9.00
COUPE MAISON AU CASSIS	14.00
Glace vanille, fruits, chantilly	
Ice-cream vanille, fruit, whipped cream	
COUPE MELBA	14.00
Glace vanille, pêche au sirop, chantilly	
Ice-cream vanille, peach sirop, whipped cream	
SEMIFREDDO	11.00
Gâteau glacé	
PROFITEROLES	14.00
BANANA SPLIT	15.00
COUPE JUVENTUS	15.00
Salade de fruits, glace ananas et chantilly	

SERVICE 15 % EN SUS

Figure 1-2 (continued)

15

would be best, but to make certain that my broken French was communi-
cating correctly.

Now it's true that being exceptionally hungry and sitting in an exotic
village square, dreaming of the romantic summer to come, may be
extenuating circumstances, but they do not account for the rejuvenating
process begun by the mere sight of my first genuine Salade Nicoise. It had
a style unlike any of the hundreds I had seen and made in America or even
Paris. Somehow ordinary vegetables like tomatoes, green peppers and
onions managed to look not just French but Nicoise. I tasted a mouthful in
disbelief, marveling that the vivid colors on my plate had vivid tastes
too. Right then, before the salad was finished, I decided that there were
exciting avenues in the culinary arts I hadn't even dreamed of. I had to
cook in Nice.

In order to create exciting food, a chef must be excited by food. Travel is
a rejuvenating process, a fountain of new ideas and pleasures. But more
than inspiration, travel offers a close look at the work of other chefs and
restaurant chains—professionals who have achieved success in radically
different markets. The guidelines change in unusual, unpredictable ways
which can only be experienced by firsthand observation. For instance, in
France there is a type of Italian restaurant which normally is a cafe-bar
with medium prices and casual ambiance. Like the Chinese restaurants in
America, these Italian restaurants have menus which are so similar that
they are practically interchangeable. The CAFE DE LA MAIRIE (The Cafe
of the Young Marrieds) was one such restaurant in Paris (Fig. 1-2).

Its menu is a classic; any item on it would make it a unique *special du
jour* in America. The authenticity of the names and their ingredients
makes it as resourceful as an Italian cookbook and, for its practical
insights into retailing, more so.

Part of the joy a chef receives from dining out is that of having someone
else do the cooking. Don't forget the kitchen crew when you are traveling.
Stop in, say hello, mention that you are a chef from wherever, and express
intest in their kitchen and food. Always ask for a souvenir menu. A quick
look at the work stations, equipment and *mis en place* provide an experience of these more practical but still interesting aspects of a chef's duties.

Travel and dine as part of the general enthusiasm for life or with the goal
of investigating a region or cuisine thoroughly. But keep travel an integral
part of the learning/experience process.

Classwork

Cooking schools and seminars can speed up the experiential process,
either at the foundation level or with specialized training. Beginning

classes build the fundamental cooking skills. For professional but nov-ice cooks, coursework broadens and deepens the understanding of accepted procedures. This provides more vital information for the mem-ory bank—creativity's resource pool. Any chef who lacks in-depth work experience in an area should consider a cooking class to round out this knowledge.

Specialized classes offer many of the same rewards as travel and may be a good substitute. An intensive course with a master chef can teach a particular style of cuisine, with all its flair of taste and presentation. A professional chef with years of work experience is in a position to absorb the subject quickly. Any chef who desires to master a particular style of cuisine, French nouvelle for instance, must acknowledge the value of training in a small class with a professional instructor.

A diploma from a recognized cooking school is one of the few paper credentials a chef can offer as proof of experience and background. For many types of restaurants, professional training is a prerequisite of employment. Appendix A is a list of some cooking schools and classes which are established enough to offer excellent experience and presti-gious credentials. Not listed are the many two- and four-year colleges which now offer culinary programs. Those can be found in traditional sources.

Work Experience

Working as a cook can be an intensely rewarding education or a routine, boring ordeal. A lot depends upon the chef and his or her attitude on how to run a kitchen, especially the delegation of specials preparation. However, the major factors determining a cooking job's interest level are the menu and the specials board. If the restaurant serves the same food every night and the original concept is mundane, the work will be rote and mechanical. The more variety and uniqueness in the menu, the more there is to learn.

Smart cooks keep a file of good recipes they have learned from each chef they have worked for. Make it a point to write down the recipe for every menu item and to save the menu. Later, this collection will serve as a personal repertoire and a handy reference. At the beginning of a career, each cook has a lot to learn from most chefs. And the reverse is also true: every chef can learn at least one thing from even the newest cook. The idea is to learn from each other, keep your guard down, and be receptive to change and to new information or techniques. The most aggressive career-minded cooks are out to absorb everything they come across, whether it be cooking or business practices. Keep in mind that the most rewarding work experiences are also the most challenging. For instance, the chef is extremely temperamental, or the co-workers curt, or the work load intense and the pay low; these are more than likely the conditions at interesting restaurants.

In a sense, a chef is a food mechanic. There are tools and heavy equipment to be mastered, myriad parts or ingredients to choose from, and a clear mental picture or blueprint of the finished product. As a mechanic, the chef has to be good with the hands, knowing all the special moves with knives, pans and big equipment like ovens and broilers. A master chef is in total control of the equipment and understands the physical and chemical limits of food and temperature combinations. These capabilities usually begin at home or in the classroom as talent but mature in the workplace, where existence depends upon speed and precision.

The ultimate in creative freedom is to have the experience and repertoire needed to create new and exciting dishes with whatever ingredients are available.

Highlights

Assertive culinarians are accomplished in two fields; their skills are a marriage of creative cuisine and business sense.

Direct competitors have definite similarities based on several characteristics; location, price, style of cuisine, dress code, service and reputation are the most significant.

When a chef goes out for dinner, a part of that experience must be the intuitive gathering of information.

Perhaps the easiest way to receive ideas about dishes and trends is to have them delivered to the restaurant on the pages of magazines.

An aggressive chef will read everything to gain a creative edge and to turn a competitive profit.

A complete chef's library should include preparatory textbooks that cover the basics well.

Pocket dictionaries offer a quick reference for ingredients and spelling without the bulk of a large cookbook.

The following categories are the ones most likely to warrant the expense of a single reference cookbook: fish, meat, fowl, pastas, salads, sandwiches, egg dishes, appetizers, soups, vegetables and desserts.

Cookbooks offer a fingertip resource but can only augment a chef's personal experience.

It is impossible to duplicate the presentation and taste of another locale. Everything is different by nature and society.

Travel offers a close look at the work of other chefs and restaurant chains, professionals who have achieved success in radically different markets.

Cooking schools and seminars can speed up the experiential process at the foundation level and with specialized training.

For professional but novice cooks, coursework broadens and deepens the understanding of accepted procedures.

An intensive course with a master chef can teach or impart a particular style of cuisine, with all its flair of taste and presentation.

A diploma from a recognized cooking school is one of the few printed credentials a chef can offer as proof of experience and background.

Keep in mind that the most rewarding work experiences are also the most challenging.

As a mechanic, a chef has to be good with the hands, knowing all the special moves with knives, pans and big equipment like ovens and broilers.

The ultimate in creative freedom is to have the experience and repertoire needed to create new and exciting dishes with whatever ingredients are available.

Chapter 2

MARKET POSITION AND COMPETITION

Introduction

There's an old maxim which states that great artists create not only works of art, but their audience as well. For innovative chefs, this is especially true. A master creates an ambiance which is reflected in their food. Before the layman knows what he wants other than "something different," a master chef sets a trend in motion, tantalizing a whole new audience of gourmand thrill seekers. The masters are the risk takers. Obviously, they feel that the rewards are great.

What about the other ninety-nine percent of professional chefs? They must be content to take little chances based on data—specific knowledge about their restaurant, its competition and its customers. In most restaurants, business supersedes art. Rather than streaking ahead with radical cuisine, restaurants strive to find their niche and fit into it. Identifying the market position is one of the first major steps in building sales volume. It cannot be considered using a haphazard dish-by-dish method but must be approached holistically, with the thorough precision of a marketing survey.

Define the Market

To define a market, consider how restaurants compete: by geography or location, type of cuisine, price, ambiance or physical surroundings, quality of food, originality and type of customer targeted. Each restaurant has, or should have, a slightly different character. Chefs consider these aspects in order to know who they are competing against and what their chances for success are. By considering each category as a feature of the restaurant market, a chef builds the composite picture of his or her niche.

Geography or Location

The geographical region in which a restaurant operates has a very strong effect on the customer's likes and dislikes. A region is influenced by the roots of its people. For instance, the long-standing rage in the Southwest has been Tex-Mex cuisine. There it is an art form. But in northern Pennsylvania it's still called Mexican food, and perogies or kielbasa are the most commonly found dishes. Each geographical location has one or two strong ethnic influences, even today when families move from region to region. The basic population retains certain characteristics in its eating habits, which are absorbed by newcomers. It takes a major migration to change a region significantly, as southeastern Florida was changed. In Colorado there are a handful of French Nouvelle restaurants; in Manhattan there are hundreds. The reasons are deeply rooted in the background of each region's clientele. The more a chef or owner tries to go against the trends of the region, the greater the risks involved. There will be a few dramatic successes, but many more quick failures.

Another regional aspect affecting consumers' eating habits is the type of community: urban, suburban, or rural. The names alone connote different lifestyles which influence how often people dine out, how much they spend, how they arrive at the dining experience, and the formality of dress and ambiance desired. It's true that good food is good no matter where it's sold. But an outsider trying to educate the clientele will be met with resistance, even dislike. A chef should study the characteristics of the region by living there. Never assume that you know better than the customers.

A location is a building in a neighborhood of the region, a very specific spot with existing traffic routes, competing restaurants and a population base. The location of a restaurant, along with its rent, is the number one consideration in a business's success. Everything else can be positive for a restaurant, but if the location is bad, the business will fail. An ideal location is one that has considerable traffic, either by foot or car, during the times of the day which the restaurant will be open. There must be a history of people dining in the area. For instance, the previous occupant was a successful restaurant or the location is in the local restaurant row. In most cases, a corner affords better visibility, which is a form of advertising, and offers other amenities like extra space for parking. In addition, in big cities, corner buildings allow more windows, inside light, and sidewalk space for cafes and extensions. The ideal location is a large corner space in a strip of popular restaurants in which the building housed a very successful restaurant for decades but changed hands a few years ago and the new management failed its customers. The proper rent to pay for this ideal location will be covered in Chapter 7.

Another definitive element of a location is its built-in competition— the number and type of restaurants operating nearby. This is strictly a commonsense factor. If a chef-owner does Italian food better than anyone west of Piemonte, but there are already three Italian places in the neighborhood, look further. The location is flawed. Don't ignore the danger flags or plan to rely on superior talent. The risk will be too great.

Type of Cuisine

Which comes first, the great location or the sumptuous menu? Except in areas where there are several excellent vacancies, the location is primary, but immediately after it, a menu must be designed for the available clientele. This creative menu will be restricted somewhat by the physical peculiarities of the new or existing kitchen. If a restaurant menu is designed before a location is discovered, then finding a spot with less direct competition to the style of food becomes the primary concern. That's when originality of concept becomes a strong asset. Deciding on a style of cuisine before signing a lease can be a waste of time; it depends on how prevalent the competition is for the proposed style of cuisine.

There are several basic cuisines which honor common ingredients, recipes and presentation styles: French Classic and Nouvelle; Italian Southern, Northern and Nouvelle; pasta; Chinese; Japanese; Cajun; Caribbean; seafood; Indian; American Indian; Mexican; Tex-Mex; California Nouvelle; American Continental; Southern American; steak houses; and fast food. Beyond the categories is a range of blends and choices as diverse as the personalities of every chef working today.

It is essential that the chef know what category the menu falls into, even if the title is evasive, like American Eclectic. That describes the food—it's eclectic. Categorization also helps a chef to pinpoint the clientele. For example, how many eclectic customers are there in any given neighborhood? East Greenwich Village in New York City may be densely eclectic, but what about the rest of the country—suburban Pittsburgh, for instance? Perhaps the entire concept is not a viable business idea. Name the food, label it, and then draw every possible generalization about the customer, decor, price, location and viability possible. Be flexible. A professional chef analyzing a restaurant menu asks the same questions as an amateur chef does when planning a dinner for four. What do the people like? The only significant difference is volume—the number of people to be pleased. A professional chef can't ignore the statistics. In the United States there are three major categories of restaurants which draw the largest clientele—Italian, Chinese and Mexican.

To be successful, a chef must sell the same food as everyone else, but in new and exciting ways. It is possible to be in the vanguard of culinary style without being overly pretentious or costly—although, for the clientele sought, it may be important to be both pretentious and costly. Competition dictates what a menu should be for any given restaurant. The person with the most experience in food sales should make the decisions or define the parameters. A restaurant's style of cuisine clicks for two reasons: it has definite, tasteful qualities which excite and satisfy, and it has the ability to attract customers.

Cooking experience, trends, competition, basic cuisines, customers, location, physical limitations of the kitchen and price structure influence a restaurant's style of cuisine. If a chef finds himself in charge of a kitchen which has little chance for success, no matter how good the quality gets, usually the menu is at fault. Its original concept did not take into consideration all relevant factors and must be reanalyzed to assess possible errors. Or, as is the case with old restaurants, perhaps the style has become outmoded. Chapter 4 contains several examples of how to spot and rectify old-fashioned menus.

Price Level

Each restaurant has an average per customer dollar figure which is the amount an average client spends on appetizers, main courses, desserts and nonalcoholic beverages. Surprisingly, this amount varies by as little as fifty cents from day to day. Lunch customers spend the same average amount, as do dinner customers, from week to week. For example, the TEXAS STAR RESTAURANT served two hundred and sixty dinner customers during its busy season and had a food receipts total of $2743. Its per customer average was $10.55. With few exceptions, the per customer average at the Texas Star will stay within $.50 of $10.50. This holds true for seasonal changes in volume. For example, during a slow period, the Texas Star had one hundred and twenty dinner customers, with a food receipts total of $1295; that is a per customer average of $10.80.

There is no trick or magic involved here. The per customer average is a function of the menu's pricing structure. This average, which has to be computed by the chef or manager, is known intuitively by the restaurant's prospective customers—especially given current trends, which have customers dining out several times per week, not only for pleasure but for business and convenience as well. The public is budget conscious. Customers know that dinner at the Texas Star Restaurant costs $15 per person, drinks, tax and tip included. If that is within their budget, the way is cleared for them to consider other aspects, such as food quality. The following chart of dollar amounts represents different levels of averge per customer expenditures for dinners in restaurants.

CATEGORY	AMOUNT
A	$50 and above
B	$20 to $50
C	$15 to $20
D	$10 to $15
E	$ 5 to $10
F	Below $ 5

Although different regions have various standards of living, according to their population's size and affluence, each of these categories is relative on a national scale.

Market Size by Average Cost to the Customer

Category A is the ultimate dining experience, or should be. Most customers will never have the money or inclination to try it. Those customers who have the money may save it for a very special occasion. The market for this level of restaurant is as large as the affluence of the local population. Occasionally, customers will travel unusually long distances for a particular chef's specialties.

Category B is much more accessible to middle-class Americans, who like to dine out on special occasions without feeling it necessary to make snide comments about the bill being more than their day's salary. Again, the average number of times a customer will dine out in this category depends upon his or her affluence, or on business and personal needs.

Categories C and D may offer the same sorts of cuisine and dining experience; the only difference is the price. The markets for these price ranges, $10 to $20, are generally strong, though there is still an element of occasion when customers dine at these levels. The element of value is now firmly in the picture. Customers in these middle ranges expect a little flair for their money and will go to the restaurants that provide it.

Category E seems downscale, but nationwide this is the level at which most repeat diners—customers who eat out instead of cook—feel most comfortable. The $10 barrier is a psychological one, but nevertheless real. This market is large, both in regular customers and in occasionals or transients. Competition is stiff too, because this is the level of restaurant which attracts the highest number of amateur owners. Value is particularly important to the customers in Category E.

Category F consists primarily of fast food and limited-service establishments. While value is guaranteed here, quality and ambiance are on the low end of the scale. Without a doubt, this market is vast and competitive.

Ambiance

This is a concern for the front-of-the-house manager, at least in execution. But the ambiance must be closely related to the type of food sold. Therefore, a chef must gauge the elements of ambiance in order to further understand the place of the restaurant in the total market. For instance, the style of service could include a white tablecloth, settings of expensive silver and china, with a floor staff of maitres d', captains, waiters and busboys. In another restaurant the staff may be dressed in cowboy costumes and serve dinner in plastic baskets. Formal or casual, there is a wide range of styles a restaurant can adopt.

The decor on the outside and inside will conform to the owner's projected style, as will the music, menu design, prices and hours of operation. At least there will be an intended style, which may or may not be realized. A chef who has worked in many kitchens or eaten in all styles of restaurants will have the experience necessary to coordinate the cuisine's presentation and style to match the restaurant's image.

Quality of Food

A restaurant which has been rated either favorably or unfavorably by one of the international, national or local food critics will find itself carrying much heavier responsibilities due to the reputation which it must now uphold. Suddenly the food becomes a serious political issue. Management will often ask whether the food is as good as it was the night "so and so" bestowed three stars. Or they may ask pointedly, "Is the food better than it was the night that so and so panned us?" It will be understood that a certain portion of the clientele are responding to the notoriety of press coverage, either positively or negatively. This is an important market issue, but only for a limited percentage of restaurants.

Most places rely on their own advertising or on word of mouth. For them quality is a matter of opinion. Remarkably, many restaurants are designed to sell mediocre food. That which goes directly from the freezer, to the fryolator, to the customer is one example. Food laden with chemicals is another. There are millions of customers who love fried food and don't care what chemicals lace their main course. What a chef has to understand is how committed the restaurant is to quality, how important quality is to its customers, and intelligently, with a cold business eye, when compromises in quality must be made.

Poor quality is a term with several interpretations. There is a vast difference between selling spoiled goods or sauces which have been burned, selling classic dishes with no classic taste, and selling lower-priced food that is done well, without chemicals. Quality is in the eye of the beholder.

Originality of Concept

In the vast market of chain and franchise restaurants, there is a lot of talk about concept. Clowns, cowboys, sea captains, actors, sports figures, pastimes, careers, music and sex are used to sell food. Theme restaurants abound on the principle that all other things are equal and that customers can be enticed by the promise of entertainment or comaraderie. This has been proven logical. But establishments which offer something other than food as the main course run the risk of being just a fad. The surefooted concept is one which relies on original cuisine in the mode of customers' tastes. It is in these types of restaurants that full-service chefs will find challenging and rewarding careers.

An original concept in cuisine is either the blending of existing styles into a new approach or the importation of a classic style from one geographical area to another. Tex-Mex food is the perfect example of the first conceptual process. Caribbean is a current popular cuisine only recently presented to middle-American customers. The success of these trends has to do with population shifts and to the increase in Americans' willingness to try new foods—two prime reasons for any new restaurant to consider adding an original flair to its classic menu.

In the marketplace, originality in style or presentation of cuisine may be the only factor separating restaurants within basic categories such as Continental, French, Italian and Chinese.

And originality does not necessarily mean eclectic. Borrowing from the old country is a way to bring new concepts to the American public—hence the smorgasbord, bistro and brick oven pizza. Originality is essential for any viable business—restaurants included. Yet many chefs discover that their restaurants have menus with nothing new to offer. Usually these establishments stress low prices, or have accepted low volume, or are more interested in selling liquor. No matter what the existing situation is, there are ways to inject originality. These methods will be covered in Chapter 6. For the purposes of the marketing survey, cast a critical eye on the entire package of retail approach, pricing strategy and originality of cuisine. These are the factors that will bring customers through the front door.

Type of Customer

Having considered all the aspects of a market profile, a chef can now see the restaurant as a composite picture whose features are geography and location, type of cuisine, price level, ambiance, quality of food and originality of concept. This composite picture isn't a room with a bar and checkered tablecloths; it is a perfect customer—the type which can be expected to frequent the restaurant most often. After completing the profile, judge the effectiveness of the restaurant's impact. How wide or narrow does this customer profile appear? It may be necessary to broaden the restaurant's appeal by temporary or permanent menu additions.

Establishing a Core Market

Use the market profile to establish a core of regular customers by giving them precisely what they expect. If the chef of an Italian restaurant has no salads on the menu because the previous chef wanted to attract a male business crowd, then he or she should realize that historically Italian restaurants have served salads and business people include both sexes, either of which may want a salad.

Put a firm focus on what type of customer the restaurant and the menu are attracting; then compare it to the type the restaurant could attract. Look for ways to broaden the restaurant's appeal by extending the base of categories—for instance, by adding salads. Also, consider current market trends. If the entire market is moving away from red meat to seafood and chicken, as it is, then menu modifications are in order.

The purpose of the marketing survey is to supply factual support and data-based direction which will aid an innovative chef's efforts to save an ailing business or build a new one. Use this survey as a checklist, starting with geography and location; then write a paragraph or two on each category to explain what is most evident about the target restaurant. Evaluate the notes in order to discover the big problems. Don't begin with preconceived issues to promote, and don't draw conclusions until every aspect of the restaurant in its market are uncovered. Give the survey a day or two to gel. Let the ideas come and go freely for a while before deciding on what the principal difficulties are. If the solutions are small and within a chef's authority, implement them at once. If the problems are severe but there are possible changes which could be helpful, consider the opposition. A chef who wants to make changes needs backup material, like a track record of success and a specific marketing report before the powers that govern will be swayed. Even with all the reasonability on the chef's side, something fickle may thwart progress. Personalities have a way of impeding the progress of any small business. A chef in a no-win situation should consider moving to a more stable position. Even with a loss in pay, it will prove more lucrative in the long run.

What sorts of judgments should a chef make about the dishes which customers expect but are not getting? The first indication that something is missing is low sales volume. Customers communicate their dissatisfaction by not returning. Don't expect the customers to complain when the food is less than they expected. When a couple go out for a casual dinner after a movie, there must be dishes for each of them to choose from or they'll never be back. Yet there are thousands of restaurants which offer only "guy food" or the exact opposite: "seeds and weeds." A restaurant with one hundred seats and a menu which is either obscure, limited or chi-chi will have a problem finding enough willing diners to make the business profitable.

Chefs must put themselves in the customer's seat, reading the menu for the first time at lunch, dinner or brunch from every possible perspective: that of a businessman at lunch, a teenager at dinner, a family of four at brunch. Ask the pertinent questions. What do these different types of people like to eat at those times? Will they find something on this restaurant's menu? This is fundamental research which seems as obvious as success and failure, but surprisingly, it is overlooked by owners and chefs alike. Chapter 4 shows subsequent procedures which utilize the market information.

Expanding the Core Market

The first step as a result of the marketing survey is to build a core of regular customers by offering a full menu of what they expect. The second step is to compete for additional clientele by offering items which broaden the restaurant's appeal, bringing it into other customers' ranges. The aim is to diversify without losing the original clientele. The easiest way to do this is to sell specials, either through sophisticated multimedia presentations or via chalk boards. Virtually every restaurant sells specials in one way or another. Even if the offerings are few and presented verbally, specials play the important role of menu expander.

In how many directions should the menu be expanded? In other words, how many specials should be run per meal shift, and what kind? Run as many or as few specials as are necessary to make the restaurant's position aggressive. Think of specials as coming from various categories rather than as a hodgepodge of cuisines. The purpose of specials sales is to accent strong points, mask weak points and compete aggressively. Therefore, specials lists should include dishes that are similar to those from the menu which sell well already; dishes which offer things not on the menu at all; dishes which balance the goods or style of cuisine; dishes which are trendy or seasonal; dishes which are priced to compete; dishes which are big profit makers; and dishes which act as price leaders or come-ons.

How specials are presented to the clientele depends on the advertising budget and the physical size of the restaurant's potential market. Are customers more likely to walk or drive by, or do they need to be attracted by the media? The answer should be obvious, though it is likely that the mode changes between lunch and dinner. People who walk by will be attracted by a specials board at the front of the restaurant. Those who drive by will notice a marquee sign. Customers who have to travel by car will be attracted by newspaper, magazine or television ads. Many restaurants advertise at movies and plays. Each region needs a tailored approach. Finally, it is best to spread the advertising budget over many media rather than concentrating on one medium or expecting the specials board to do all the work. A diversified approach here will help to broaden the market.

An important component in the assessment of a market is the proper classification of all competing restaurants, especially the successful ones. Before chefs can successfully market their menus or specials, they must know precisely how the competitors are approaching the problem of menu design. Many restaurants in the area will be only fairly busy; others may be failing miserably. Part of a market analysis is to provide the reasons for each place's failures.

The following is an example of how a chef caught and reversed the downhill trend of his restaurant with a market survey which indicated the need for menu changes.

Chef Jack had been the chef at *BARON'S* for over ten years. He had built the business from a friendly bar with hamburgers to a busy pub which specialized in steaks, chops and burgers. For several years, Baron's had three or four turnovers a night. Then business began to slacken, gradually but with marked regularity. Chef Jack checked and rechecked his recipes; they were of the same high quality which had meant success in the past. He also watched the quality of preparation and the presentation of his cooks, even to the point of asking the floor staff to critique the food. Everything seemed in order. There was no problem severe enough to warrant the present downturn in sales. For the first time in years, Chef Jack took a good long look at the competition. It was remarkable how it had changed. Some of the old mainstays, restaurants which had been Baron's leading competitors, were gone. One by one, the owners had retired, sold out or been pushed out. A whole new style of restaurant was thriving. Whereas before there had been other steak houses and chophouses offering fancier service to compete against, now Baron's was the only steak house around. The nearby competition was six or seven coffee shops and delis, four mid-range American-Continental places, a seafood specialty house, one Chinese, one Taiwanese, two Japanese, and the newest, right next door, a Tex-Mex restaurant which had a large Southwestern-style bar area. Two of the places had outside cafes and light, airy fronts. Baron's looked like an English pub from the outside; its ambiance was dark and cool. The neighborhood had changed, too. It was undergoing gentrification; the surrounding apartment houses were being remodeled and sold as coops and condominiums. Some buildings had been torn down to make room for new high-rises.

Chef Jack had to admit that Baron's looked antiquated. But it was supposed to be an English pub; that was part of its charm. Everything was in order except the food receipts. If Chef Jack hadn't had so much to lose (he'd accumulated raises and benefits through a ten-year run of success), he would have left the worries to the owner and continued to turn out high-quality food, as he had always done. But being well paid, he had prosperity at stake, so he took a few days to worry about the business. During that time, he read cooking and restaurant business magazines. Every day on the way to work he stopped to study the menus of his competition, expecially that of the most successful, the Tex-Mex place. In the final analysis, Chef Jack had to admit that Baron's was lagging behind the current eating trends, and although it had a strong position as the only steak-chop house around, it would have to reach other types of customers. He took two simple dishes as starting points: the introduction of home-made soups and fresh salads as daily specials. These were added to the existing specials, which were primarily fish and chicken and had never totaled more than two per night. The immediate response was strong enough to keep both new items on as regular specials and to start Chef Jack thinking about other ways to reach the new types of customers who had moved in.

A marketing survey can be as formal or informal as the chef who does it. However, the written form is bound to be more complete and has the long-term benefit of existing a year later to act as a reference. But as most chefs are not inclined to be bookish business types, an informal look around the neighborhood may be all that is ever done. This is poor chef's management, the sort that puts the restaurant's profitability at risk.

Chef Jack was smart. He took a close look at the problem areas within a few months of his restaurants's slide from the top. It is much more common to be the chef of a place with severe problems which no one can seem to pinpoint or solve. To begin with, a chef who finds himself at the head of a restaurant with a mediocre to low sales volume must assume that the preceding chefs were old-schoolers who steered by the anti-quated seat-of-the-pants method. Collect hard facts, and then formulate a plan of action to turn the business around. Be as radical as necessary, but remember that for each menu deletion a customer will be lost and that the ultimate goal is to build business, not reduce it. Don't be caught in the glory game of trying to turn a pub into a supper club. The purpose of the market analysis is to help build the factual basis for change.

Long-Range Planning

Once the new and improved menu has been visualized, it is a good idea to devise a way to get from the present menu to the desired one. A plan covering six months or longer is necessary for many reasons. It keeps the ultimate goals in clear view. It helps to gauge progress or stagnation and to give the chef a perspective on his or her present position, which may be sorely needed during a long period of retraining and reorganization. But the best use of the plan is as a guide, laying out the goals in a step-by-step manner from beginning to end, as clearly and usefully as the rungs of a ladder.

Another important reason for a long-term plan is that in the process of delineating goals, a restaurant's limits become obvious. A clear-cut plan of procedures eliminates a lot of error by providing reasonable alternatives before crises occur.

Today's markets are rapidly expanding and changing in response to Americans' current enlightenment about cuisine and their desire to dine well. Established restaurants must be aware of national moods and trends, as well as shifts within their local market. The future will bring concepts which are still unheard of, but which will entice scores of dining customers.

Highlights

In most restaurants, business supersedes art.

Rather than streaking ahead with radical cuisine, restaurants strive to find their niche and fit into it.

To define a market, consider how restaurants compete. A region is influenced by the roots of its people.

The more a chef or owner tries to go against the trends of the region, the greater the risks involved.

Another regional aspect affecting consumers' eating habits is the type of community.

An outsider trying to educate the clientele will be met with resistance, even dislike.

The location of a restaurant, along with its rent, is the number one consideration in a business's success.

The ideal location is a large corner space in which the building housed a very successful restaurant for decades but changed hands a few years ago and the new management failed its customers.

Another definitive element of a location is its built-in competition — the number and type of restaurants operating nearby.

Location is primary, but immediately after it, a menu must be designed for the available clientele.

To be successful, a chef must sell the same food as everyone else, but in new and exciting ways.

Competition dictates what a menu should be for any given restaurant.

A restaurant's style of cuisine clicks for two reasons: it has definite, tasteful qualities which excite and satisfy, and it has the ability to attract customers.

A restaurant which has little chance for success, no matter how good the food quality is, usually has a faulty menu.

The ambiance must be closely related to the type of food sold.

A chef must gauge the elements of ambiance in order to further understand the place of the restaurant in the total market.

What a chef has to understand is how committed the restaurant is to quality, how important quality is to its customers, and intelligently, with a cold business eye, when compromises in quality must be made.

The surefooted concept is one which relies on original cuisine in the mode of customers' tastes.

An original concept in cuisine is either the blending of existing styles into a new approach or the importation of a classic style from one geographical area to another.

No matter what the existing situation is, there are ways to inject originality.

The purpose of the marketing survey is to supply factual support and data-based direction which will aid an innovative chef's efforts to save an ailing business or build a new one.

The purpose of specials' sales is to accent strong points, mask weak points and compete aggressively.

Spread the advertising budget over many media rather than concentrating on one medium.

An important component in the assessment of a market is the proper classification of all competing restaurants.

The purpose of the market analysis is to help build the factual basis for change.

Once the new and improved menu has been visualized, it is a good idea to devise a way to get from the present menu to the desired one—a long-range plan.

Established restaurants must be aware of national moods and trends, as well as shifts within their local market.

Chapter 3

THE ROLE OF CREATIVE SPECIALS

Introduction
Specials Fulfill a Need
Holiday Specials
Weekly Specials
Lunch Specials
Dinner Specials
Highlights

Introduction

If you are the owner or chef of the perfect restaurant, one which has reached its full sales potential and is profitable without specials, why change? So few operations are able to generate continuous enthusiasm based upon their menu alone that when it happens, the management is wise not to tinker. However, virtually every restaurant has room for improvement. Specials are a management tool with uses much more diverse than simply offering cheaper prices. A creative chef can outdistance the competition with a sophisticated specials program.

Specials Fulfill a Need

Every menu has its problems. They are inherent because of the way the menu is designed and the way outside influences change the season-to-season variables in customers' needs. This chapter shows how specials offer solutions by:

1. Rejuvenating interest and increasing sales.
2. Offering a greater variety of styles and dishes.
3. Countering seasonal deficiences in the menu.
4. Serving in a research and development capacity.
5. Providing an effective form of advertising.
6. Increasing the restaurant's profit by outselling unprofitable menu items.

The form in which a special is presented is relatively unimportant, though some studies show that customers prefer to have the specials explained by the staff. The final results should be the same whether the customer is given a mimeographed list, sees a chalk board or electronic sign, or hears a verbal description. These considerations are a question of style for the front-of-the-house operation.

The type of special is very significant, however. Each kind has an impact which is best suited to a specific type of problem. Consider the effective uses of the various types: holiday, weekly, lunch, and dinner specials.

Holiday Specials

No matter how successful or stylized a restaurant's menu is, it can benefit from a holiday or one-time special. Here's an example of how it works.

ROUTE 66 is a theme restaurant which has been a busy lunch and dinner spot since it opened about three years ago. The menu is a one-page laminated billboard. It is big, with a full range of dining options. Route 66 has never run a special of any sort. But this year, one of the managers believes that staying open on Thanksgiving Day could be a wise move. The restaurant has always closed in the past, but it's obvious that the area's competitors will do well that day. Should they just open the doors following a word-of-mouth campaign? Not if they want to do their usual high volume. Route 66 needs a one-time special—a holiday special. It should be an all-inclusive dinner for one, two or the family, depending on the regular clientele's makeup. The dinner should have a few hooks or gimmicks which will lure customers from their usual festive retreat—for instance, undercutting all the competitors' prices per dinner by a dollar. Offer a choice of original dinners which, like those on the usual 66 menu, are highly stylized and stress quality. The dinners should be all-inclusive but should not rely on the all-you-can-eat aspect. The specials should be advertised for at least three weeks before Thanksgiving. Use any method which will reach prospective customers, especially those used by the competitors who have been running specials for years. In small towns, this special makes an effective newspaper ad. Where a restaurant is supported by foot traffic, a poster board sign is an excellent announcement.

An assertive chef can push sales to new levels by running holiday specials as often as possible, or at least once a month. In low-volume periods, they may be just the perk needed to influence the month's percentages (pc's).

One-time specials work on the same principles as the restaurant itself, i.e., customers are attracted by the promise of high quality, reasonable price and good service. What will not work is the misapplied use of another eating establishment's style. For instance, a corner coffee shop trying to promote a Mardi Gras night with gumbo, blackened redfish, beans and rice and beignets will not attract business. It would be better off putting a sign in the window which says "Blue Plate Special Daily." That approach would support the existing menu's style rather than confusing it.

The most prevalent misuse of the one-time special is a version of the antiquated "all-you-can-eat" fish fry. This used to be a feature of Friday night dining, and some restaurants are still trying to peddle the idea. Take a look at the "Weekend Dinner Mania!" sign, which is reproduced exactly as it was run by a struggling restaurant (Fig. 3-1). It has a number of classic mistakes which makes it an exercise in futility.

The first strategic error, which has the power to practically negate the entire campaign, is the use of the words "all you can eat." With a few exceptions, such as groups of college men or runners just finished with a marathon, no one wants to eat all he or she can. No one. As a matter of

---

ALL YOU CAN EAT!

WESTERN STYLE BBQ RIBS   9.50
INCLUDES: SALAD, POTATO, ROLLS & BUTTER

WEEKEND
DINNER
MANIA!

PRIME RIB AU JUS   10.75
INCLUDES: SALAD, POTATO, ROLLS & BUTTER

PLUS: ALL YOU CAN DRINK AFTER 4 P.M.:
BEER, WINE, SANGRIA, SODA

Figure 3-1. Dinner mania! Specials board.

fact most people spend time and money trying to lose the weight caused by the little they have eaten. What's more, customers don't even want a dinner which includes potatoes, rolls and butter. So, unless the price is low enough to warrant eating an average portion of ribs or prime rib (the customer's one heavy meat meal of the week), the special will have no affect whatsoever. The promotion of an unpopular concept is the second major fault and signals the end of this special's appeal. The price is fair for an all-you-can-eat meal but too high for the average. To prove the ineptness of Dinner Mania's management team, another restaurant in the same area has built its Friday night trade by selling Prime Ribs for $8.95. True, the portions are smaller and no free drinks are included, but customers buy them out every weekend. Dinner Mania remains empty and its managers puzzled as to why no one likes their great deal.

Weekly Specials

Once-a-week specials have a big chance for success. As a matter of fact, brunch, which has become an American tradition, started as a breakfast deal designed to get lazy Sunday customers out of the house and into the restaurants.

Brunch menus are usually shortened breakfast-lunch versions of the restaurant's regular menus. As such, they need the added range which specials give. During the ongoing week-to-week, year-to-year struggle for brunch clientele, it's essential to remember the customers' attitude. They are up, but they haven't eaten yet, nor have they had their morning coffee. They're driving or walking around in the worst of moods. There had better be something exciting waiting for them at the end of the pre-coffee Sunday morning trek. Fifty percent of these customers will order Eggs Benedict anyway. But they won't be the member of the group who decides where they're going. The leader will be the person who ends up ordering banana pancakes, or eggs exotica or fruit whatsit. Specials have a strong drawing power because they add excitement. They rejuvenate the menu every week.

Consider the example of LA DOLCE VITA, a fairly busy Italian restaurant with moderate prices (see Fig. 3-2). At $6.95 their brunch is competitive, especially considering that other moderately-priced restaurants in their area charge $7.95 and give only one free drink. Pricewise, La Dolce is supercompetitive.

What about the menu? It is laid out well: the breakfast items first, Eggs Benedict right on top. The salads express the Italian cuisine of the

LA DOLCE VITA

Brunch Menu

Served From 12:00 to 3:00 P.M. Saturday and Sunday

All Items Are 6.95

Includes: Unlimited Champagne or 2 Drinks

(Bloody Mary, Screwdriver or Wine)

Eggs Benedict

Country Breakfast

2 Eggs Any Style, Bacon or Sausage, Muffin & Fresh Fruit

French Toast

Bacon or Sausage & Fresh Fruit

Three-Egg Omelette

2 Ingredients: Procuitto, Mozzarella, Bacon, Swiss, Ricotta,
Onion, Mushrooms, Tomato, Olives, Spinach

House Salad

Ceasar Salad

Arugula & Endive Salad

Fettucini Alfredo

Fuscilli Primavera

Linguini Vergine (Al Olio)

Linguini Con Spinaci

Penne, Ricotta e Procuitto

Tortellini Papalino

Ask Waitress About Our Weekly Special

Figure 3-2. La Dolce Vita. Brunch menu.

restaurant, though it is hard to imagine making a meal of two drinks and a house salad. It is probably elaborate and worth the price. The second half of the menu is reserved for pastas, each of which sounds appetizing and has a fantastic price. But is pasta a brunch item? It is a perfect lunch item and many people will want to eat lunch on the weekend, so it seems to fit will with the Italian brunch theme. The argument that pasta is too filling for a major concentration (one-half) on a lunch or brunch menu could be proven wrong by the exception—a restaurant which specializes in pasta.

The focus and range of La Dolce's brunch menu err by being too narrow. To make matters worse, they offer only one special per week; they admit it right on the menu.

In La Dolce's strong effort to keep the Italian influence of their restaurant, they have forgotten the main purpose of a brunch menu—to offer a breakfast-lunch selection. They have offered a lunch-dinner selection with the obligatory "eggs." Even in doing this, they have missed opportunities. What about the fritata—an excellent Italian egg dish which is known to Americans but doesn't appear? At least one of the egg dishes should be an omelette or another inventive version of Eggs Benedict which utilizes recognizably Italian ingredients. The major fault of the menu is the total lack of sandwiches, which Americans eat for lunch, brunch or dinner. Italians have many tasty versions. Every twosome or group which considers La Dolce for brunch will include the occasional individual who wants a hamburger but will settle for an interesting, hearty sandwich. On Saturdays, the sales for sandwiches and salads are stronger than those for egg dishes. This recognized customer need is left unfulfilled by La Dolce. Although it would be better to modify this brunch menu by adding a fritata, some Italian sandwiches, and heartier salads, the narrowness of the menu can be countered with a full specials list. Include six or seven items which will broaden the menu's appeal, such as a fritata du jour, three sandwiches, an egg dish and a salad. These specials should be displayed prominently wherever customers are deciding whether to come in.

In actuality, La Dolce has a specials board, a large sandwich board, set up on the sidewalk. Their clientele are mostly on foot. But on the board, instead of listing a diversity of specials or even the one promised special, "Unlimited Champagne" is scrawled. That is the wrong focus. La Dolce's champagne approach uses their most effective advertising spot to say, "The best thing about our place is that you can drink a lot of champagne." Nondrinkers will not care—they may even be offended—and, many of the drinkers are after stronger drink than bubbly. La Dolce's brunch gimmick misses the mark.

The following is a basic list of brunch items which will fulfill La Dolce's and most restaurants' brunch special's needs:

Soup du Jour (hot or cold, depending upon the season).
Seafood-Egg Dish.
Salad Entree (which utilizes meat, fowl and/or fish).*
Sandwich Platter
Cheese- or Vegetable- or Herb-Egg Dish.
Seasonal or Trendy Egg Dish.
Dessert du Jour.

Lunch Specials

Daily specials are a particularly active form of competition in many areas of the United States. Population centers, with their high concentration of restaurants, favor this casual form of comparison shopping. A chef's creativity and price structure savvy face the most direct competition they will ever encounter. Entire neighborhoods wage price wars over the favors of a few hundred lunch customers. For the average American-Continental restaurant, specials make the difference between high and low volume.

For example, consider the lunch menu from *THE EMBERS,* a moderately priced Continental-broiler restaurant with a solid dinner trade (see Fig. 3-3). Despite the regular evening trade, the lunch business has been mediocre.

Though the individual dishes lack originality of any distinctive flair, the overall range is very good. The selections offer real choice in a number of categories which are important for lunch. Judging from the dinner volume, the quality is probably good and should be reasonable at lunch, too. There are, however, three problems which should be countered by a specials list: the lack of any seafood dishes, the poor selection of sandwiches (two), and a general problem with the boring style of the menu items.

Consider the actual lunch specials list used by The Embers (see Fig. 3-4).

This specials list illustrates why the French and Italians do not consider American food a legitimate cuisine. The Embers' day chef has paid lip service to the specials list, with a half-hearted selection of four mundane, unoriginal and unappetizing dishes. For a list to be this poor, a manager, a day chef, a head chef and an owner must each have had a hand in some sloppy or lazy decision making. Surprisingly, many specials lists are just like this, undescriptive and boring.

---

* In the fall and winter, substitute a crepe or pasta dish.

THE EMBERS

LUNCH MENU

Cold Soup du Jour 2.75

Hot Soup du Jour 2.75

Appetizers

Buffalo Chicken Wings 4.75

Chicken Fingers 3.50

Potato Skins 2.75

Shrimp Cocktail 6.95

Salads & Pastas

Avocado Stuffed with Chicken Salad 6.50

Hearts of Palm and Dressing 4.25

Spinach Salad 6.25

Chef Salad 6.50

Green House Salad 2.50

Egg Fettucini, Vegetables, Garlic & Cream Sm 5.25 Lg 9.25

Spinach Fettucini, Fontina & Walnuts Sm 5.25 Lg 9.25

Meat Tortellini in Tomato Sauce Sm 5.25 Lg 9.25

Open for Lunch 11:30–3:00

All Major Credit Cards Accepted

Entrees

Breast of Chicken in Mustard & Wine Sauce 9.25

Breast of Chicken with Herbs 9.25

Grilled NY Steak with Peppercorns 12.75

BBQ Baby Back Ribs ½ 7.95 Full 12.95

Baby Lamb Chops Grilled and Marinated with Fresh Basil 11.75

Our Lunch Specialty —

Broiled Chicken Cutlet Sandwich 4.50

Hamburger Platter with Fries 4.50

Eggs & Specials

Omelette and Fries 6.75

Fritata 6.95

Quiche and Salad 5.95

Guacamole and Chips 2.75

Nachos 3.75

The Embers is Available for Private Parties.

Figure 3-3. The Embers. Lunch menu.

THE EMBERS

LUNCH SPECIALS

Mushroom Ravioli in Tomato Sauce   6.95

Mushroom & Swiss Omelette   4.95

Broiled Filet of Sole   8.75

Turkey Club Sandwich   6.25

Figure 3-4. The Embers. Lunch specials.

What should The Embers or any restaurant with a standard Continental menu do? Attack the problem of boring food head on by presenting highly creative dishes—nothing elaborate or heavy, but food which solves the problem of what to have for lunch. An American restaurant which continues to serve the same style of food it did the day it opened is in a dangerous rut. It runs the risk of being eclipsed by newer or more competitive places which offer a quick, clean meal coupled with a little pizzaz. That's the best combination, the one which will attract new customers while retaining the old ones.

A lunch specials list must address two needs: the customer's hunger and the menu's deficiencies. Despite the changes in customers' tastes from region to region, there are certain dishes which Americans want to eat for lunch. And despite the shortcomings of a particular restaurant's lunch menu, there are certain dishes which should be sold. That list is the same and should include all or most of the special categories listed below. Modify the list to adjust the radical regional tastes or severely deficient lunch menus.

One Hot Soup du Jour.
One Cold Soup du Jour.
One Salad Special of Entree Size Year Round.
Add Another Salad Entree in Summer.
A Light, Boneless Chicken Entree.
A Seafood Entree.
A Pasta Entree.
One or Two Sandwich Specials without Fries.
One or Two Desserts du Jour.

Lunch specials should be light, seasonal, and trendy or creative. They need not be full meals. In highly competitive areas, start the list with a loss leader (see Chapter 10). Once the format for the specials list has been established, offer those same categories of food every day. The customers have to get used to buying a special sandwich or pasta, for example. After the list is established, it will work as a draw.

Dinner Specials

Dinner customers have larger appetites, and therefore a larger range of dishes which they will consider for a meal. For that reason, an evening specials list allows more flexibility. It is less dependent upon customers' needs, or at least it seems so because the needs are all-inclusive. A dinner list is more reflective of the restaurant's menu faults and emphasizes what the owners wish to promote. Restaurants which specialize in steaks or seafood, for instance, may do very little or no menu balancing with their specials list. Instead, they may reinforce their already strong position by offering creative versions of different steaks or seafood, as the case may be. Common sense dictates that successful specials lists for steak houses, seafood places and theme restaurants should include seasonal or trendy dishes, either loss leaders of profit makers, or finishing touches to already successful upscale menus. A well-established chef must have worked out the balance problems in the original menu by revision, trial and error. After years of refining the printed menu, a chef is able to concentrate on specials that are mouth-watering come-ons. Tantalizing food descriptions are an effective form of daily advertising.

Consider the case of LES TROIS POMMES, a successful dining establishment which is priced in the $40-per-person range. Its clientele is regular and established (see Fig. 3-5).

LES
TROIS
POMMES

DINNER

Appetizers

Soup of the Day	3.50
Soup Du Poisson Provence	4.95
Salad Mixte	3.25
Tomato and Warm Mussel Salad	4.95
Camembert and Brie Croutons	4.50
Fresh Lobster Claw Salad	6.50
Pistou Salad Au Gratin	3.95
Blanquette of Snails and Leeks	6.25

Fish

Fish of the Day	P.A.
Mesquite Grilled Swordfish	15.95
Mussels in Tomato and Caper Coulis	8.95
Baked Sea Scallops Nantau	11.95

Pasta

Pasta of the Day	P.A.
Lobster Ravioli in Garlic, Butter and Walnut Oil Sauce	12.95

Entrees

Mesquite Grilled Free Range Game Hen	14.95
Grilled Chicken in 3 Citrus Marinade	9.95
Chicken Fricassee Burgundy	10.95
Roast Chicken Supreme with Paté and Strawberries	10.95
Grilled Duck with Gin and Juniper Glaze	13.95
Steak Tartare	12.75
Grilled Lamb Steak with Rosemary and Lemon	13.95
Filet Mignon Medallions with Roquefort	16.95
Double Lamb Chops with Tomato and Tarragon Hollandaise	17.95

Entree Salad

10.95 or 12.95

A Melange of Red Leaf Lettuce, Roasted Red Peppers and Toasted Walnuts Topped with your Choice of Warm Poached Lobster or Warm Grilled Chicken Breast

Desserts

Peach Melba	4.50
Creme Brulee	4.50
Profiteroles	4.25
Fresh Pineapple Flambé	4.50
Strawberry-Chocolate Genoise	4.50

Figure 3–5. Les Trois Pommes. Dinner menu.

The selection includes several recipes ranging from Classic to Nouvelle French styles, with a few American additions. The presentation is Nouvelle. The appetizer and entree selections are creative and diverse, establishing a broad range of appeal. The pastas are an extra touch for this French-style menu and, like the entree salad, further extend the market base. The fish category, however, is minimal. Today's customers emphasize two dishes, chicken and fish. Apparently the chef of Les Trois Pommes is well aware of that, for the evening specials list is fifty percent seafood (see Fig. 3-6)—a perfect balance to a nearly perfect menu. Even in the highly successful restaurants, menus have limitations due to selection and style. The deficiencies may be temporary, due to seasonal changes or eating trends, but they exist nonetheless.

What happens if the deficienies of a menu are not immediately apparent? A general specials list offering a dish for every taste would serve to attract customers and pinpoint what they are buying most often. The list on the following page is an all-purpose dinner special's list.

LES TROIS POMMES

Specials List   June 6th

Grilled Calves Liver with Sage Oil and Strawberry Vinegar	12.95
Grilled Salmon Filet with a Citron Creme and Vegetable Pearls	16.95
Cold Poached Halibut with Green Sauce	14.95
Chou Crout (Chicken and Sauerkraut)	10.75

Figure 3-6. Les Trois Pommes. Specials.

Soup du Jour (Hot or Cold in Season).
An Entree Salad (in Spring and Summer Months).
A Pasta Entree.
A Chicken Dish.
One or Two Seafood Dishes.
A Meat Dish.
Two Desserts du Jour (One Chocolate, One Fruit).

Fowl varieties, appetizers and vegetable entrees must be considered as additional selections, not as replacements for any of the basic items. Any switches reduce the range and depth of appeal within the market.

The simplest most obvious solutions are often the best—fish specials by the restaurant whose menu lacks a seafood selection, for instance. But the specials list can be a possible source of future problems. A case in point is the restaurant where over fifty percent of the dinner volume is generated by the specials list. Chefs who evaluate this sales pattern as a testament to the success of their creative genius are turning a blind eye to a potentially severe fault. The restaurant's menu is too weak to attract a steady clientele. One slip on the specials list, and the total volume would take a sudden dip. When chefs lose their touch, even temporarily, a precarious situation occurs. Customers have no old favorites from the menu to sustain their patronage. Specials must never supplant the menu as the primary focus. They are like the fine controls on a color television; they are meant to be adjusted only after the set is warmed up.

Highlights

Specials are a management tool with uses much more diverse than simply offering lower prices.

Specials offer solutions by:

1. Rejuvenating interest and increasing sales.
2. Offering a greater variety of styles and dishes.
3. Countering seasonal deficiences in the menu.
4. Serving in a research and development capacity.
5. Providing an effective form of advertising.
6. Increasing the restaurant's profit by outselling unprofitable menu items.

An assertive chef can push sales to new levels by running holiday specials at least once a month.

One-time specials work on the same principles as the restaurant itself, i.e., customers are attracted by the promise of high quality, reasonable price and good service.

Specials have a strong drawing power because they add excitement.

Specials should be displayed prominently wherever customers are deciding whether to come in.

For the average American-Continental restaurant, specials make the difference between high and low volume.

A dinner list is more reflective of the restaurant's menu faults and emphasizes what the owners wish to promote.

After years of refining the printed menu, a chef is able to concentrate on specials that are mouth-watering come-ons.

Even in highly successful restaurants, menus have limitations due to selection and style.

The deficiencies may be temporary, due to seasonal changes or eating trends, but they exist nonetheless.

Specials must never supplant the menu as the primary focus.

Chapter 4

QUALITY CONTROL AND MENU ANALYSIS

Introduction

The ultimate aim of quality control is to build popularity, for without it, sales and profits lag.

In the worst of all possible situations, a chef finds himself the newly appointed head of a very unpopular restaurant. Several major problems will become immediately evident, including a dour staff. The food will be the worst offender, but other issues, such as faulty pricing and poor menu design, will compound the difficulties. An ironic aspect of this situation is that a restaurant often serves mediocre food for years at a profit; then, for no seemingly good reason, sales dry up. The restaurant has slipped across the fine line separating mediocre from poor. At that point, a return to mediocrity will be insufficient to improve the profit picture. A complete overhaul is necessary. The owner and old-timers among the staff and customers may want a return to mediocrity. Those were comfortable days.

So, if you were hired to turn around the business, dig in for a long campaign.

The First Stage

Quality control often becomes a political issue and should be approached carefully, surreptitiously, at first. Chefs must employ solid detective work to understand the entire situation and to build their case.

A chef in a new position may be too busy with ordering, cooking and management to spend enough time on an in-depth analysis of quality. Here is a simple format which should be considered as the first stage.

Approach the question of quality in an orderly fashion in your head, if not on paper. There are four major areas where quality can sag: purchase and handling of raw products, house recipes, food preparation procedures and line production. On a daily basis, spend time in each area to pinpoint the problems. Not all quality control problems are of the same intensity. The established chef of a successful restaurant will encounter no resistance when they effect a change, while the new chef of an empty restaurant will be met with paranoia and skepticism. However, a chef *must* assume responsibility for the quality of the food from purchase to final disposal. If that means an in-house struggle with the maitre d', whose great-aunt's recipe for duck a l'orange is a dead end, so be it. Prepare to do battle. An experienced chef will have laid out the ground rules with the owner during the overly enthusiastic hiring talk. An essential part of a chef's job is to be the standard bearer of high quality.

Purchase and Handling of Raw Products

In most restaurants, the chef buys all foodstuffs. But the chef should also take care that what has been ordered is being delivered. A visual check is necessary to verify brand names, size of units, and freshness, especially in the case of meats, fish and vegetables. How to keep the food fresh before usage is an important topic which is discussed at length in Chapter 9. For purposes of quality control, remember that any spoiled food must be thrown away. Never try to save money by using raw goods of questionable quality.

A chef must be personally involved with every aspect of the kitchen's operation. Make it a part of the daily schedule to check in food, to observe handling or storage procedures and to make changes where necessary.

Relations with suppliers can be tricky, so they should be left to the person with power to hire and fire—the chef. For example, consider two commonly purchased items which have short shelf lives but need separate management tactics in dealing with their purveyors.

Chopped meat comes in a variety of grades and qualities, which, of course, dictate its price. As with all other raw goods, the right quality must be chosen for each particular menu's needs. A 90–10 mix of high-grade chuck steak may be too expensive for an American restaurant with a large burger volume but low prices, especially when the perceptible taste difference is minimal. An 80–20 blend of fresh chuck may even have a better "hamburger flavor" and can be sold at a lower price. Based on the restaurant's needs, a verbal contract is developed between the chef and purveyor for a specific quality of chopped meat. Its color and texture are established when the first sale is made and are reinforced with each subsequent delivery. Substandard (gray or fatty) meat should be refused immediately and replacement demanded from the person who made the original sale. If the company is unable to deliver the right quality, it must understand that it is breaking the original agreement. Put the pressure on. If the purveyor cannot come through, fire him. Don't be mollified with conversation.

The right chopped meat purveyor doesn't send out gray or fatty product— ever. A gross infraction of this standard is cause for dismissal. For example, one Friday my chopped meat supplier delivered over one hundred and fifty pounds of gray meat. I rejected it and fired the purveyor even though he had been delivering to us for over a year. Because this sort of mistake isn't a result of human error but rather of poor management, it will definitely happen again. I decided not to be a partner of a company with problems. No chef should.

Fresh fish are another raw good with a short shelf life, sometimes shorter than that of chopped meat. The standard for dealing with a fish purveyor must be less strict in policy, though not in effect. Some companies deliberately try to sell off quantities of bad fish. Their sales pitches should be ignored; never buy from them (see the section "Tricks of the Trade" in Chapter 11). The best fish dealers will have an occasional bad day. However, the burden of responsibility is on the chef to check each fish delivery and to reject any questionable product. The supplier's management will come to know a chef's standards by watching the returned goods. Not to return poor-quality product sends the wrong message and compounds the problem. The ideal fish purveyor will provide same-day replacement. Find that supplier even if it means firing a few in the search.

House Recipes

Nothing is to be gained by immediately changing every recipe on the menu, even if the new chef feels that it's warranted. The disruptive backlash would cause an overriding negative effect. Here is a perfect opportunity for the chef to build confidence among the staff, both floor and kitchen. Use an informal marketing technique to discover which menu items are least popular. Asking the bartenders, waitpersons, owners, customers and line cooks will give a rough picture of which items are good and will identify the dishes which need immediate change. If the overall consensus is that a recipe is bad, change it. Upgrade the quality of the ingredients and flavors. The house recipes must be analyzed for correctness of style or execution and, of course, taste before any real strides can be made in the following steps of the production process.

Food Preparation Procedures

At the beginning of a turnaround campaign, it may be more effective to do a number of menial tasks quickly and efficiently by yourself to support the total reeducation of the preparation staff. In that way, things will be accomplished with maximum proficiency while preparation cooks and helpers either adopt the new program or begin to appear obstinate in their constant inability to do it the "new" way.

Up to fifty percent of the flavor can be lost during the preparation process by inept cooking techniques. Know the best ways to make stocks, soups and salads; to trim meats and roast; to par boil; and even to operate the slicer. Every chore must be analyzed for its end result—the quality of the food. Nine times out of ten the preparation cook will be task oriented, rarely thinking of the food as food, something to be eaten and enjoyed. Ex-dishwashers who are learning their trade from the bottom up are the worst offenders. They tend to operate by strict recipe instructions without ever tasting the final product—and, what's worse, without knowing what taste should ultimately be achieved. A chef in the first months on a new job or a chef spot checking for problems should be a taster. Someone must taste every item produced. If the staff hasn't been trained to do it, then the chef must.

Prepared foods must be cooled properly for storage. Of course, any preprepared foods must be kept in clean, tightly sealed containers. A breakdown in any stage of this process can result in sporadically or consistently poor quality.

Line Production

In the first days on a new job, when the chef has limited time to spend on each area of concern, it is difficult to do more than make one's desires known. Often the main source of poor quality from the line is a person whose attitude or skills are below standard. The most time-consuming aspect of quality control is isolating the problem workers and obtaining the evidence to correct their mistakes. Cooks are notorious for doing things exactly the way the chef wants them done when the chef is around, and then letting quality slide when the chef is absent. Stand outside the kitchen during peak hours, ideally without announcing your intentions, and watch the plates going out. Are the recipes being executed correctly? Are they garnished? Are the portions too large or too small? Is the presentation consistent with the style of the restaurant? Are there any complaints about orders coming out too slowly? What do the plates returning to the dishwasher look like? Are any plates being rejected completely? Three nights spent outside the kitchen door will act as a warning to the cooks that things are changing. More importantly, they will see the chef's personal concern with quality. They will be doing their best during those three nights. This will give the chef an opportunity to educate the wait staff as to what is below standard and what should not be served, i.e., sloppy plates without garnish. It is also an opportunity to taste sauces. This will be valuable later, when a general revamping of line recipes may be in order. The most effective change comes from on-the-spot implementation of style and technique. Raise the quality by showing or instructing. Constantly reeducate to establish the policy as a strict one. It is important to be as diplomatic as possible when dealing with a new staff. One of the problems to watch for is a bad attitude. Be aware of any resistance to your changes or directions. It is helpful for a chef to question the floor staff about the quality of the food during shifts or hours when he or she is not present. Remember, there may be personality clashes between some kitchen and floor staffers, so always double-check. Develop inter-restaurant intelligence sources—remote sets of eyes and ears which will aid the chef without being devisive.

The most difficult part of being a chef is telling a moody cook to do a plate differently—for the hundredth time. Cooks will play dumb or feign naiveté while they try to wear down the chef. In this situation, personal conferences, kitchen meetings, and then reprimands with the owner or manager present may be necessary. But the staff still may not sense the chef's personal stake in the new quality until someone is fired. Here's a quip which works well as a warning: "Do it my way, or hit the highway." Often kitchen staffs are strangely dependent upon a person whose skills are poor. It may seem a hardship to fire a workhorse—a cook who works six or seven busy shifts per week for instance—but the sooner the poor-quality centers are removed the better.

Quality Control Maintenance

Since quality control is such an important aspect of a chef's responsibilities, it should be a daily part of his or her schedule. Informally at least, the previous four divisions of quality control must be routinely considered, beginning the first week of a new chef's reign and continuing every week thereafter.

In smaller restaurants where the sales volume is lower, it is better to monitor the popularity of menu items by looking at the dupes, noting which items do not sell, and following up with daily inspection of the refrigerators to spot stale goods. That process is an essential part of a chef's quality control efforts.

Menu Analysis

In larger restaurants, those which sell over a million dollars worth of food a year, quality control needs assistance from management tools which are much more formalized. Because of the time needed to implement them, it is best to schedule an in-depth menu analysis of sales during the slower periods of the year. However, a new chef will want to do an analysis as soon as possible. With few allies at the beginning, the numbers will supply the backup needed to convince the owner and managers of the changes needed. The two-week menu analysis provides a data base from which policy can be formulated. In a larger operation, seat-of-the-pants piloting isn't enough. The menu designing process must be rooted in contemporary business practices. No one should effect a major menu change without first answering the questions: What's really selling? and Where do we make our money?

Study the following basic forms for the two-week menu analysis:

Form A	Beginning Inventory
Form B	Item Sales Record
Form C	Dollar Sales Record
Form D	Dollar Purchase Record
Form E	Weekly Menu Analysis
Form F	Ending Inventory
Form G	Two-Week Menu Analysis

FORM A   Beginning Inventory

Restaurant Name:		Date:	Time:	
TYPE OF GOODS	UNITS ON HAND	UNIT COST	DOLLAR AMOUNT	TOTALS
Meat:				
Fish:				
Vegetables:				
Pasta:				
Frozen foods:				
Dairy:				
Dry Goods:				
Desserts:				

FORM B   Item Sales Record

Restaurant Name:		Date:	Shift:
MENU ITEM	QUANTITY SOLD	MENU ITEM	QUANTITY SOLD
Appetizers:		Entrees—Meat:	
Salads:		Entrees—Fish:	
		Entrees—Fowl:	
Pastas:			
		Entrees—Other:	
Sandwiches:			
		Specials du Jour:	
Side Dishes:			
		Brunch or Breakfast:	
Desserts:			

FORM C   Dollar Sales Record

Restaurant Name:

DATE	DAY SHIFT	NIGHT SHIFT	SUBTOTAL	TOTAL

FORM D   Dollar Purchases Record

Restaurant Name: Week Beginning: Week Ending:

MEAT	FISH	DAIRY	PASTA	FOWL	VEGTS.	FROZEN	DRY GOODS	DESSERTS	BAKED

FORM E   Weekly Menu Analysis
(Use this heading on Form B)

Restaurant Name: Week Beginning: Ending:

MENU ITEM	QUANTITY SOLD	MENU ITEM	QUANTITY SOLD

FORM F   Ending Inventory
(Use this heading on Form A)

Restaurant Name:		Date:	Time:	
TYPE OF GOODS	UNITS ON HAND	UNIT COST	DOLLAR AMOUNT	TOTALS

FORM G   Two-Week Menu Analysis
(Use this heading on Form B)

Restaurant:	Period Beginning:	Ending:	
MENU ITEM	QUANTITY SOLD	MENU ITEM	QUANTITY SOLD

Procedures for the Two-Week Analysis

Step One: Do the preanalysis setup, which involves informing other management and the owners that the analysis is scheduled. The individuals who are responsible for the cash register tapes and closeout sheets must be aware of the analysis, especially the need for daily access to the sales records. A final setup procedure is to get copies of the necessary forms. These include one Form A, fourteen Form B's, two Form C's, two Form D's, two Form E's, one Form F and one Form G. The number of Form B's needed is decided by the number of shifts per day, the number of times a cash register is closed and the sales figures totaled. For most restaurants this occurs twice a day, once for the day shift and once for the evening shift. Variations may include one shift for restaurants which open for one meal only and three or four shifts for twenty-four-hour operations. It is an important part of the analysis to total these shifts separately.

Step Two: Using Form A, take a beginning inventory of all goods in house. Even estimate the amounts of prepared food. Shorthand notes to yourself will be precise enough, because the first inventory is important as a comparison to the ending inventory. The inventory information will be used to calculate how much of each product was used during the two-week period. Compute the complete totals of each inventory item and category, using the prices actually in effect when the goods were purchased. This involves looking through some old invoices.

The inventory must be taken before the first shift of the analysis begins and after the last shift of the analysis ends. Any other time would be too inprecise.

Step Three: Begin the actual data recording process. This involves Forms B, C and D.

The information for Form B is obtained by going through the customer checks, one shift at a time. Take the first shift's stack of checks. Begin at the top, and mark the appropriate row for every item sold. After the entire shift's stack has been recorded, total each item individually. This includes all specials which are temporary menu items. The totals in the "Quantity Sold" columns can be subtotaled by menu categories: appetizers, entrees, sandwiches, salads, specials, desserts, etc.

Form C is simply a record of the food sales in dollars for every shift. Use the number which generally accompanies the customer checks—in other words, the official food sales total.

Form D is an important aspect of the analysis procedure in that it supplies the raw data for determining the cost of goods sold. Be thorough in this aspect of record keeping, and make certain that you can have access to the invoices for the entire two-week period.

Step Four: Continue the procedure in step three until the first week is completed.

Step Five: At the end of week one, there will be fourteen Item Sales Records filled out. Combine the totals for each item and record the amounts on Form E, the Weekly Menu Analysis.

Total Form C, the Dollar Sales Record, and Form D, the Dollar Purchases Record.

Continue with new forms the second week of analysis just as directed for week one in step three. Complete the week of record taking.

Step Six: Using Form F, take an ending inventory of all stock and prepared goods, just as the beginning inventory was prepared.

Step Seven: There will be fourteen Item Sales Records completed during the second week. Combine the totals of each item and record the amounts on Form E, the Weekly Menu Analysis.

Combine the totals from the two Form E's on Form G, the Two-Week Menu Analysis.

Total the second week's Form C, the Dollar Sales Record, and Form D, the Dollar Purchases Record. Compute the total sales for the two-week period and the total purchases for the same period.

Step Eight: Calculate the cost of goods sold during the two weeks by using the following formula:

Beginning Inventory + Purchases − Ending Inventory = Cost of Goods Sold

For the purpose of analysis, it may be necessary to calculate specific costs of menu items—fish or chicken, for instance. Or it may be desirable to know the actual cost of those menu items which sell well or poorly. Use the same formula to figure those costs. For example:

Beginning Fettuccini Inv. + Fettuccini Purchases −
Ending Fettuccini Inv. = Cost of Fettuccini Sold.

Beginning Swordfish Inv. + Swordfish Purchases −
Ending Swordfish Inv. = Cost of Swordfish Sold.

Beginning Chix Cutlet Inv. + Chix Cutlet Purchases −
Ending Chix Cutlet Inv. = Cost of Chix Cutlets Sold.

Step Nine: Analysis, the translation of the numbers into clear business facts. The most obvious, concrete conclusion to be reached concerns the best-selling menu items; they will jump off the sheet with their high totals. This information is extremely useful when deciding how to expand or repair a faulty menu, because it clearly shows what the customers like best at the present time.

Another obvious type of analysis which can be safely used as an element in the chef's argument for making changes is to pinpoint those items that have not sold at all. These items have no appeal, no drawing power, and are certainly a waste of menu space. They also contribute to other forms of waste by causing ingredients to stagnate.

Marginal sellers are trickier. Before deciding to drop an item from the menu because of poor sales, calculate the cost of the goods sold, their percentage of the total food cost and their contribution margin (see Chapter 13). A contribution margin is calculated by subtracting an item's cost from its menu price. Always a dollar figure, the contribution margin is especially useful during menu analysis; it provides a look at an aspect of profitability which is otherwise slighted. For example, an item with a relatively high menu price, such as swordfish in the previous example, has a poor food pc, around fifty percent. However, its contribution margin is high and gives a true gauge of the item's profitibility. The sale of one unit of swordfish brings in over five dollars, which is over four times greater than a hamburger's sale.

Another complicating factor in the decision-making process is the comparison between food pc and sales volume. A low food pc combined with a high sales volume is a highly profitable situation, but what about an item which has sluggish sales and a moderate food pc? A closer analysis is needed to determine the item's overall contribution to the restaurant's gross sales and gross profits. This is where a calculation of the contribution margin is essential. The bottom line in the restaurant business is total profit. Therefore, each item sold must provide maximum levels of sales and return.

The menu analysis is best used to pinpoint best-sellers, poor sellers and profit or loss centers. These data are then used to define a menu's future. Consider two examples. The first is a successful pub-restaurant which has been losing sales volume for six to nine months. The second is a new, trendy restaurant and watering hole which opened to big fanfare but never reached one-third of its sales potential.

In the first example, Rafferty's was a college bar with pub food that added more and more main dishes to satisfy its customers. The menu had expanded and remained a constant success for seven years. At the pub's peak each seat turned over two and one half times a night. Recently, poor business had caused the chef to consider changes for the first time in years. How should Chef Gary proceed? A menu analysis to highlight the eating patterns of the existing clientele is the first step. Review the menus for Rafferty's (see Figs. 4-1 and 4-2). Then study the results of a two-week analysis.

RAFFERTY'S PUB

MUNCHIES

Zucchini Sticks	SM 1.25 LRG 2.50
Mozzarella Sticks	1.95
Onion Rings	SM 1.25 LRG 2.50
French Fries	SM .75 LRG 1.50

Potato Skins Stuffed Your
Way   3.25

Sauteed Mushroom Caps   2.75

Chili Con Carne   SM 1.85 LRG 2.50
   Topped w/Cheddar .40 extra

A Crock of French Onion Soup
   Au Gratin   2.25
   Soup Du Jour   SM 1.60
         BOWL 2.25

BURGERS 'N BITES

Hamburger 2.95	Platter	3.55
Cheeseburger		3.35
Platter		3.95
Bacon Cheeseburger		3.75
Platter		4.35
Chili Burger 3.95	Platter	4.55
Campus Club Sandwich		4.25
Bacon, Lettuce & Tomato		2.95
Grilled Cheese, Bacon & Tomato		3.95
Chicken Salad Sub w/Melted Cheese		3.95
Tuna Salad Sub w/Melted Cheese		3.95
Grilled Ham & Cheese		3.25
Turkey-Turkey Sandwich		3.25
Spaghetti	SM 1.25 LRG 2.50

SALADS

Spinach Tossed Salad	SM 3.25
	LRG 5.25
Julienne Chef Salad	
	SM 4.00 LRG 5.75
Quiche and Salad	4.50
Chicken Salad Supreme	4.25
Tuna Salad Supreme	4.25

MAIN COURSES

Mushroom Sliced Steak Platter	4.95
Cheese Steak Platter	5.50
Chopped Steak	5.25
16 oz. Ribeye Steak	9.25
House Ribeye Steak	6.25
Veal-Oreganato	6.25
Chicken-Oreganato	5.75
Country Fried Chicken	3.95
Fish Fry	3.95
Filet of Sole	5.95
Broiled Bluefish Filet	5.50
Mussels Marinara	3.95

DESSERTS

Triple Chocolate Cake	1.95
Apple Pie A La Mode	1.95

PASTA

Fettucini Alfredo	4.95
Tortellini	5.25
Ravioli in Meat Sauce	4.75

OMELETTES

A Whipped 4-Egg Omelette with One Ingredient, Toast & Fries	3.25
Each Additional Ingredient	.75

(Sorry, No Personal Checks)
(Free On-Campus Delivery)
(Take Out Service)

Figure 4-1. Rafferty's Pub. Menu.

RAFFERTY'S Two-Week Menu Analysis
(10/5/87 to 10/18/87)

MUNCHIES:

Zucc. Sticks	SM 67	LG 19
Mozz. Sticks		155
Onion Rings	SM 52	LG 14
French Fries	SM 75	LG 36
Skins		79
Mushrooms		43
Chili	SM 66	LG 43
French Onion		113
Soup	C 121	B 72

BURGERS 'N BITES:

Hamburger	258
Cheeseburger	183
Bacon Burger	109
Chili Burger	47
Club Sandwich	126
BLT	82
Grilled Cheese	67
Chicken Sub.	53
Tuna Sub	37
Grilled Ham and Cheese	3
Turkey	52
Spaghetti	SM 45 LG 32

PASTA:

Fettucini Alfredo	68
Tortellini	47
Ravioli	12

OMELETTES: 21

SALADS:

Spinach	SM 3	LG 28
Chef's	SM 57	LG 14
Quiche		26
Chicken		41
Tuna		13

MAIN COURSES:

Sliced Steak	80
Cheese Steak	49
Chopped Steak	5
16-Oz. Steak	31
House Steak	54
Veal Oreganato	41
Chicken Oreganato	66
Fried Chicken	39
Fish Fry	28
Sole	49
Bluefish	37
Mussels	21

BRUNCH:

Breakfast Special	103
Eggs Benedict	138
Granola	69
Steak and Eggs	37

DESSERTS:

Chocolate Cake	107
Apple Pie	62
Du Jour	161

SPECIALS:

Meat	134
Fish	186
Fowl	164
Pasta	172
Vegetable	88

RAFFERTY'S For Brunch
Served 10-4   Saturday and Sunday

LJVE JAZZ

The Breakfast Special   4.75
  A Choice of Three Eggs Scrambled, Poached, or
  Fried with Bacon or Ham, Hash Browns and
  Toast

Eggs Benedict   4.95
  Served with Hash Browns

Hot Granola Served with Fresh Fruit, Yogurt
  and Bran Muffin   4.50

Steak and Eggs   4.95

Figure 4–2. Rafferty's Pub. Brunch menu.

Rafferty's Dollar Sales Record

	DAY	NIGHT		DAY	NIGHT
Oct. 5	456	692	12	368	658
Oct. 6	412	813	13	417	712
Oct. 7	419	674	14	373	756
Oct. 8	561	719	15	543	843
Oct. 9	642	1,175	16	614	1,118
Oct. 10	863	1,276	17	829	1,197
Oct. 11	1,028	957	18	1,001	807
Subtotals	4,381	6,306		4,145	6,091
Subtotals		10,687			10,236
Total					20,923

Rafferty's Dollar Purchase Record (Totals)

Week Beginning: 10/5/87   Ending: 10/11/87

MEAT	FISH	DAIRY	PASTA	FOWL	VEGTS.	FROZEN	DRY GOODS	DESSERTS	BAKED
110	403	353	85	393	791	67	1012	211	180

Week Beginning: 10/12/87   Ending: 10/18/87

MEAT	FISH	DAIRY	PASTA	FOWL	VEGTS.	FROZEN	DRY GOODS	DESSERTS	BAKED
1001	363	473	89	375	853	36	618	158	164

Beginning Inventory — Ending Inventory

+215	+110	−75	−18	−65	+115	+10	−236	+42	−5

Cost of Goods Sold

1896	656	901	192	833	1529	93	1866	327	349

Total Cost of Goods Sold = 8642 or 41.3%

Interpreting the data can become confusing, leading to conflicting conclusions. Analyze the raw figures in an orderly fashion, without any preconceived plans. List the best sellers, the zero sellers, the marginal sellers, the profit centers and the loss centers. After considering the data-based answers to the questions about where the profit originates, Chef Gary can decide on effective changes for the future.

Best-Sellers

The best-sellers are easy to spot:

Entrees: (1) Sliced Steak, (2) Chicken Oreganato, (3) House Steak

Sandwiches: (1) Hamburger, (2) Cheeseburger, (3) Club

Salads: (1) Large Spinach Salad, (2) Small Chef's Salad

Pasta: (1) Fettucini Alfredo

Appetizers: (1) Mozzarella Sticks, (2) Soups, (3) Potato Skins

Desserts: (1) Du Jour

The other obvious best-sellers are hidden in the specials category, which was responsible for twenty-five percent of the entree sales volume. If Chef Gary had wisely kept a list of Rafferty's best-selling specials, they would be prime candidates for addition to the menu. But at least the chef will know what types of things are selling. Gary says that his customers are affected by general trends and fads: more fish and chicken, less meat; pasta sells well if it is creatively presented, but not in the classic approaches. For a time, anything done in a Mexican or Cajun style was a hot special; now that seems to have broadened into a general curiosity for stylized tastes.

One way to pinpoint the best-sellers of a menu is by calculating the popularity index of categories and specific items. (A popularity index is a percent ranking obtained by dividing the number sold of a specific menu item by the total number of items sold.) For example, the total number of menu entrees sold, including large salads and all sandwiches, was 1885. The major categories had popularity indexes which ranked as follows:

1. The total number of meat entrees on the menu is twelve, approximately thirty-eight percent of the total entrees, or thirty-two. During the two-week period, meat entrees from the menu accounted for fifty percent of sales — nine hundred thirty-nine meat entrees sold. Meat sold considerably more strongly than its menu placement.
2. Fowl entrees comprise sixteen percent of the menu, with six dishes. They made up twenty percent of the total sales volume, with three hundred seventy-seven entrees sold. Fowl also outsold its menu placement.
3. Fish accounts for sixteen percent of the menu entrees, with five listed. The total number of fish entrees sold during the two-week period was one hundred sixty-four — only nine percent. This is a considerable drop from the normal outcome, which would generally be the same percentage of sales as the percentage of total entrees on the menu.
4. Pasta had a similar drop. It accounted for nine percent of the total entrees on the menu, with three. Yet, during the analysis period, it

accounted for only seven percent of the total entrees sold, or one hundred twenty-seven.

Before reaching any conclusion, finish the best-sellers' analysis with a look at the strongest aspect of Rafferty's sales — the specials. A total of seven hundred forty-four were sold. Fish sold the most at twenty-five percent. Pasta sold twenty-three percent, fowl twenty-two percent and meat eighteen percent — almost an exact reversal of the menu's sales.

From the best-sellers' analysis, one can deduce that the meat dishes on the menu are well disposed and well received. Fish and pastas sell strongly off the specials board but are not selling effectively as menu items in their present form. Chicken is showing a similar record of mediocre menu acceptance and good specials board sales.

Poor Sellers

The poor sellers were not immediately apparent at Rafferty's, but there are a few dishes which should be considered close. The Small Spinach Salad, the Ham and Cheese Sandwich and the Chopped Steak each sold five or fewer in the two-week analysis. That's low enough to fall into the zero category, especially considering that every other menu item has a quantity sold of twelve or above. Mark these poor sellers for replacement.

Marginal Sellers

The marginal dishes at Rafferty's need individual consideration, including a look at their profitability. These dishes include the Mussels, Large Chef's Salad, Tuna Salad Supreme, Ravioli and Omelettes.

MUSSELS: Even though the total number sold is low (it is the least favorite appetizer) mussels are a great profit item. Chef Gary checks his notes; there were $24.75 worth of mussels used during the two weeks, and $82.95 in sales. That's a food pc of 29.8 percent, well below the Rafferty's average of 41.3 percent. Mussels cannot be immediately ruled out. Save the question for the final considerations, when the overall thrust of the menu is analyzed.

LARGE CHEF'S SALAD: With only fourteen sold compared to fifty-seven of the small chef's salads, it would seem that a large chef's salad is simply not a good idea. Chef Gary takes a long look at the actual dish. It is huge, almost embarrassingly so. Its profitability is the same as that of the smaller more successful salads. It gets penciled onto the delete list.

TUNA SALAD SUPREME: While this is a poor seller and could be taken off the menu for that reason, the matter is complicated by the Tuna Sub Sandwich, which uses the same tuna salad in its base. To delete the salad menu item would probably cause a large waste factor in tuna salad. In addition, the added variety of tuna is needed in the already sparse salad section. The solution is to enhance the Tuna Supreme's popularity by changing its presentation, perhaps even the basic recipe. Test the recipe. Is it the best one possible? How can the platter be dressed up? Perhaps the addition of artichoke hearts or walnuts or avocado will help. Make the change soon, and track its success.

RAVIOLI: Perhaps the meat sauce approach is too common or old-fashioned; maybe the sauce is bland. Or it could be that the ravioli is simply the poorest seller in a small, underdeveloped category. Chef Gary checks his notes. The cost has been minimal, around $25 for sales totaling $57. That's a food pc of 26 percent, much lower than the 41.3 percent average. Keep ravioli in mind for replacement or a different presentation.

OMELETTES: One of eight major categories, its sales record is the worst. Perhaps the solution is to diminish its importance by placing it after Quiche on the menu. The profitability will always be good, and eggs are used in house. The final question is style. Does the inclusion of omelettes on Rafferty's menu in any way reduce or confuse the style? Absolutly not, omelettes are in keeping with a pub-restaurant style. Find another place for it on the menu.

The preceding eight dishes were immediately affected by the analysis and constitute one-quarter of the total entrees. That is a healthy impact. But before moving on to analyze the profit and loss centers, consider the other entrees which were not selling that well: Sauteed Mushrooms, Quiche, 16-Oz. Ribeye Steak, and Steak and Eggs. Their general acceptance is good; probably a recipe or presentation change will make these dishes more popular. Don't hesitate to make these kinds of changes after thinking through the possible effects—positive or negative.

Profit and Loss Centers

Profit centers are those items on the menu whose popularity and profitability coincide. The second most important aspect of the analysis is that it identifies the dishes which account for the restaurant's existence. Surprisingly, this is a fact which many owners and managers fail to uncover—where the money comes from.

Rafferty's menu ran a 41.3 percent food cost during the two-week analysis period. Chef Gary's goal is to pinpoint the menu items whose food pc was in the low thirties or twenties. Any item in the forties must be considered a loss center. No menu can support more than two or three of these profit losers, no matter what the rationale. Since no one can predict exactly which menu items will be the profit or loss centers, make a list of each category and dish to be analyzed; then compute their cost of goods sold by investigating the data: Beginning Inventory + Purchases − Ending Inventory = Cost of Goods Sold.

Divide the cost of goods sold by the total dollars received for the corresponding categories or individual items. (Menu Price × Number Sold = Dollars Received.) Not all the calculations are possible for each menu item, but the categories and major dishes are easily discernible with the available information. Use a simple form to list the categories and items; then calculate the food costs, as on RAFFERTY'S analysis of profit and loss centers.

RAFFERTY'S Profit and Loss Centers (10/18/87)

MENU ITEM	COST OF GOODS SOLD	DOLLARS RECEIVED	FOOD COST (%)
Pasta (Inc. Specials)	192.00	1,480.00	13.0
Chicken Cutlets (Inc. specials)	544.00	1,735.00	31.4
Tuna	89.00	201.00	44.3
Turkey	289.00	704.00	41.1
Hamburgers and Chopped Steak	468.00	1,996.00	23.4
Sliced Steak	283.00	696.00	40.7
16-Oz. and House Ribeyes	301.00	625.00	48.2
Sole	132.00	292.00	45.2
Bluefish	56.00	203.00	27.6
All Fish Specials	468.00	1,122.00	41.7
All Meat Specials	369.00	924.00	39.9
Veal	184.00	256.00	71.9
Chocolate Cake	88.00	209.00	42.1
Apple Pie	60.00	121.00	49.6
Du Jour	179.00	362.00	49.4
Fish Fry	41.00	111.00	36.9
Fried Chicken	52.00	154.00	33.8
Totals	$3,795.00	$11,164.00	33.99%
Without Pasta or Chicken	$3,059.00	$7,949.00	38.5%

Pasta, hamburgers, bluefish and chicken. If Rafferty's sold only those items, the raw food pc (the cost of goods sold unadjusted for vegetables, dry goods and incidentals) would be 23.3 percent, a full ten points below the average for all entrees. These four categories and the menu items in them are the profit centers. Another interesting fact brought out by the data is that $9759 of the sales volume, or 45.6 percent comes from the sales of appetizers, salads, brunch and the remaining sandwiches not analyzed.

The loss centers—Veal Oreganato, Desserts, 16-Oz. and House Ribeye Steaks, Sole and Tuna—sell moderately well. Their high food pc's cannot be automatically blamed on the menu price, however. It may very well be that the food is being handled poorly, causing old sole, for instance, to go into the garbage. Waste is the primary cause of profit loss. The other one is the staff consumption. Perhaps the night staff is eating half of the desserts du jour and the dishwashers are having steak twice a day.

A plate cost analysis would be essential to discover the new menu price for Veal Oreganato and the tuna items. This topic is discussed in Chapter 10.

Final Analysis

Having confirmed Rafferty's best-sellers, zero sellers, marginal sellers, profit centers, and loss centers, the next step is the final one—to define the menu's future. How will Rafferty's menu have changed in one, two or more years? Will the cuisine be Italian-American, American steakhouse, or Continental? This decision should never involve a radical turnaround in the menu's style, but rather a slow movement by the addition of profit items, or popular ones, and the deletion of unpopular and unprofitable dishes. Again, the ultimate goal is to build sales volume and lower food costs. Since a primary portion of a menu's changes will depend upon the chef's experience and repertoire, it is Chef Gary's task to utilize the data to introduce an improved version of Rafferty's pub menu. For the purpose of this example, consider Chef Gary to have a complete list of successful specials which are prime candidates for menu slots. This is how he chose to develop the menu.

APPETIZERS: Mozzarella Sticks price raise to $2.25. Addition to the menu of Guacamole and Chips at $3.25.

SALADS: Drop Small Spinach and Large Chef's salads. Raise prices of Small Chef to $4.50, Chicken Salad and Tuna Salad to $4.75. Include avocado on Tuna Salad Supreme. Introduce the Taco Salad at $4.75.

PASTA: Drop Ravioli. Add Spaghetti Carbonara at $4.95. Add Chicken, Fettucini and Mushrooms in White Sauce at $4.95.

SANDWICHES: Drop Ham and Cheese. Raise Club Sandwich to $4.75, Turkey Sandwich to $3.95. Add Rafferty's Grilled Chicken Sandwich at $3.95. Raise all burgers $.40.

ENTREES: Drop Chopped Steak and Veal Oreganato. Raise Sole to $6.25, 16-Oz. Ribeye Steak to $9.95 and House Ribeye Steak to $6.95. Add Shrimp Parmagiana at $6.25. Add Chicken Pizzaiola at $5.75.

OMELETTES: Raise the basic price to $4.25.

DESSERTS: Raise Triple Chocolate Cake and Apple Pie to $2.25. Raise Specials Desserts to $2.50.

BRUNCH: The only possible change would be a $1.00 price raise for entrees. This depends on the quality and popularity of the present product. A decision must be made by Chef Gary after firsthand investigation.

Chef Gary has taken a conservative approach by staying within the Italian-American style for entrees and enhancing the areas which have proven reliable—pasta and chicken. The one radical decision to drop Veal Oreganato was countered by a bold decision to add another possibly popular item—Shrimp Parmesan. For profit reasons, that seemed an essential change.

Now consider the second example, a theme restaurant named ROUTE 66. It is new and trendy, a spot where young moderns are expected to meet, eat and water down. The first three months it opened were successful in both bar and food sales. Then the slump began, with bar sales off one-third and food sales barely alive. After the seventh month of the slump, the owners fired the opening chef and promoted Sous Chef Rich to the number one job. Little change has occurred in sales. How should a chef or consultant solve this severe business problem? First, study the menu (see Fig. 4-3).

This is one of the few examples of a menu which has it all—trendy food, reasonable prices, a strong theme, a full selection, and real food, not simply chi-chi imitations. Common sense should dictate the procedures

ROUTE
66

Starters

Blue Crab and Green
  Onion Fritters   6.95
Chicken Tenders with
  Two Salsas   4.95
BBQ Baby Back Ribs   5.95
Channel Flippin' Nachos   4.50
  Your Choice of
  Toppings — Special
  Beef Jalapenos.
  Shrimp. Salsas. BBQ
  Chicken
Shrimp & Black Bean Sopa
          cup 3.75   bowl 5.95
Chunky Guacamole and
  Blue Corn Chips   4.95

Salads

Greens & Tomatoes 2.25   4.95
Wilted Spinach & Bacon   5.50
Avocado Stuffed with
  Seafood Salad   6.95
Albequerque's Taco Salad 7.95
Marty's Choice   6.95
  A Smoked Chicken
  Salad with Pecans.
  Pimentos & Scallions

Detour

Corn Bread   1.50
Cottage Fries   1.50
Mashed Potatoes &
  Chicken Gravy   1.95
Fried Yams   1.50
Corn on the Cob   1.50

Sandwiches

Sloppy Jose   5.95
Double Smokey Burger   6.75
Two Mesquite Grilled
  Patties on an Onion
  Roll w/Slaw and
  Cottage Fries
C.L.T. Grilled Chicken. 5.25
Lettuce and Tomato
  Served with Cottage
  Fries
Combo Special   9.95
  BBQ Shrimp and Chicken
  Kebobs Served with
  Choice of Two
  Vegetables

Main Plates

Slow Roasted Chicken   8.95
Texas BBQ Chicken   8.95
BBQ Baby Back Ribs   11.95
Blue Crab Enchiladas   9.95
Southern Fried Brook
  Trout   9.95
Spicy Fish Cakes with
  Three Tartar Sauces   8.50
Chicken & Shrimp
  Chimichangas   9.95
Chicken Fried Steak   10.95

Rest Area Ahead

Black Bottom Pie   2.50
Key Lime Mousse Torte   2.50
Walnut & Raisin Bread
  Pudding with Whiskey
  Sauce

Call for Free Delivery

Figure 4-3. Route 66. Menu.

of any menu analysis. In this case, it appears that the menu is strong. The fault, more than likely, is in the execution and presentation of the recipes. A two-week menu analysis is designed to uncover the facts which common sense can't reveal. Why spend valuable time to discover that nothing is selling well? In other words, don't undertake a menu analysis simply for form, as a business show. Use your cooking and management experience to solve all the obvious problems; then begin the in-depth analysis.

Highlights

The ultimate aim of quality control is to build popularity, for without it, sales and profits lag.

There are four major areas where quality can sag: purchase and handling of raw products, house recipes, food preparation procedures and line production.

An essential part of a chef's job is to be the standard bearer of high quality.

The chef should make it a part of the daily schedule to check in food, to observe handling or storage procedures and to make changes where necessary.

Use an informal marketing technique to discover which menu items are least popular.

The house recipes must be analyzed for correctness of style or execution and, of course, taste before any real strides can be made in the production process.

Up to fifty percent of the flavor can be lost during the preparation process by inept cooking techniques.

A chef in the first months on a new job or a chef spot checking problems should be a taster.

Often the main source of poor quality from the line is a person whose attitude or skills are below standard.

The most effective change comes from on-the-spot implementation of style and technique.

In smaller restaurants where the sales volume is lower, it is better to monitor the popularity of menu items by looking at the dupes, noting which items do not sell, and following up with daily inspection of the refrigerators to spot stale goods.

In larger restaurants, those which sell over a million dollars' worth of food a year, quality control needs assistance from management tools which are much more formalized.

The two-week menu analysis provides a data base from which policy can be formulated.

No one should affect a major menu change without first answering the questions: What's really selling? and Where do we make our money?.

The menu analysis is best used to pinpoint best-sellers, poor sellers and profit or loss centers. These data are then used to define a menu's future.

Profit centers are those items on the menu whose popularity and profitability coincide.

Waste is the primary cause of profit loss.

Additions and deletions should never constitute a radical turnaround in the menu's style, but rather a slow movement by the addition of profit items, or popular ones, and the deletion of unpopular and unprofitable dishes.

towel. Place on a high flame. Add one-fifth of a cup of soya oil. Add one tablespoon each of garlic and ginger. Brown evenly. As the oil begins to smoke, add equal portions of zucchini, squash, pepper and onion—one cup uncooked. Toss over a high heat, searing the vegetables until cooked medium. Deglaze with about one-quarter of a cup of the sherry-soy sauce mixture. Sprinkle in one rounded tablespoon of sesame seeds and toss. Remove the bluefish from the oven. Pour sesame primavera over the fish. Garnish and serve.

PAN-FRIED REDFISH ROLLED IN CORNMEAL WITH COLD TEX-MEX TARTAR SAUCE

Fish

5 lb. Redfish Fillet	½ dozen Eggs
1 lb. Cornmeal	2 T Salt
5 cups Cooking Oil	1 T Tabasco
2 cups Flour	

Use the three to four-ounce fillets of redfish. They usually have no bones. The skin may be left on. Store covered with a damp towel until service. Makes ten to twelve orders.

Beat the eggs well, adding the salt and tabasco to the blend. Cover and refrigerate.

Tex-Mex Tartar Sauce

1 cup Mayonnaise	¼ cup Sweet Pickle Relish
2 cups Sour Cream	1 Lemon
¼ cup Chopped Red Onion	1 T Lea & Perrin's Sauce
¼ cup Chopped Jalapenos	1 T Salt

Place the mayonnaise and sour cream in a mixing bowl. Add the jalapenos, red onion, pickle relish, Lea & Perrin's Sauce and salt. Squeeze in the juice of one lemon, but be careful that the texture doesn't get too runny. Another note: Whenever using pickled jalapenos, wash and dry them well. Occasionally the pickle juice will break or overseason the sauce.

On the Line. Heat cooking oil in a saute pan until it begins to smoke. Quickly place the rolled red fillets in the oil, skin side up. (The fillets are first patted with flour, dipped in the egg mixture and rolled in cornmeal.) Cook until brown, then turn the fillets. Cook at a moderate heat. When the fillet is white and flaky, plate it. Garnish and add a large dollop of Tex-Mex tartar sauce.

Pastas

FETTUCINI WITH GARLIC, FRESH DILL AND PIMENTO

5 lb. Fettucini	4 cups Olive Oil
1 cup Chopped Garlic	1 cup Butter
2 cup Fresh Dill	6 T Salt
2 cups Pimento	3 T White Pepper
1 cup Soya Oil	

If dried pasta is used, blanch it in oiled, salted water until it is almost al dente. Cool, drain and oil it. Store any pasta, dry or fresh, covered with a damp towel to keep the ends from drying.

Chop garlic. Clean the dill. Julienne the pimento. Place the separate ingredients in containers; cover and refrigerate until service. Makes twelve servings.

On the Line. Using a pasta strainer, drop one portion of fettucini into slowly boiling water which has been oiled and salted. At the same time heat one-third of a cup of olive oil in a saute pan. Add one tablespoon chopped garlic. Brown at a moderate heat. When pasta is al dente, drain the water and add it to the pan. Add two tablespoons of pimento and two tablespoons of dill. Toss. Add one tablespoon whole butter, and sprinkle on salt and pepper. Plate and garnish.

ASPARAGUS TIPS, PROCUITTO AND LINGUINI CARBONARA

5 lb. Linguini	1 lb. Whole butter
6 bunches Asparagus	12 Eggs
½ lb. Procuitto	6 T Salt
3 qt. Heavy Cream	3 cups Grated Parmesan

If dried pasta is used, blanch it in oiled, salted water until it is almost al dente. Cool, drain and oil it. Store any pasta, dry or fresh, covered with a damp towel to keep the ends from drying.

Peel the asparagus stems and cut away any hard, pulpy ends. Cut each stalk on a slant, making pieces about one-half inch long. Wash and drain. Saute the asparagus pieces in whole butter with a sprinkle of salt and pepper. Cool, cover and refrigerate until service.

Slice the procuitto thinly, then cut into julienne strips. Cover and refrigerate until service.

Makes twelve servings.

effort of an experienced chef, cheap cuts of meat can be made more valuable. Expensive cuts can be made to yield a greater than average profit, as in the recipe for Sirloin Steak Kebabs.

Other principles which are valid guidelines, despite the occasional exception, are:

1. Time invested in preparation reduces the food costs.
2. Labor costs can be used to supplant food costs.
3. Using food from cans or the freezer adds to the cost when compared to executing recipes from scratch.
4. Elaborate recipes call for more steps and ingredients. With few exceptions, moderately complex recipes are likely to cost less than complicated ones.

Dishes which cost less than twenty-five percent to produce are hard to find. Great care should be taken to ensure that each of these dishes served is at peak quality every time. Careful attention to the quality of high-profit specials is imperative. This will keep sales strong, allowing the dish to be repeated as often as once a week. It also increases the likelihood that a high-profit dish will move to a permanent place on the menu. There its effect on the profit picture will be even more positive.

Highlights

Every dish on the menu is responsible for generating a profit, and the more profit each dish makes, the more profitable the restaurant is.

Chefs must be able to create their own high-profit recipes based on changing variables.

To create profitable dishes, start with economical kinds of meat, fish, fowl, pasta and vegetables.

The most ordinary Continental restaurant could excel by offering creative alternatives.

Moderately priced restaurants compete through their quality, price and service.

Small amounts of expensive items can be used to dress up dishes, thereby raising the sale price without substantially raising the cost per plate.

Another variation of economical food usage is to use items which sound expensive but are not.

Through the skill and effort of an experienced chef, cheap cuts can be made more valuable.

Expensive cuts can be made to yield a greater than average profit.

Careful attention to the quality of high-profit specials is imperative.

Chapter 6

CREATING TRENDY DISHES

Introduction

Trendy food is popular food which either becomes or embodies a specific style of cooking and presentation. At one time, even the classics were trendy. And perhaps when they're rediscovered in some now remote corner of the world, they'll become trendy again. So much depends on opinion. A large part of what is considered trendy is a purely personal observation. In the Southwestern United States, for instance, Tex-Mex cuisine is "hot." In the Southern states, no one is thinking about any form of Mexican food. Soulful seafood still reigns.

Trends Are Temporary

Trends tend to come and go with the seasons; in that sense, they contain an element of a fad. But as with any fad, a given number of people will remain enthusiastic indefinitely. Vegetarian restaurants are a good example of a fad which had a heyday, peaked and subsided. The best of the vegetarian restaurants are in business today because they are smartly competitive and sell their food expertly.

During a trend's hour in the spotlight, every Continental restaurant with a specials list will be offering a dish or two in the new style. Customers will love them, demand them, then six months later turn up their noses. That's the nature of a trend.

The Components of Creativity

A chef must be able to offer trendy dishes while they're popular, and not simply as a copy artist. This is either the hardest or easiest thing for a chef to master, depending upon talent, experience, training and creative ability. The last element is the elusive one. It's the quality that separates the master chefs from the mechanics. But think about the situation realistically. What is the possibility that the grand chefs of the world are creative geniuses? Perhaps only a few of the very top ones are. What percentage are they of the total number of chefs? Five percent? Two percent? That controversial question is better left to the French and Italians. The point is that at least ninety-five percent of the world's chefs are not creative geniuses, but they use creativity in very ingenious ways. While it is not possible to formulate the process of creating trendy dishes, the elements of the act are definable and totally accessible to the professional chef.
The components of the process are:

A chef's creative experience.
The season of the year.
The raw goods.
The style of the trend.

These four components form the process of creating trendy dishes. Consider each aspect separately to understand how they work together.

A Chef's Creative Experience. This is certainly the most important component because it exerts the greatest influence on the creative process. If a chef has no experience with food (see Chapter 1 for a complete discussion on developing creativity), the creations will be too derivative or eclectic. These are opposite ends of the spectrum; at one end, the derivative dishes are uninspiring, possibly boring; at the other end, the eclectic dishes are too obscure to be popular.
Years of work and dining experience give master chefs the creative edge in developing their dishes. But the odd truth is that the majority of chefs lack creative flair no matter how long they have been in the business. There needs to be an awareness and concentration on the chef's part to incorporate the elements of creative discipline into the daily routine.

The Season of the Year. The popularity of a dish will depend largely on how well it is targeted for the seasonal eating habits of the local customers. If it is July 1 in Miami Beach, creatively stuffed pork roasts will never appeal with the power of a seafood entree. Basic common sense applies here. Choose foods and styles which enhance the qualities of the season. The best way to keep abreast of seasonal foods is to ask questions at the vegetable market. Fruits and vegetables are the most seasonal of foods, and the purveyors will be happy to discuss what's in season, available and cheap.

The Raw Goods. Trendy cuisines have some specifications as to what types of food can be adapted to fit the style. These specs are classic and are found in the culture and history of the region from which the trend originated. Calves liver wouldn't be used as a Cajun dish, for example. The Cajuns didn't have much access to this raw good, or recipes for it would be included with other repertoires. Therefore, the raw goods—fish, meats, fowl, vegetable, fruits and spices—must be from the same genre. If the spices and herbs are not available, it may be impossible to create in that style. It is often the products available which dictate how a dish will be prepared. When the chef opens the refrigerator looking for leftovers to sell as creative specials, he or she may see oysters, have ginger and leeks on hand, and get several good ideas for Chinese or California Nouvelle creations. The creative process is aided by the abundance of raw goods in all varieties.

The Style of the Trend. The more a chef knows about a style, the better the creations will embody it. Cooking techniques change from trend to trend. These techniques, which may be as simple as putting flour in first instead of last, may radically change the taste of the dish. Regional techniques give classic flavor and authenticity to a chef's creations. The best way to learn about them is by firsthand experience. Cooking and eating in the region or with a master from the region are the best ways. But as one chef noted, "You don't have to be from Detroit to know how to drive a car." An experienced chef can get a feel for a style from a cookbook, an article or simply a look at a menu. But the more chefs investigate, the greater their range will be, and the better the creation will taste.

Presentation does half of the job for the chef. If it looks Chinese on the plate, the chances are much greater that it will taste Chinese. How could anyone expect to capture the essence of California Nouvelle cuisine while serving huge quantities of food garnished with a parsley sprig? The guidelines for presentation are as strict as the cooking techniques. In fact, they are rooted in the same history and culture. It is the way meats, fish, fowl and vegetables are cut before being cooked which dictates how they will look on the plate. Original garnishes add the finishing touch by uniting the elements of the dish, enhancing its culture and adding color.

Marketing Concepts

The creative process must be complemented by an equally mysterious feat—the naming of the dish. Madison Avenue has turned marketing into a science of appeal and competition. On a local scale, a chef's menu competes with other menus by exhibiting the hidden qualities of a "hot" cuisine. Trendy dishes have to capture that certain flair which is part of the reason why the public has embraced it—it sounds interesting, appealing, appetizing, different and exotic. The name has to work for the chef. It must establish the quality of a particular trend with words, just as the presentation does with vision and the technique does with taste. Each trend has its trick phraseology. This will become clearer in the examples which follow.

First, a few do's and don'ts in naming dishes. Never confuse obscurity with originality. Obscurity does not sell; it confuses. A dish must be easy to envision. There are exceptions to the rule; Shrimp Tschopatoulos, for example is a well-known Cajun dish with a weird name. But that is a classic dish and name. A chef's creations are not promoted by a formal, proper name.

The easier a name is to read and pronounce, the better the dish will sell. Alliteration in names is a powerful selling tool.

Consider the following examples. Each are creations which work within the specific trendy cuisines: Southwestern, Cajun, Caribbean, California Nouvelle and American Chinese.

Southwestern Cuisine

BAKED CHICKEN BREASTS MONTEREY WITH SUPREME SAUCE SERVED WITH SPANISH RICE PILAF

From the same tradition which brought us Chicken Kiev and Chicken Cordon Bleu comes the Southwestern version—Chicken Monterey. This dish is trendy because its ingredients are recongized by customers as being part of this new cuisine. The presentation style is classic except for the Spanish Rice Pilaf, which adds the taste, color and look of the Southwest.

Chicken

10 lb. Chicken Cutlets	5 lb. Bread Crumbs
2 lb. Monterey Jack Cheese	½ cup oregano
1 cup Jalepenos	½ cup Basil
1 cup Cilantro	¼ cup White Pepper
5 lb. Flour	¼ cup Salt
2 Dozen Eggs	

Trim all fat and cartilage from the chicken breasts. Divide them at the breastbone seam. Pull off the tenderloins and retain for another day. Pound out the breasts with a meat hammer.

Shred the Monterey Jack and toss it with the chopped jalapenos and cilantro. Place two to three tablespoons of cheese mixture inside of a chicken cutlet. Fold and mold the chicken around the cheese to make a uniformly stuffed breast. Place on a metal sheet pan. Stuff each breast. Place the pan in the freezer.

For the breading process, prepare three trays: one with flour, the second with whipped eggs and the third with bread crumbs, fresh oregano, basil, salt and pepper.

After one hour, remove the chicken breasts from the freezer. Bread them through the flour, egg wash and bread crumb trays. Finish each breast. Refrigerate until service. Makes fifteen servings.

Supreme Sauce

2 Whole Chickens Chopped	2 Chopped Shallots
2 bunches Parsley	½ cup Olive Oil
1 bunch Celery	1 Qt. Heavy Cream
3 balls Garlic	¼ cup Salt
2 Leeks	¼ cup White Pepper
2 White Onions	1 cup Flour
1 cup Clarified Butter	1 Liter White Wine

Roast the chicken and mirepoixed vegetables for one hour in a very hot oven. Heat the olive oil in a stock pot, and then brown the chopped shallots. Add the chicken and mirepoix. Stir often. When the pot and ingredients reach a high temperature, add the flour. Continue to stir. Add the clarified butter. Stir to brown the flour, and then add the white wine. Add two gallons of hot water. Reduce the liquid until about two quarts remain. Add the heavy cream. Boil. Salt and pepper to taste. Reduce to proper thickness. Strain and retain until service.

Peel, seed and medium chop the cucumbers. In a stainless steel bowl, mix the cucumbers, jalapenos, shallots, sugar and salt together. Add the lime juice. Refrigerate.

On the Line. Heat two ounces of bacon grease in a saute pan. Flour two chicken cutlets and place them in the pan. When brown, turn the breasts. Add one-half tablespoon of chopped garlic and one-quarter cup each of onion and green pepper. Sprinkle on one teaspoon of oregano and one teaspoon of paprika. Add one tablespoon of cilantro and one-half cup of tomatoes. Finish the chicken breasts on a sizzle platter in the oven. Toss the vegetables and cook over a very hot flame. Deglaze with four ounces of rum. Reduce. Add two ounces of tomato juice. Salt and pepper to taste. Pour sauce on a plate. Place the chicken breasts on top. Garnish with lime wheels and a dollop of cucumber relish.

CARIBBEAN SEAFOOD FRICASSEE WITH BAKED COCONUT YAMS

To use the words *Caribbean* and *seafood* in the same name is almost redundant, so strong is the association between them. *Fricassee* sounds French but is familiar to Americans. In all, the name combines popularity, familiarity and the exotic. Execution of the recipe is practically the chef's prerogative. The baked coconut yams add a Caribbean touch to strengthen the presentation.

Fricassee

2 lb. Medium Shrimp	6 cups Sliced Mushrooms
2 lb. Sea Scallops	1 cup Chopped Parsley
2 Monkfish Fillets	1 qt. White Wine
1 cup Chopped Garlic	1 qt. Heavy Cream
1 cup Chopped Shallots	¼ cup Salt
4 cups Flour	Louisiana Hot Sauce
Clarified Butter	1 Dozen Eggs

Peel, devein and wash the shrimp. Wash and drain the scallops. Clean and portion the monkfish into one-ounce pieces. Makes twelve servings.

Yams

10 Yams	1 tsp. Salt
4 cups Coconut Cream	1 tsp. Pepper
¼ cup Butter	1 tsp. Ground Clove
¼ cup Honey	½ cup Shredded Coconut

Peel the yams. Boil them slowly in a pot with the coconut cream, butter, honey, salt, pepper and clove. Cook the yams until tender, remove
them from the liquid and cover them at room temperature. Continue to
boil the liquid. When it becomes a thick syrup, strain the mixture into
a container.

On the Line. Roll the yams in shredded coconut and bake in a low oven
until the coconut is toasted. Heat the butter in a saute pan. Lightly flour
two- to three-ounce portions each of shrimp, scallops and monkfish.
Place in the hot butter. Add one-half tablespoon each of garlic and
shallots. Add one-half cup of mushrooms. As the seafood nears doneness,
deglaze with three ounces of white wine. Add salt and hot sauce to taste.
Reduce. Add four ounces of heavy cream and one egg yolk.

Plate the fricassee and garnish with a sprinkle of chopped parsley. The
baked coconut yams should be served on a small side dish with their
syrup. Garnish with a cinnamon stick.

GRILLED TENDERLOIN MEDALLIONS IN ST. MARTENS HERBES
WITH SCALLIONS AND RICE PILAF

For beef lovers who haven't tried the latest taste trend, this recipe offers a
gentle introduction to the region, with two of its classic tastes and the
traditional technique of marinating meats with herbs.

Tenderloin Marinade

2-7 lb. Filet Mignon	½ cup Malt or Balsamic
2 cups Pureed White Onion	1 cup Dark Rum
½ cup Pureed Chive	1 T Paprika
¼ cup Pureed Garlic	½ T Cayenne
½ cup Fresh Oregano Leaves	1 T Salt
1 cup Peanut Oil	

Trim the fat and sinew from the two tenderloins. Then cut four-ounce
medallions.

Prepare the marinade by mixing together the onion, chive, garlic,
oregano, oil, vinegar, rum, paprika, cayenne and salt. Liberally coat each
medallion with the herb marinade. Cover and refrigerate until service, at
least two hours. Makes approximately twelve servings.

Pilaf

3 cups Rice	1 T Curry Powder
3 bunch Scallions	½ lb. Butter
1 cup Chopped Red Bell Pepper	1 T White Pepper

Rinse the rice to remove dirt and excess starch. In a sauce pot, saute scallion rondelles and chopped red peppers in a little butter. Add the rice and cover with water. Add the remaining butter, curry, salt and pepper. Steam until tender. Keep warm until service.

On the Line. Remove two medallions from the marinade and scrape off excess herbs before placing the meat on the grill. Cook to the correct temperature (rare to well). Plate the steak and a portion of rice pilaf. Garnish with chive shoots.

California Nouvelle Cuisine

PASTA PARCELS STUFFED WITH CHICKEN, MUSHROOMS AND RICOTTA IN PIMENTO CREAM

All the classic principles of pasta which the Italians developed are at work here, but in a new and very delicate way. The parcels resemble green gift packages, exactly like popcorn balls which have been wrapped in cellophane and tied at the top, leaving a gathered bunch of wrap spraying up in a cone shape. The unusual look of the pasta is further complemented by a chicken stuffing and the light cream sauce—both departures from American pasta habits.

Parcels

4 sheets Spinach Pasta	1 T White Pepper
6 3-lb. Chickens	1 cup Cognac
2 cups Fresh Basil	½ cup Chopped Garlic
8 cups Chopped Mushrooms	½ cup Chopped Shallots
4 cups Riccota	1 T Salt
1 cup Parmesan	4 oz. Oil

Season and roast the chickens until the meat is pink. Allow them to cool. Remove all skin, bones and cartilage. Break the meat into small pieces with your hands. Do not chop. Heat two large saute pans with olive oil, shallots and garlic. When the oil is hot, add the mushrooms. Toss over a very high flame. Salt and pepper. Add the basil and chicken. Continue to toss over the high flame until the natural juices from the mushrooms and chicken have evaporated. Deglaze with the cognac. Flambe. Take the mixture away to cool, and then shred the chicken and mushrooms into a large mixing bowl. Add the ricotta and parmesan. Mix well. Salt and pepper to taste.

Find a round object six inches in diameter to use as a pattern. Roll out the pasta sheets, one at a time, and cut as many pasta circles as possible, approximately forty-eight pieces. Spoon a golf ball-size dollop of stuffing directly into the center of a pasta round. Wet a pastry brush with lukewarm water; then wet the outer rim of the pasta round to one inch wide. Delicately lift the pasta, wrapping the balled stuffing and crimping the top as described. This recipe makes twelve servings of four parcels each— smallish portions, just right by Nouvelle standards. Refrigerate until service.

Sauce and Garnishes

4 qt. Heavy Cream	1 T Salt
1 dozen Egg Yolks	1 T White Pepper
½ cup Chopped Shallots	4 pints Cherry Tomatoes
1 T Chopped Garlic	1 cup White Wine
½ cup Pureed Pimento	2 T Butter

In a sauce pan, slowly heat the butter; then brown the garlic and shallots. Deglaze with all of the white wine; then reduce out the liquid. Add the heavy cream, salt and pepper. Add the pureed pimento. Bring to a boil and reduce for one-half hour. Strain the cream into a large mixing bowl. Stir frequently until the cream has cooled evenly. Whip in the egg yolks, which have already been beaten. Keep cool until service.

Peel the cherry tomatoes, being careful to retain their shape.

On the Line. Prepare a poacher of salted water deep enough to submerge the parcels. Cook the pasta al dente. Heat a portion of the pimento cream in a small sauce pan. At the last moment, drop four cherry tomatoes into the sauce to warm them. Plate the sauce. Plate four parcels. Drop one cherry tomato into the cone of each parcel. Serve.

GRILLED CHICKEN SUPREME AND WHITE EGGPLANT MARINADE IN FRESH BASIL AND TOMATO COULIS

One of the interesting trademarks of Nouvelle cuisine from any region is the lengthy, descriptive language of its titles. The wording is very plain even though some of the words, which are French, appear proper or ultrasophisticated. They are merely foreign, and their meanings are common. For example, *supreme* refers to a boneless chicken shoulder, and *coulis* means crushed.

The grilling of chicken has been taken up by California Nouvelle chefs with such enthusiasm that they seem to have invented the technique. In fact, it embodies an aspect of the trend—light, healthy dining.

Chicken and Eggplant Marinade

6 Large Roasting Chickens	1 bottle California Chablis
24 White Eggplants	1 qt. Olive Oil
2 White Onions Chopped	1 T Salt
4 Lemons	½ T White Pepper

Cut twelve supremes, with the skin and first wing bone left on. Prepare the marinade by mixing the wine, oil, salt, pepper, garlic, roughly chopped onions and lemon cartwheels. Trim the sides of the eggplants by cutting two flat planes of skin away. Leave a band of peel and the dark green stem on the eggplant.

In a deep square pan, lay alternating levels of chicken, marinade, eggplant, marinade and chicken. Cover and refrigerate for at least two hours. Makes twelve servings.

Coulis

24 Ripe Tomatoes	½ cup Red Wine
¼ cup Chopped Garlic	¼ cup Butter
¼ cup Chopped Shallots	2 T Salt
1 cup Fresh Basil Leaves	1 T White Pepper
1 T Sugar	

Peel, seed and roughly crop the tomatoes. Heat the butter in a large sauce pan; then brown the garlic and shallots. Add the tomatoes. Keep the pot covered to retain as much liquid as possible. When the tomatoes begin to boil, add the red wine, sugar, salt and pepper. Cook slowly, covered, until the pulp is tender. Cool and puree. Cut the basil leaves into fine slivers and add them to the coulis. Refrigerate until service.

On the Line. Grill one supreme, two white eggplants and two lemon wheels from the marinade. Grill each separately, to be done simultaneously. Heat eight ounces of coulis and plate in a flat circle. Nestle the supreme on the coulis. Flank with the eggplants. Connect with lemon cartwheels. Garnish the supreme bone with a paper foot. Serve.

POACHED HALIBUT FILLET BOUCLEE IN EGGS OF SALMON
SERVED WITH LEEKS PUREE

Part of the appeal of any trendy cuisine is the snob factor or, more nicely put, how sophisticated the food appears to the aficionados. California Nouvelle relies on upwardly mobile, well-traveled, credit card–carrying clients. Not everyone wants an elegant dinner in chi-chi surroundings, but those who do are willing and able to pay for it. The word *bouclee* speaks to these types of customers. It reminds them of their business trip to Paris or prepares them for that future vacation to the South of France. Today, Americans enjoy being experts on food. Gourmands will try every new restaurant which pops up to interpret the latest trend. Using the peculiar terms of the cuisine—like *bouclee*, which literally means "buckled" but is translated as "smothered"—enhances the entertainment factor.

Ingredients

5 lb. Halibut Fillet	2 qt. Fond de Poisson
2 oz. Salmon Eggs	6 Large Leeks
1 cup Creme Fraiche	1 Pound Butter
12 Egg Yolks	¼ cup each Salt and White Pepper

Portion the halibut into six- or seven-ounce servings. Wash, dry and cover. Refrigerate until service. Beat the egg yolks and mix well with the creme fraiche. Keep refrigerated.

Trim the leeks, and cut them into thin rondelles. Wash and dry. Saute the leeks in butter, salt and pepper. Puree the leeks. Cool and put aside until service.

Fond de poisson is a heavy fish stock, almost a base. Its recipe can be found in most French cookbooks. These ingredients make twelve servings.

On the Line. Poach one portion of halibut in the fond. While poaching, ladle four ounces of fond into a small sauce pan. Heat to a boil.

Heat one-half cup of leeks; then form it into a fluted mountain on a plate. Keep hot. Place the cooked halibut next to the leeks. Remove the reduced fond from the heat. Add one tablespoon of salmon eggs and one tablespoon of the creme fraiche-yolk mixture. Stir rapidly and pour over the fish. Garnish with three peeled cherry tomatoes.

and reduce over a high flame until the liquid has completely evaporated. Add the heavy cream and reduce for thirty minutes. Add the ginger and continue to reduce at a medium boil. Salt and pepper to taste—a little spicy. Strain the cream, and allow it to cool. Add beaten egg yolks to the cream. Refrigerate. Saute the asparagus tips in butter and salt until they are half-cooked. Cool, cover and refrigerate until service.

On the Line. Pour eight ounces of ginger cream into a saute pan. Heat over a moderate flame. After the cream begins to boil, add the lobster meat— four ounces—and one-half cup of asparagus. Cook the pasta in salted water, strain well and add to the boiling cream. Toss, plate and garnish with toasted almonds.

Trends and Profits

Trendy foods are one of the glamorous aspects of cooking and restaurant work. The majority of cooks and chefs seem to prefer working in chi-chi, white tablecloth dining clubs rather than the more retail-oriented eateries, even if it means making less money or working more hours. The professional chef must be wary of the prime pitfall of trendy foods and restaurants —popularity does not not necessarily mean profit. The trendiest restaurants in town this season may be gone in two years.

If you are considering adding a new type of trendy dish to the specials list at your restaurant, consider these cautionary postscripts to the glory of trendy cuisine. Test trends slowly with a few specials which can build a following. Create enthusiasm for trendy dishes by considering them the vanguard; do your best work there. And at the beginning of a trend, underbuy rather than overstock. Plan on selling the product out. Waste for any reason is disastrous. Too much unwelcome originality can ruin a restaurant's profit picture first and its following second.

Highlights

Trendy food is popular food which either becomes or embodies a specific style of cooking and presentation.

Trends tend to come and go with the seasons; in that sense, they contain an element of a fad.

A chef must be able to offer trendy dishes while they're popular, and not simply as a copy artist.

While it is not possible to formulate the process of creating trendy dishes, the elements of the act are definable and totally accessible to the professional chef.

A chef's creative experience exerts the greatest influence on his or her ability to keep up with trends.

Regional techniques give classical flavor and authenticity to a chef's creations.

The guidelines for presentation are just as strict as the cooking techniques.

The names of trendy dishes have to capture a certain flair, making them sound interesting, appealing, appetizing, different and exotic.

Never confuse obscurity with originality.

The easier a name is to read and pronounce, the better the dish will sell.

Alliteration in names is a powerful selling tool.

Popularity does not necessarily mean profit.

Too much unwelcome originality can ruin a restaurant's profit picture first and its following second.

Chapter 7

CREATING MENUS AND OPENING RESTAURANTS

Introduction

Menu creation is the first crucial step toward a viable business—the profitable restaurant. It involves the most sophisticated skills a chef can offer and is the most difficult area to master. Menu creation, like dish creation, is an exciting part of the chef's career. Ironically, it is reserved for only a minority of chefs. Many owners of new restaurants consider menu design easy and approach it with little or no experience. Perhaps that is the reason so many restaurants open and close without having a chance of success. Only one out of three newly opened restaurants is believed to survive. The other two-thirds are failures, representing lost life savings and investment dollars. Sad.

Menu design should be a team effort, initiated by the most qualified member of the group—the chef or chef-owner. But regardless of who leads the design work and how experienced the owners, managers and their spouses are, there is a procedure which will ensure that all the key business questions are being addressed. When followed, the creative process has a structure to which its energies can conform. The primary purpose of menu design is to produce a package which will please the customers. Too often new owners are more concerned with satisfying egocentric needs.

Image Definition

"Too many cooks spoil the broth," an old adage which brings to mind a warning for restaurateurs. Too many owners spoil the restaurant. Equal partners waste time and money by vacillating on fundamental issues such as whether to have pink tablecloths and leopard-spotted walls or no tablecloths and dark walnut walls. Both ideas may or may not work. A chef designing the menu has the awesome task of pinning down the owners on all the details. This should be done in the acquired location, with all the owners present. Most new menus can't be designed until the location is actually obtained because food preparation depends significantly on equipment and spatial limitations. Often the style of the menu is limited by the amount of ready cash available for equipment and the existing kitchen's layout and equipment. Despite the owners' declaration to build Club Chi-Chi, when they see the price, realism will lower their expectations.

Call a special meeting to address the agenda. The format is a question-and-answer period chaired by the chef, whose purpose is to define the front-of-the-house operation. Include these questions on the list of essentials: What is the restaurant's name? The number of seats? How close together are the tables? Tablecloth or covering? Flowers or vases? Will there be a bar? How big? A juke box, tapes, radio or television? Sports or music? What kind of music? Video games? Men or women waitpeople? How will they be dressed? Will there be other wait staff? Will there be a host or maitre d'? Is there a specific motif and decor? Finally, and perhaps the most important issue, what kinds of customers do the owners want to attract? Will they be coming from the neighborhood or from further away? How will they dress? Will they pay with cash or a credit card?

The chef not only gets a feel for what the restaurant will be like when it's actually running, but also helps the owners make these decisions at an early stage, when they are valuable in putting together a cohesive, viable concern. To use an extreme example, how many customers would be attracted by a barbeque ribs and chicken restaurant which had a tuxedoed maitre d' and white tablecloths? A funny combination, but others just as foolish are made often enough to keep the failure ratio at two to one.

Develop a picture of the prospective customers based upon the information given by the owners. And if there are changes in policy, be certain that you are informed.

Kitchen Design

Spatial limitations are a prime consideration which should be completely understood before the first appetizer is decided upon. The ideal situation is to know the space first, but there are many new restaurants which have developed their entire menu before the space is located—restaurant groups, for instance. In those cases, the kitchen must be designed to serve the menu. That may or may not be easy. Sewage lines, heating ducts and doors have a way of being in the wrong place and of being immovable.

Take the case of *MUMBLES,* an expanding restaurant group. The menu is set; each location uses virtually the same layout, with very few changes (see Fig. 7-1). The menu is large, and so must be the line crew: three or four cooks and an expeditor at peak business hours. For the Mumbles kitchen design, the chef must consider each aspect of food handling: ordering, receiving, stocking, hot food preparation, cold food preparation, prepared food storage, line storage, the types of line cooking done, i.e., the cook's stations needed, pickup points, the dupe system, entrances to and exits from kitchen, the dishwashing, dish storage areas and garbage disposal. Because all these activities go on at once during a restaurant's operation, they must live in a chef's imagination, enabling the chef to see everything going on at once. The goal is a massive organization of the kitchen tasks which occur both simultaneously and in series.

The existing space for Mumbles had three obstacles—two square columns containing sewage pipes and electrical conduits, and the rear exit, which could not be moved because of the building's lobby (see Fig. 7-2). Additionally, the owner insisted that the wall from the rear exit toward the restaurant front must stay. That left enough space to fit a full-line kitchen, but the preparation kitchen and main storage areas had to be allocated to the basement level. The projected seating capacity was two hundred fifty.

The designing chef obviously needs a complete understanding of the equipment. Without it, wasted space is always a problem, which will be manifested as an equipment problem. No matter what the chef does, there won't be enough room for all the necessities. In the Mumbles renovated kitchen (Fig. 7-2, After), there is sufficient work space for a saute cook (1), broiler cook (2), salad cook (3), expeditor (4), pot washer (5), and dishwasher (6). The floor staff is free to move between the two doorways, picking up food, dropping off dishes and picking up glasses. Even beverage and bread areas could be designed into the service setup area. The greatest shortcoming, from the line cooks' point of view, was the shortage of ample refrigeration space inside the kitchen itself. The preparation kitchen in the basement is a common though awkward solution to spatial limitations. It causes wasted time during peak business hours. The

American Express, MasterCard and Visa accepted

mumbLES

| | Downtown 603 2nd Ave. and 33rd St. 889-0750 | Midtown 1491 2nd Ave. and 78th St. | Uptown 1682 3rd Ave. and 91st St. 427-4355 | 772-8817 |

APPETIZERS

Soup du Jour	cup 1.95	bowl	2.50
French Onion Soup Gratinee			2.95
Chili	cup 2.50	bowl	2.95
topped with cheese	cup 2.75	bowl	3.50
Mussels Possilipo			5.25
Mozzarella Pizziola			3.50
Stuffed Potato Skins			3.95
Chicken Fingers			4.50
Stuffed Mushrooms			3.75
Mexican Nachos			3.50
Guacamole and Chips			4.25

SALADS

Fresh Spinach Salad			5.25
Chef Salad			5.95
Caesar Salad			4.95
House Salad	small 2.25	large	5.25
Mumbles Chunky Chicken Salad Platter			6.75
Tuna Salad Platter with Avocado			6.75
Taco Salad with Guacamole			6.95
Quiche du Jour and Salad			6.25
Choice of Dressings-Bleu Cheese .50 extra			

SANDWICHES

Mumbles Over-Stuffed Club Sandwich with french fries	6.25
Bacon, Lettuce and Tomato	4.25
Grilled Cheese with bacon and tomato	4.95
Chicken Salad topped with melted cheese	6.50
Tuna Salad topped with melted cheese	6.50
Fresh Turkey Sandwich	5.95
Grilled Chicken and Avocado	5.95

PASTAS

Fettucini Primovera with Olive Oil and Garlic	7.50
Fettucini Alfredo with Broccoli	7.50
Linguini with Shrimp and Broccoli	8.50
Linguini with Clam Sauce	7.25
Linguini with Veal and Mushrooms	8.95
Tortellini Carbonara	7.95
Linguini Marinara or "House" Style	6.25
PASTAS SERVED WITH HOUSE SALAD	

MUMBLEBURGERS

A 1/2 pound burger served on a toasted english muffin with lettuce, tomato and pickle

Hamburger	4.95	platter 5.95
Cheeseburger	5.50	platter 6.50
Bacon Cheeseburger	5.95	platter 6.95
Chili Burger	5.95	platter 6.95

MUMBLES PUB FAVORITES

Mumbles Sliced Steak Sandwich	6.95
Cheese Steak Sandwich	7.50
Chopped Steak - 16 oz.	7.95
Honey Dipped Fried Chicken	6.50
Fish and Chips	6.50
Omelettes	
A fluffy omelette made with the ingredient of your choice, and served with a toasted english muffin	4.95
Each additional ingredient	.75
PUB FAVORITES SERVED WITH FRENCH FRIES	

ENTREES

Sauteed Chicken Breasts and mushrooms in a marsala wine sauce	8.95
Sauteed Chicken Breasts Francese	8.95
Chicken Parmagiana	8.95
1/2 Broiled Spring Chicken	8.25
New York 16 oz. Boneless Shell Steak	14.95
Jr. Shell Steak	11.95
Grilled Swordfish Steak with soy-mustard-ginger dipping sauce	10.95
Broiled Filet of Scrod	7.95
Shrimp Parmagiana	8.95
Loin of Veal Medallions in fresh Basil Piccata	9.95
Loin of Veal Medallions and Mushrooms in fresh Chive and Mustard Brown Sauce	9.95
Veal Parmagiana	9.25

ENTREES SERVED WITH SALAD AND CHOICE OF VEGETABLE

SIDE ORDERS

French Fries	small	1.75	large	2.25
Onion Rings	small	1.75	large	2.75
Fried Zucchini	small	2.95	large	3.95
Garlic Bread				1.25
Linguini				3.25
Broccoli				1.95
Stir-Fried Vegetables				1.95
Baked Potato				1.75

BEVERAGES

Coffee	1.00	Soda	1.00
Tea	1.00	Milk	1.00
Iced Coffee	1.25	Iced Tea	1.25
Brewed Decaf	1.25	Juice	1.25
Hot Chocolate	1.50		

FROZEN TROPICAL DRINKS

Pina Colada, Melon Colada,
Strawberry Daiquiri, Banana Daiquiri
in season

INTERNATIONAL COFFEES

Irish, Mexican or Jamaican topped with whipped cream	
Espresso	1.75
Cappucino	2.25

DESSERTS

Cheesecake	2.75
Pecan Pie (hot or cold)	2.75
Carrot Cake	2.75
Chocolate Chocolate Chip Cake	2.75
Dessert du Jour	

MUMBLES BRUNCH

Every Saturday, Sunday - till 4 PM
3 eggs, any style, with choice of steak, bacon, ham or sausage.
Served with french fries or home fries and a toasted english muffin or bagel

Eggs Benedict	7.95
Eggs Florentine	7.95
French Toast, with bacon or sausage	7.50
All of the above served with Bloody Mary or Mimosa and coffee or tea.	

Side Orders:	Steak	1.95	Ham	1.50
	Bacon	1.75	Home Fries	.75
	Sausage	1.75	Bagel	1.00

CHEF'S SPECIALS LISTED ON THE BLACKBOARD DAILY

Figure 7-1. Mumbles. Menu.

112

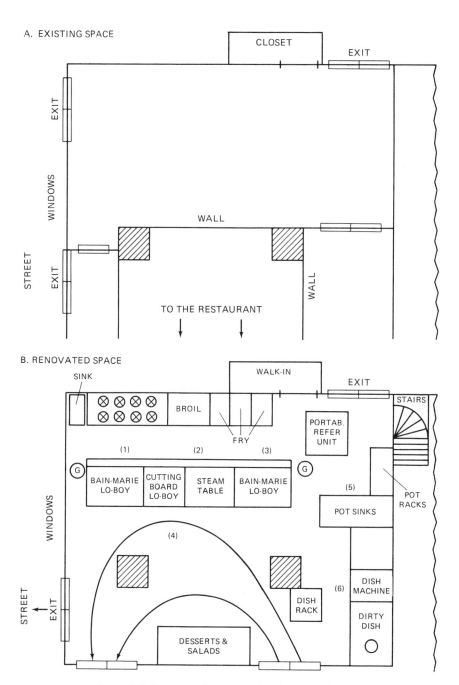

Figure 7-2. Restaurant kitchen design: before and after.

113

closet converted into a walkin kitchen is large enough to supply one service with prepared foods. The portable refer unit moves into play during the rush hours to keep foods at arms' reach.

The key to efficient kitchen design is knowledge of the number of staff work spaces necessary to handle the peak volume. It is also necessary to know what each worker needs in terms of accompanying machinery, overhead work space, tabletop space, refrigeration square footage and garbage access. A poorly designed kitchen will be a grueling work experience from which the best cooks will run.

Another type of kitchen-menu design problem is the reverse of that of Mumbles restaurant, where the kitchen must fit the menu. In this common opening situation, the restaurant kitchen has been completed. The designing chef is inheriting an old kitchen which the new owner would like to paint and put into service. Its limitations can be great enough to cause a business failure, which may well be why the space was available in the first place.

Consider THE SPOT—a restaurant venture by first-time owners who have found a good, cheap location. They hope to have $100,000 as seed money, but as yet have no budget. In other words, there may be considerably less capital. The kitchen is small and the equipment filthy (see Fig. 7-3).

The owners have decided to attract a casual, late-night crowd. In their words, they would like a menu with a lot of appetizers an interesting things to eat—"sort of like California Nouvelle, but with bigger portions." The owners favor Southwestern cuisine. The designing chef's dilemma is to reconcile a very idealistic menu with the reality of a runway kitchen smaller than that of most private homes.

The first step is to list the pluses and minuses in the kitchen's layout and equipment. The single strong point is the grill. It is modern and can be the center of a repertoire such as the owners desire. The major drawback is the lack of space, and the primary space stealer is the dumb waiter. Another problem is the lack of sufficient refrigeration to support the grill and the stove during peak hours. (The Spot seats fifty inside, with a planned outside cafe seating of twenty.) Also, the fryolator in the center of the pickup window is a monolithic obstacle stubborn enough to make any chef pull out his hair in frustration.

The first order of business is to have a heart-to-heart chat with the owners. Be honest; let them know that without $10,000 to $20,000 for renovation, the kitchen will never service seventy seats. In the scheme of things, $10,000 is considered a bargain. The new kitchen layout must be agreed upon before menu design begins. There must be logical working stations for two cooks and a dishwasher. One cook will never be able to serve seventy customers during a rush period, nor will two cooks be able

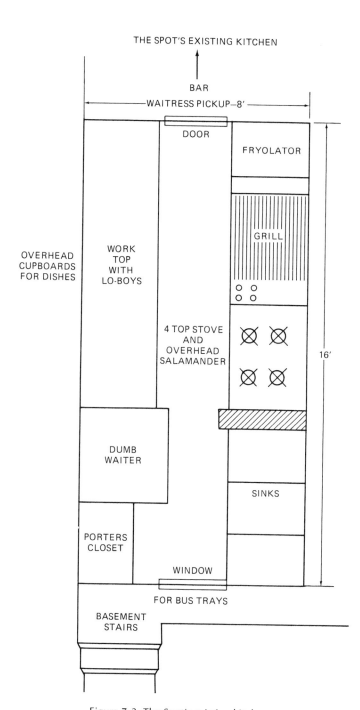

Figure 7-3. The Spot's existing kitchen.

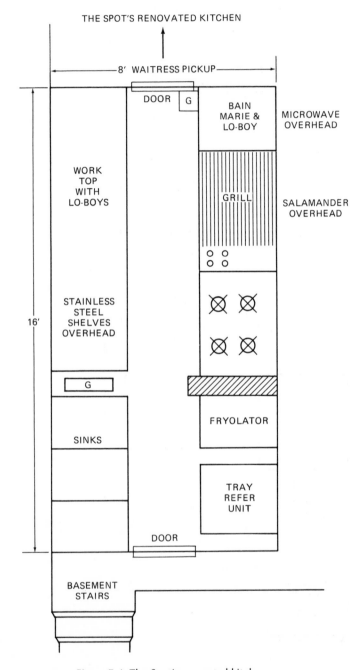

Figure 7-4. The Spot's renovated kitchen.

to work by crossing paths in the narrow space. Study the remodeled kitchen in Fig. 7-4.

With the limited space, it is essential to remove all noncooking elements. And in this instance even the dumb waiter must go. Originally conceived as a timesaving device to link the upstairs and downstairs kitchens, it is simply too cumbersome. The remodeled plan provides sufficient space for one or two cooks to use the equipment and prepare the plates. The added refrigeration is designed for backup and to ease the pressure around the pickup window by making the first countertop refrigerator less crucial to the production process. After a reasonable kitchen layout is assured, menu design can proceed.

The Market Survey

The location of the new restaurant may or may not be prime; what kind of food can be sold successfully becomes the essential question. A chef can contribute to the profitability of an opening by correctly gauging the area's potential market in terms of both numbers of customers and types of cuisine. Virtually every location can become a successful restaurant of some sort. Take a realistic look at the area, and decide what kind of restaurant it can support. You will need a map or sketch of the area and a pad to take notes about the other restaurants in the neighborhood, town, or other field of competition. The field of competition is the area in which the potential customers live.

The procedure is simple. Visit all restaurants in the area. Mark them on the map with a number code, so that the location can be matched with the information which must be noted for each coffee shop, drive-in, pizzeria, and restaurant. List the hours of operation, style of cuisine, types of food, price range from appetizers to entrees, number of seats, ambiance, types of customers and number of customers.

After the preliminary visit to record all the basic data, plan to make several return visits to gauge the area's peak business hours. Find out which restaurants are doing the heaviest volume and when. It will be very clear which places are most successful. Consider them the direct competition. Try to define the reasons for their success.

Analyze the data from a purely objective point of view, with no preconceived opinions about what style of restaurant will work. Is there an overabundance of one or two styles of cuisine? Are there any open markets? Perhaps the location is prime for a popular or trendy cuisine which has proven successful in other areas.

Trends

What's hot around the country? How will national and regional eating trends affect this restaurant? Gain complete knowledge of the current trends by studying recent issues of food and regional magazines.

How does the restaurant compare geographically with the areas of influence? For instance, do the restaurants in the field of competition feel the effects of trendy restaurants in New York, Los Angeles, San Francisco and other large cities? If there is an influence from the big towns, how quickly does it take a style to reach the popular stage in the area? Perhaps trend-setting menus are risky business for the target location. Are there any trendy restaurants at all in the area? If not, is that because some have been tried and have failed? Trends are peculiar to each geographic region and need special investigation to measure their viability.

The Owner Factor

No owner wants to finance a restaurant in which he or she has no say about the menu's design, and rightly so. This is one of the rewards of ownership—to see a bit of oneself reflected in the new creation. For most owners, the new restaurant is their baby—a product of years of dreaming, working and saving. A chef's role should consist of developing a creative menu in the owner's image. The best way to do that is to ask a lot of questions about what kind of food the owner likes to eat. Is it different from the kind the owner wants to sell? How? Is it possible to have a meal in an existing restaurant which serves the kind of food that the owner wants in the new place? That is the ideal meeting place. It will inspire the owner and give the chef a perfect opportunity to ask specific questions as the food is brought to the table.

Involving the owner in the early stages of the creative process is of primary importance. Not only does it strengthen the owner–chef working relationship, it lessens the possibility of false starts on the menu. These are time wasters which can necessitate the duplication of effort. Find out what the owner is specifically looking for, after the information discussed in the previous sections is understood. Then if the owner is moving into a dead end, such as a pizzeria on a block that already has two, or a Tex-Mex restaurant in an area with four successful competitors, the chef will be in a position to speak authoritatively if the situation is negative.

Later stages of the menu creation are better left to the chef. If the owners have had professional experience in cooking or marketing food, however, their participation must be encouraged. But for the most part, a

chef working alone will design the most comprehensive plan for attracting customers—in other words, creating a tantalizing menu. After the first
draft of the menu is completed, the owners can decide to reject specific
dishes, sauces or other items. But if the chef has worked closely with the
owners to know their desires in a menu, the approval/changes process will
be short and smooth.

The Profit Motive

As a final step before beginning to work on the actual menu, print a card
in bold letters and place it in front of you wherever the menu will be
created. The card should read, "Who will buy this dish?" Answer this
question for every dish created in order to understand the entire range of
clientele which the menu must satisfy. What time of day will men, women
or children order the dishes being designed? Are these results in keeping
with the desired customers and hours of operation?

By including individual dishes with popular followings, the overall
menu will be popular. The experience gained through years of eating and
cooking good food is as important as that achieved by years of selling
food. Ironically, a dish can sound delicious, look tantalizing and taste
marvelous, but not sell well. Some basic ingredients have limited appeal.
No chef can make liver a big seller no matter how it is prepared. Be
reasonable and business minded in the design process. Even in the most
creative moments, when the chef's inspirations take form, one must remember that a restaurant is still a buy-and-sell business. If the menu does not
establish a clientele, there will be no restaurant in which to create.

The pricing of menu items will be discussed at length in Chapter 10.
Remember at this early stage not to design a menu with such expensive
ingredients that it ends up pricing the restaurant out of the market.

La Grande Carte

For an experienced chef, menu design begins as a process of elimination.
There are some styles and dishes which are immediately ruled out because
they conflict with the background data which has already been gathered.

Review all the information one last time, and begin to make decisions.
Consider the following factors: image, kitchen design, the market, trends,
the owner's desires and the profit motive. These variables should now
have definite characteristics and should be uppermost in the chef's mind
as he or she gets a feel for the menu's design.

Often one restaurant will have more than one menu, including separate cartes for breakfast, lunch, dinner, brunch, supper and snacks. Factors which influence this choice of presentation are kitchen space, style of cuisine, formality of service and individual preference. The important matter is that a group of menus for one restaurant should be uniform in style, price and presentation. They must appeal to the same clientele, but at different times of the day or week.

Start with a list of every sort of course category conceivable: appetizers, soups, salads, pasta, fish, meat, fowl, vegetables, breads and sandwiches. Make another list which indicates the way the food is cooked—on the grill or broiler, for example. For each menu, some items will be completely wrong; eliminate them. Proceed with the remaining categories by estimating the number of dishes desirable in each.

After deciding on the appropriate menu categories, begin to build a list of specific dishes. What remains is the purely creative process of menu design, one of the most rewarding aspects of a chef's career. The interpretation of data and the application of experience result in as many different conclusions as there are qualified chefs to do the design.

For example, reexamine The Spot's situation. The kitchen has been remodeled. The owners' wishes are known: "Like California Nouvelle, only with bigger portions." Add a definite Southwestern influence. A late night crowd. Casual. Singles. Pink tablecloths and leopard-patterned walls. Friendly atmosphere with great music. "Some spontaneous dancing would be happening," reports one of the owners. They're in it for the money, but would like to be trendy too. The only hitch is the market survey. While the neighborhood is capable of supporting one more restaurant, it is in fact in an area undergoing gentrification, the best and busiest existing restaurant is right across the street and it has a Cajun-style menu. It would be senseless to start another similar style of restaurant, i.e., Southwestern, so close to a strong competitor. The neighborhood is upwardly mobile, but the population concentration hasn't reached its peak. In a year or two, after the streets have been completely renovated and the coops filled, the area will need a sophisticated restaurant with pink tablecloths and California Nouvelle cuisine. For the present, an informal atmosphere, service and menu will score the most direct hit. If the owners are adamant about having Southwestern or California Nouvelle food because that's their only reason for getting into the business, they must be made aware of the likelihood that they will fail. Nevertheless, the trend toward Southwestern food is strong and may not conflict with Cajun, so they opt for that style anyway. The chef's creation satisfies them perfectly (see Fig. 7-5). It's sophisticated, fun food with California Nouvelle and Southwestern influences.

The Spot

Nachos Chips with 3 Salsas 4.25

Shrimp and Black Bean Sopa . . . .
                                 cup 3.95   bowl 5.95

Skewed Chicken and Pineapple Glazed with
  Honey-Garlic 4.95

Fried Calamari with Basil & Tomato Sauce 5.25

Bourbon Marinated Filet Mignon & Mushroom
  Kebobs 5.95

Camembert and Roasted Red Pepper Toasties . . .   3.95

Deep Fried Monterey Jack Sticks
  w/Hot Tomato Salsa 4.50

Salad Dressings: Balsamic Vinegar & Olive Oil
                   Vinaigrette
                   Creamy Roquefort
                   Honey-Mustard

Warm Chicken Breasts over Greens with Papaya,
  Avocado and Pine Nuts 6.95

Shrimp Taco Salad 8.95

Fettucini in a Country Pesto Sauce 7.95

Sauteed Chicken Breasts in a Tomato Coulis
  with Fresh Cilantro 8.95

Spinach Raviolis with Seafood Stuffing in a
  Shallots, Fresh Tomato, Tequilla and
  Cream Sauce 9.95

Grilled Swordfish Steak with Avocado and Red
  Onion Relish 10.95

Super Burger Deluxe 4.95
  A Super-Lean 8 oz. Burger on an Onion Roll
  Served with Hand-cut French Fries,
  Lettuce & Tomato

House Salad A La Carte 1.95

Desserts: Coconut Chocolate Mousse Cake. 3.25
         Hazelnut Raspberry Torte 3.25
         Dessert Au Jour 3.50

Figure 7-5. The Spot. Menu.

Selecting Equipment

Opening a new restaurant is not simply a matter of designing the menu. A chef has to decide on the right equipment and tools. What to buy and how many of each are decisions which can save time and money during operation or just the reverse—cause wasted motion and supplies. Keep abreast of the changes in equipment, and discover new machinery by reading the ads in restaurant business magazines and by visiting equipment showrooms.

Nothing saves time like a complete checklist. Every chef should develop their own. Appendix B is a list which in most cases will include every piece of equipment and tool that a new restaurant will need. The list is so comprehensive that many items will be unnecessary for specific restaurants. It is especially useful when preparing the budget for the new owner.

Budgeting Future Expenses

The budget is a breakdown of projected expenses—in this case, the costs for restaurant or kitchen startup. It should be organized like an outline, with major categories and elements from those categories specified in a few words.

The following is the basic budget format, including headings.

Kitchen Startup Budget (October 1987)

CATEGORY		COST	TOTALS
I. Renovation			
A. Kitchen Design		$1,000.00	
B. Electrician		2,000.00	
C. Gas—Plumber		2,000.00	
D. Carpenter		2,000.00	
E. Cleanout		500.00	
F. Heavy Equipment		10,000.00	
	Total		$17,500.00
II. Menus			
A. Design By:			
1. Chef		$1,000.00	
2. Graphic Artist		200.00	
B. Mechanical Layout		200.00	
C. Logo Design		800.00	
D. Printing		500.00	
E. Covers		200.00	
	Total		$2,900.00

III. Restaurant Supplies
   A. Kitchen Tools (Pots, $3,000.00
      Pans, etc.)
   B. Plates, Bowls, Cups   2,000.00
   C. Silverware   500.00
   D. Paper Products   2,000.00

            Total $7,500.00

IV. Food Stocks (Through the First Week of Operation)
   A. Meat $3,000.00
   B. Fish   1,400.00
   C. Dry Goods   5,000.00
   D. Dairy Goods   400.00
   E. Vegetables   2,000.00
   F. Pastas   600.00
   G. Breads   200.00
   H. Desserts   400.00
   I. Miscellaneous   200.00

            Total $13,200.00

V. Staff (Through the First Week of Operation)
   A. Chef $4,000.00
   B. Sous Chef   1,200.00
   C. Line Cooks   5,000.00
   D. Prep Cooks   1,600.00
   E. Dishwashers   2,400.00
   F. Porters   1,500.00

            Total $15,700.00

Total for All Startup Costs $56,800.00

This sample budget is designed to show all the items which a chef may be responsible for estimating. The dollar amounts only show the form. Although traditionally chefs do not order menus or paper goods, eventually they will be asked to do so by one owner or another. It is inevitable, so be prepared with an overall understanding of the category.

The budget can be an important owner-management tool if it is complete. If it doesn't cover everything, including miscellaneous expenses, it becomes practically useless. Be thorough when estimating expenses. Get bids if necessary. And don't forget to include the chef's wages in any startup budget. The chef will often be working for weeks before any of the other staff is hired and long before the owner or manager has set up the payroll system, so be clear in dealing with the patron right from the beginning.

Estimating Food Sales Volume and Expenses

The parameters for these estimates are wide. Many variables can cause great fluctuations in sales volume: initial fanfare, walkouts, the weather, complimentary meals to pay for poor service. A year or two after beginning, the sales volume and expenses can be projected within one thousand dollars. That estimate is based on past records. But in the first few months, and especially in the first week, the only figures available are based on the number of seats, the hours of operation and the menu prices.

Let's return to our example restaurant startup, The Spot. These are the known facts. There are seventy-five seats with the cafe and fifty seats if the cafe doesn't open. There are five lunch shifts, two brunch shifts and seven dinner shifts until 2 A.M.

Begin by calculating the average customer's food bill. The menu is moderately priced, with entrees between $4.95 and $10.95. A straight average of entree prices, computed by adding $4.95 and $10.95 and dividing by 2, equals $7.95. This amount agrees with the concentration of menu entrees in the $7.95 to $8.95 range. Though most entrees are priced above $7.95, burger sales will more than likely keep the average lower. To this figure add $1 for beverages, $1 for desserts and another $1 for appetizers. The total is $10.95. That is the estimated average amount which will be spent by every customer who buys a full meal. The brunch dollar average per customer will be within a dollar of the brunch cost—in this case, $8.50. Thus, $7.95 is a reasonable estimate. The lunch crowd will be using the same menu, but the chef plans to run a lot of specials in the $4.95 to $6.95 range. Calculate the lunch total per customer at $6.95. With all of the estimates, the customers buying just a beverage or appetizer will not be counted as covers. The next step is to calculate the number of entrees sold during the first week. For a seventy-five-seat restaurant like The Spot, which is moving into a neighborhood with a medium lunch trade, future success must be judged on the basis of the sales volume of other restaurants in the area. The notes made during the market survey should indicate how many covers the competing restaurants are doing for each shift—lunch, brunch and dinner. The most successful restaurant, the Cajun place across the street, does about seventy-five lunches a day. A low estimate for The Spot would be twenty lunches per day. A high estimate is sixty. Rather than figuring an average, calculate both high and low to get a range. Brunches at the Cajun restaurant run approximately one hundred to one hundred and fifty on Saturdays and around two hundred on Sundays. The Spot's outside cafe will be the only one in the area, so they will score well at brunch. Estimate between ninety and one hundred and thirty Saturday brunches. Consider Sundays to be almost as busy as the competition. Estimate between one hundred and fifty and two hundred.

The best way to work up the estimate is with a chart which has a block for each shift. Fill in the estimated entrees sold—high and low figures—and then total the estimates and multiply by the dollar per customer estimates—$10.95 for dinner entrees, $7.95 for brunch entrees and $6.95 for lunch entrees.

Entree Estimates

MON.	TUES.	WED.	THURS.	FRI.	SAT.	SUN.	TOTALS	
LUNCH AND BRUNCH PROJECTIONS								
20-60	20-60	20-60	20-60	20-60	90-130	150-200	100-300	L
							240-330	B

MON.	TUES.	WED.	THURS.	FRI.	SAT.	SUN.	TOTALS	
DINNER PROJECTIONS								
80-100	90-110	110-140	110-140	130-160	130-160	80-100	730-910	D

DOLLAR ESTIMATES
100-300 Lunches × $ 6.95 per Average = $695 to $2,085
240-330 Brunches × $ 7.95 per Average = $1,908 to $2,624
730-910 Dinners × $10.95 per Average = $7,994 to $ 9,965
Total Estimated Food Sales = $10,597 to $14,674

A spread of $10,000 to $15,000 may seem gigantic, but as a guestimate, it is the best projection available. Remember, the variables are intricately woven together. The Spot's competition has a greatly fluctuating dinner volume, depending upon the day of the week. No matter how enthusiastic the new management team is, estimates for Sunday and Monday nights must be low. Again, the only way to estimate is to assess the competition's volume and then compare your possible impact with their present drawing power. Will the new restaurant be taking a slice of every other place's clientele or drawing a new crowd into the neighborhood? Is this a sure thing? Probably not; estimate low, below what the most successful competitor is doing. The Spot's estimated food sales volume of between $10,000 and $15,000 is wide but viable. The chances for great success and failure are just as wide. What if it rains all week?

First-time owners love to ask, "How much money will we make?" With the estimated food sales volume figure, this can be easily calculated. Of course, the figure is a rough estimate, but the ballpark number will be helpful to management, nonetheless. Assume a food cost of forty percent for the first few weeks; forty percent of $10,000 to $15,000 is $4,000 to $6,000. Remember, this is *after* startup costs, which may include a huge dry goods order. The first week's projections allow the owners to figure the overall earnings potential of The Spot after they have added liquor sales to the volume and subtracted their operating and fixed expenses.

Highlights

Menu design should be a team effort, initiated by the most qualified member of the group—the chef or chef-owner.

Develop a picture of the prospective customers based upon the information given by the owners.

Spatial limitations are a prime consideration which should be completely understood before the first appetizer is decided upon.

The key to efficient kitchen design is knowledge of the number of staff work spaces necessary to handle the peak volume.

With limited space, it is essential to remove all noncooking elements.

After a reasonable kitchen layout is assured, menu design can proceed.

The location of the new restaurant may or may not be prime; what can be done successfully becomes the essential question.

Take a realistic look at the area, and decide what kind of restaurant it can support.

Analyze the data from a purely objective point of view, with no preconceived opinions about what style of restaurant will work.

Gain complete knowledge of the current trends by studying recent issues of food and regional magazines.

Trends are peculiar to each geographic region and need special investigation to measure their viability.

A chef's role should consist of developing a creative menu in the owner's image.

Involving the owner in the early stages of the creative process is of primary importance.

Even in the most creative moments, when the chef's inspirations take form, one must remember that a restaurant is still a buy-and-sell business. Do not design a menu with such expensive ingredients that it ends up pricing the restaurant out of the market.

The interpretation of data and the application of experience result in as many different conclusions as there are qualified chefs to do the design.

The budget is a breakdown of projected expenses. It should be organized like an outline, with major categories and elements from those categories specified in a few words.

The only way to estimate sales is to assess the competition's volume and compare your possible impact with their present drawing power.

In the first few months, and especially in the first week, the only figures available are based on the number of seats, the hours of operation and the menu prices.

PART 2

FOOD PERCENTAGES (HOW TO KEEP FOOD COSTS LOW)

Chapter 8

PURCHASING

Introduction

This chapter highlights the often ignored partner of the creative process: the profit motive. It focuses on the largest cost of the restaurant business —food purchasing. Perhaps the owner of a four-star club is more interested in cuisine and style than the chief executive officer of a fast food chain. But be assured that the owner of Club Chi-Chi is concerned with profits and is watching the expenses closely, just as the fast food management team is concerned with quality control and image. All restauranteurs are business people.

A successful restaurant makes a profit from season to season, year in and year out. Those who profess to be in it for the glory of Haute Nouvelle are generally on their way out of business. The best-paid chefs have become excellent performers in the fields of both business and cuisine, either by taking on the dual role themselves or by working in a team with a tough kitchen manager. The more expertise a chef can apply to these two aspects, the greater the demand will be for his or her services.

The restaurant business is a cycle that begins the moment the chef picks up the phone to place an order. If that first step is ill-conceived, the profit margin begins to lose *percentage points,* a term heard as often in the kitchen as *bechamel.*

The goal is to buy the highest quality or the right quality for the lowest price. Here's how.

Forms and Procedures

New chefs must take immediate and total charge of the duties assigned only to them. Before lifting one saute pan, take some time to get organized, even if it means starting a day early. Many people on the staff are there to cook, but only the chef should order food. If others are doing this, stop them. This is too important a task to be delegated, at least at first.

Begin with a few simple procedures and forms. Write down the specifics in logical fashion. Later, after daily repetition has committed inventory lists to memory, anyone may feel confident winging it. But in the beginning, work on paper—no excuses.

In a small restaurant, the inventory may be listed on one or two sheets of paper. In that case, use a heading to make sure that all the pertinent data is there (see Fig. 8-1).

There are different ways to use the inventory sheet. (1) Group items by type—meat, fish, dairy, etc.—or alphabetically by item. (2) Group items by purveyor, i.e., everything purchased from X in a cluster. (3) List items in the order in which they are found in the storage facilities. Each restaurant is different. Find the system that works best for you and stick to it.

The "Par" column should have the minimum amounts kept on hand, as well as the maximum amounts to be ordered. Keep these pars up to date. The minimum par is the amount needed from one delivery day to the next. For once-a-week purveyors, this means that there should be at least one week's supplies on hand after the delivery man has left. How high the maximum par goes depends on the advantages and disadvantages of bulk buying for each specific item. For instance, what is the total dollar outlay? Does it amount to an extra point of food cost this month, just to save $100?

Inventory Sheet		Date		
ITEM	PAR	DELIVERY DAYS	PURVEYOR	SALESMAN

Figure 8-1.

That's not a very good sale, but here's a trick: Take advantage of sales that offer savings of ten percent by making a large purchase and withholding the payment until the next monthly cycle. This allows the savings to take full effect before the cost occurs, a perfect situation. Shelf life and storage facilities are other major considerations.

The inventory sheet works well for a small menu, but for a big operation a more streamlined approach is necessary.

Think of it as a purchasing system. Two functions will determine how a large inventory is broken down into smaller, more easily manageable classifications: first, how often a particular item should be ordered (daily, once a week, two or three times a week, or monthly); and second, which purveyor the item comes from and how often he delivers.

Frozen foods, dry goods, and all items with a shelf life of more than one week are best categorized by the purveyor (see Fig. 8-2).

Meats, fish, breads, and all items with a short shelf life, or those which are ordered daily, should be grouped together (see Fig. 8-3).

Use the bottom of the page or card to note the names of other purveyors who offer the same services or special sales.

Five- by eight-inch cards kept in a recipe box are the handiest. All the chef has to do is flip through the cards, pulling out those on whatever

XYZ CORP. (MARTY OR STEVE) Call Monday for Wednesday Delivery	212-555-1632
ITEM	*PAR*

Figure 8-2.

FISH			
ITEM	*PAR*	*PURVEYOR*	*PHONE NO.*

Figure 8-3.

WEEK ENDING OCTOBER 2				
MEAT	FISH	DAIRY & VEGETABLES	DRY GOODS	BAKERY
WS 115	FN 237	JJ 37	PP 32	BUX 90
CW 862	VP 121	DRU 273	CAL 725	ENG 72

Figure 8–4.

purveyors and daily inventory items are needed on any specific day. The unnecessary paperwork is automatically eliminated.

One of the chef's primary responsibilities is to check prices. For a new chef, an extensive round of comparison shopping is essential because inherited buying procedures are not usually the most economical. Begin by making a list of the twenty-five largest items, those which account for the most dollar volume in purchases. Get three price quotes for each item; then compare the prices, but don't be fooled into accepting the lowest quote. Check the goods by getting samples and cooking with them. It is surprising how often the best goods cost less. Have the patience necessary to find that great price.

Set a budget, a goal, an amount of spending which is the top limit. This should be based on food sales. For instance, if the restaurant does $20,000 worth of business per week in food sales and the owner has used the number forty percent frequently, the goal is a spending ceiling of $8,000 per week.

Use a weekly purchases sheet to divide the items into five or six major categories. Then, as the goods arrive, record the dollar amount of each invoice and the purveyor's initials (see Fig. 8-4).

At the end of the week, total each column. Write the number in the box at the top of each column. Keep this data on hand while recording other important numbers, too. Even on the bottom of the same sheet, keep a daily record of food sales. If the restaurant has a lunch and dinner service, there will be a change in the registers and a record of sales. Write them down (see Fig. 8-5).

DAY OF THE WEEK	DAY SHIFT	NIGHT SHIFT	SUBTOTALS
MONDAY	584	1216	1800
TUESDAY	622	1987	2609/4409
WEDNESDAY	892	2207	3099/7508
THURSDAY	725	1612	2337/9845

Figure 8-5.

With purchase and sales figures on the same sheet, it's simple to get an idea of what the week's food cost percentage will be. Watch for a pattern to emerge. After four weeks of analysis, or even sooner, estimate the spending limits for each category. Base these goals on the first four weeks of actual spending, but modify them to come under the boss's desired food percentage. However, setting a goal that is $200 less than the previous week's doesn't necessarily make it a reality.

What is the lowest food cost percentage that anyone has ever gotten at the restaurant? Can it be beaten? This system is a first step toward getting the spending under control. It provides the big picture. How the goal is achieved is part of a later chapter.

Each type of product purchased is unique, including many problems and facets. It is helpful to consider them separately.

Meat and Fowl

John, a salesman for a large meat distributor, calls on Chef Andre, the new chef at Restaurant des Etoiles. John says, "I see you buy chopped meat. How much do you pay? We have the best-quality beef, and I'd like to give you a really good price."

What does Chef Andre do?

Tell John he's too busy to talk prices?

Tell John he's happy with his meat man now and say good-bye?

Tell John his current price?

John the salesman is on a fishing expedition. He'll pump Chef Andre for information and then offer prices a nickel a pound lower just to get a new account. John knows that his main office will eventually push the price back up; that's not his concern.

Here's how Chef Andre should handle the situation. (Incidentally, the chef of a busy restaurant can expect to meet these salesmen regularly — as many as five a day.) He should not assume that he has the best meat man in town, nor should be take a chance on buying inferior meat. He can call the salesman's bluff with a trick question — for instance, by asking John to quote a price for a specific brand of bacon or turkey breasts. John will say, "What are you paying now?" Chef Andre should answer, "I asked you first." Nine times out of ten, the salesman will answer, "I'll have to call you later. I've got to check this price in the office." Chef Andre should be willing to talk prices, but only about those items on which there can be absolutely no question of quality. Cyrovaced meats completely trimmed or brand names of a specific weight are the safest.

When the low-ball salesman walks in the door offering to sell the whole cow for a nickel off, don't be perturbed. Run the meeting with these goals in mind, and then cut it off quickly. The goal is to make a large purchase of a safe item on credit. To be too busy for every salesman who comes in is the same as saying that there is no room for improvement. An attitude like that comes from a poor manager.

From the regular meat man, the absolute minimum to expect is unvarying quality and next-day service at market prices. In any given area, there are several meat distributors who have built their businesses on just such principles. Another tough part of the chef's job is to find them. But once they have been found, plan on developing a long-term relationship with them.

Variables that influence the price also determine how much work or handling the meat will need. Are any fat, trim or bones included in the per-pound price? How long will it take to clean it up? What is the bottom line, the yield, the price per pound after handling? Does a trimmed, more expensive cut end up being cheaper?

Every menu calls for different grades and types of meat. Experiment with likely alternatives, not just to find the cheapest possible cut. Sometimes a better cut costs the same or even less.

Fish

There are two categories of fish to think about: the ones on the menu, which must be kept in stock, and those used only on the specials board.

Generally, when a fish purveyor's business becomes large enough to handle all types of seafood at the lowest prices, the service begins to slip. It's best to use a number of companies. One may have excellent prices and fresh quality for the restaurant's menu items. Use him for these fish, and get to know the other kinds of seafood he gets at a good price. But for variety of catch and price, call around. Get to know salesmen at two or three other markets whose quality can be trusted.

An important word of caution: Always ask for the fillet price. This is the price without the head, bones, etc., which is usually double the whole-fish price. It is a much more accurate gauge of the final per-plate cost.

Get to know the types of seafood indigenous to the local area. Find out their seasons, and use them often. This is the type of fish to have on the menu.

Generally, frozen fish are not as desirable as fresh ones, but some may prove better. South American shrimp, a frequently frozen item, are cheap and of top quality. This is one of the few seafoods which can be purchased in bulk at a saving. Liberal freezer space pays for itself. Experiment with different types of frozen fillets, lobster, crabmeat, and so on.

Dairy Products

Selection, freshness, price and dependability are the important variables when dealing with milk companies. Does Company X handle all the items used in the restaurant? Do the products arrive with a freshness date four or five days away? Are the prices in line with those of the local milk industry? Does the company deliver precisely what was ordered and on time? The answer to each of these questions should be yes.

Vegetables

Some vegetables spoil or brown quickly, especially in the summer months. Others last for over a week without problems. Have a vegetable company that will deliver at least six days a week, no matter how small the order. It is a good idea to stock only enough of the highly perishable vegetables to last for one day. Then, rather than guessing what will be sold during the dinner rush, presuming that the chef works days, call in the vegetable order first thing in the morning. Next-day delivery from the vegetable company is a must. Many provision purveyors will supply vegetables, dry goods, meats, virtually everything. Of course, they ask a higher price for some items, so be careful. But it's a good idea to do a small percentage of the purchasing from such a supplier. Bulk purchasing of vegetables is possible, though it usually requires calling a day ahead to an independent operator or larger company—one that either has a warehouse in the local market or a truck that goes there every morning. Make two, sometimes three heavy purchases a week from this type of purveyor. This purchasing strategy is ideal for getting the lowest prices and the freshest product. It's simply a matter of finding the purveyors to work with.

Vegetable companies seem to have as many salesmen in the field as meat companies. In addition, it is certain that, once a week, someone with a van full of tomatoes, garlic and zucchinis will show up with a great offer. These people are generally more trouble than they are worth; freshness is too important a factor to risk. But if a super deal comes along, take it, provided the goods can be inspected. Allow no sight-unseen purchases from these fellows. If a salesman keeps showing up—or, what is even more perturbing, keeps calling—do something like this: Get him to quote a losing price on one or two items, and then order as much as the restaurant will use before it goes bad. Don't order anything else, though; that will encourage the salesman. Without a full list of items to deliver, the vegetable company will lose interest. Their plan is to get new accounts by offering below-market prices and then gradually return prices to normal in a few weeks. Turn their strategy against them, without being vindictive about it, and get vegetables cheaply at the same time. This works especially well during periods of peak sales.

Dry Goods

There are so many dry goods items to be purchased that the inventory list may be nearly equal in length to that of all the other goods combined. It doesn't make sense to believe that one purveyor will have the best prices for everything. Nor is it cost effective, in terms of time and salary, for a chef to get quotes for cases of salt or tabasco—items that don't cost much to begin with.

Make a list of the twenty-five items from the dry goods inventory which represent the highest dollar volume in purchases. For these items, comparison shop. Call salesmen from several companies, opening lines of communication and inviting new quotes. The key to making this strategy work is to be flexible. Divide the dry goods business among the salesmen who offer low prices on high-volume items. These salesmen will understand that when they offer a good deal or new prices, they've got a sale. When prices go up, call the salesman to ask why.

Question brand name superiority. Is the quality so much better that it is worth the drastically higher price?

Buy in bulk whenever this will make a difference in the price. A bulk purchase generally represents an amount equal to what the restaurant uses in five to six weeks.

Does the restaurant need every item on the inventory list? Are some things used infrequently? Remember, for every inventory item there is a waste factor. The more items, the more waste.

Pastas

Buying pasta is totally different from buying any other item because price has almost no relation to quality. A dried import which tastes great in Naples may cost two to three times the price of the domestic brands, but has been traveling in cardboard for a month. The taste has been lost. The best pastas are fresh, and because they're made nearby, they're cheaper, too.

With such an abundance of choices in all three categories—dried domestic, dried imported and fresh domestic—there exists the perfect pasta, one which can be handled easily in the restaurant's kitchen and meet cost requirements too.

Breads

An item as inexpensive as bread can still be a big problem. The main consideration is freshness. Selection, price and the days of delivery are important parts of the bread purveyor's job, but if the loaves don't arrive fresh, look for a new bread man. And the best baker in town may not have a sophisticated order-delivery system. The third time in a month that the delivery is wrong should be the last. If the chef has to spend time asking where the bread is, the entire restaurant is suffering.

Desserts

If desserts are priced too high, they sit. If the staff has ready access to them, they will be eaten. These considerations affect dessert purchasing. The best plan is to offer desserts as a service to the customer. Try to make a fifty percent profit on those purchased by tightening access and offering desserts from a variety of successful sellers. Fresh fruit can be dressed up to become a fancy dessert at a fantastic profit.

Desserts are not an item to scrimp on. Beware of independent purveyors who may be baking at home; they have a tendency to sell their mistakes rather than to absorb the loss as a good business practice. High-quality desserts at reasonable prices do exist, however. It's simply a matter of finding them.

Specialty Items

The little touches that dress up a menu—special oils, little cans of vegetables or fish, exotic mustards—are all very expensive. Be certain not to buy something for its unique name. Unique taste is what's important, and often that taste can be reproduced with in-house goods, domestically and cheaply.

Highlights

Purchasing is the beginning of the food sales cycle and is the greatest concentration of dollars in the restaurant business.

The chef plays a dual role as master of cuisine and profit maker.

Use a well-thought-out purchasing system, including inventory lists, purveyor information, food prices, inventory pars and shelf lives.

Budget as a means of controlling spending.

The regular meat deliverer should be able to deliver two or three staples of fresh quality without problems.

The type of fresh seafood available in each region of the country varies. Learn the varieties, their quality and their prices.

Freshness is the key when purchasing seafood.

When dealing with milk companies, the important factors are selection, freshness, price and dependability.

Learn the shelf life of each vegetable.

Use one vegetable purveyor who delivers directly from the market, without a warehouse, retail store or middleman. Use another vegetable purveyor who offers same-day delivery.

Be flexible. Buy bargains.

Dry goods are more easily substituted; therefore, more effective comparison shopping can be done.

Concentrate on getting the best prices for the highest dollar volume of goods.

Question the superiority of brand names.

Buy in bulk.

Every item purchased has a waste factor. Begin to reduce waste by not buying unnecessary items and luxury items.

Buy fresh pasta locally rather than dried imports. The taste will be better and the cost less.

Watch the bread deliveries closely. Often the best baker can't get it to the restaurant fresh.

Desserts must be exceptional.

Spend money on specialty items to dress up the menu's look or taste —but wisely!

Chapter 9

INVENTORY CONTROL

Introduction

Food handling is a significant part of a chef's duties and one which is wide-ranging, beginning the moment food enters the restaurant and ending only after it is served. The two major components of successful inventory control are implementation of the handling techniques peculiar to each item and the organization of foodstuffs within the allotted space. Let's begin at the check-in process and then move slowly through the storage system of a restaurant which handles hundreds of items weekly.

The Check-In

The drivers or delivery men who bring the ordered goods into the restaurant are, in most cases, the only company representatives a chef actually sees. Usually, orders and price quotes are given over the phone. The driver in fact is the purveyor's ambassador, and he can do a lot to ensure the success of the restaurant–purveyor relationship. It is important to have a good rapport with drivers, but it is essential to receive the goods which were actually ordered. Don't let your socializing lose its purpose. At the time of check-in, inspect each part of the order. Is it fresh and undamaged? Is it exactly the brand which was ordered or a comparable substitute? Politely explain whenever part of a shipment must be refused. A consistent pattern of acceptance or refusal of goods will educate the driver to the chef's standards, and if the chef has a developing friendship with this ambassador, he will watch out for that order at the warehouse before it leaves the dock. Often the mere offer of a sandwich can make a difference in a driver's attitude and in the chef's ability to get the goods right the first time.

Invoices should be checked for correct prices to ensure that they are consistent with the original quotes. All computations and additions should be double-checked, too. Report any errors or discrepancies to a company representative well before the end of the next payment cycle. Some companies require time to issue credit memos or, in the case of large purveyors, time to route the information through a system involving salesmen, office workers and computers.

The next and final step of the check-in process is putting the food away. The sooner this is done, the better, so any confusion about who actually does this should be minimized by a clear delineation of responsibilities. The chef may not be the person who puts the goods on the shelf, but he or she must do a follow-up inspection of the storage facilities to ensure that the goods were put in the correct place and, as is the case with most perishable goods, that they were stored properly.

Raw Food Storage

The constant arrival of raw goods necessitates a system to ensure that the old goods are being used first; this is called a *rotation process*. In a large restaurant where the food is put in storage by more than one worker and taken for use in the kitchen by any number of cooks and helpers, a clear-cut method is essential. Basically, the rotation process is a geographical game — a systemized storage and retrieval system which depends primarily upon the space available. If the storage space is poorly lit, cramped, damp and dirty, some of the product being stored will be lost or spoiled. If it is well lit, clean, dry and large enough to give each inventory item a specific place, the probability of waste is reduced. These are also the best circumstances in which to take inventories and make orders. The basic idea of the rotation system is to put the oldest goods in the place where they are most likely to be taken first. That means on top and in front. Dating the old leftovers can be helpful as a management tool to ensure that the staff is in fact using the oldest goods available. The best-protected products come in boxes, wrappers or bags and have a shelf life of about one week. These are easy to date and are usually stackable. Products like fish, vegetables and meat were not created to be stacked, however. Here more than ever, geography comes into play. If there are two, three or more walk-ins, as in large restaurants, the perishables to be used next must be kept in the box closet to the line and preparation kitchen. Keeping the new meat, fish or vegetables in the front box and the old goods in the back box will cause the system's breakdown. The storage/rotation system must be patterned after the preparation/cooking routine. The result of storage should be that after the new product is put away, the easiest, quickest way for a possibly illiterate worker to get more of it is to take the old product. Effective chefs provide the system for staff members who are hired to supply physical labor. After implementation, a chef's role in the rotation process should be one of overseer—checking the shelves to ensure that the system is being followed. With the rotation process, the old adage becomes a law: A place for everything and everything in its place.

Handling Techniques for Raw Foods

Highly perishable goods may need attention once or twice a day to ensure that they are being kept in the way which most extends their shelf life. A mistake in handling by an inexperienced staff member can spoil food within a mater of hours. Food being maintained incorrectly needs immediate attention. There are conflicting opinions about how best to store some items. For instance, two chefs I worked with spent an hour each afternoon arguing about whether or not the mayonnaise should be refrigerated. Obviously these chefs worked in Europe. In the United States, there is no question; mayonnaise is covered and refrigerated. Vast differences in storage techniques exist between the continents and even within the United States. The techniques which follow have been proven successful.

Meats and *fowl* are best kept when they are covered completely so that no air touches the flesh. Plastic bags and Cryovac work well because they lock in blood or oils which coat the meat, lubricating it from the air. Cuts of meat which are bony have less blood and can be kept covered with a wet cloth. This keeps the flesh from drying out. A temperature of 33°F is optimum to maintain freshness without freezing. Often a city health department has definate guidelines for temperature standards; be certain that your refrigeration units comply.

Frozen meats and *fowl* are often dry and gray after they're thawed. But if frozen meats must be used, remember that their shelf life is extremely short—two or three days. Keep them covered with a wet towel.

Fish which has been fileted must be covered with a damp towel to keep the flesh from drying. But it should never be wet; water replaces the natural fish oils and flavors. Trays with drain holes are made to keep fish at their peak. A temperature between 32°F and 35°F retards the aging process. Once fish has been allowed to get warm, its texture becomes mushy and its shelf life is shortened by ten to forty percent.

Whole fish last longer than filets because it has the benefit of the natural skin covering to protect the flesh from the deteriorating effects of oxygen. These fish can be kept like fillets, in trays with drain holes covered by a damp cloth, or in ice chests and drawers which have constant drainage.

Frozen fish have a very short shelf life—one to two days. It is important that thawed fillets be kept out of water and covered with a damp towel. Shrimp and other shellfish will keep a little better in the freezer because of their protective shells, but there is no doubt that the flavor will be lost. The longer fish has been frozen, the more flavor it has absorbed from the freezer air. Items which have been frozen for too long no longer taste like fish. They taste like freezer. They cook poorly too. These long-frozen fish will shrink during thawing and cooking process due to loss of water— sometimes losing as much as seventy-five percent of their original size. Frozen fish must be used with caution.

Vegetables are much cheaper than fish, meats, or fowl, but they still deserve the best care possible. They too can lose flavor and shelf life if they are not pampered. With few exceptional items which need special care, vegetables store the longest in dry, closed cardboard or wooden cases at around 40°F. The most common items which need additional handling are:

Parsley. Store at 40°F with stems down in one to two inches of water and ice on top.

Watercress. Store at 40°F with leaves down in two inches of water and ice on top.

Scallions and Leeks. Store at 40°F with roots down in one to two inches of water.

Broccoli. Store in a closed case at 40°F. Put ice on top to allow a constant drip of ice water through it.

Herbs. Store at 40°F. If the herbs have flexible living stems, place them down in one to two inches of water. If the stems are dry and brittle, put ice on top of the herb bunches and drain the water daily.

Tomatoes. Store at room temperature until the desired ripeness is reached; then refrigerate at 40°F. The longer tomatoes are kept in walk-ins, the more moisture they absorb. To preserve the flavor of tomatoes, it is much better to refrigerate them as little as possible.

Avocados. Store at 80°–90°F to ripen. If possible, use before refrigerating. Avocados absorb liquid from the damp air of a walk-in or refrigerator. Keep them tightly covered to avoid watery texture and flavor loss.

Vegetables, meats, fowl and fish which have stored well for two to seven days have a radically reduced shelf life after the preparation staff begins to carve, chop and cook. Special procedures are needed to handle them correctly.

Handling Techniques for Prepared Foods

There are three guidelines which are helpful to remember:

1. Prepare foods as close to the time they will be served as possible.
2. Guard against temperature variations. (Keep hot things hot and cold things cold.)
3. Know the effects the air will have on the prepared food in order to retard them.

Individual food products need specific techniques to ensure the best possible care. These procedures vary slightly but, for the most part, are commonsense solutions to the problems above. Professional chefs concerned with lowering food costs must have mechanical skills and experience, too. They should know which coverings react well, both physically and chemically, with the foodstuffs: plastic or stainless steel containers, paper, plastic or aluminum wraps.

Specific Problems

In most cases, restaurants with a heavy dinner volume have a low lunch volume, and vice versa. The tendency of the cooks after a busy shift will be to throw away small amounts of sauces and even cuts of meat and fish, especially if the goods were specials. The staff must be trained to save all leftovers, no matter how small the amount. Here is an example which highlights the importance of the "no throw-away law."

Chef Connie of Ma Petite Chou does approximately one hundred dinners on week nights. The menu is Continental French, and she offers a selection of seafood specials each night, totaling about six. Her sauces are an eclectic blend of Classic and Nouvelle styles. Chou's lunch trade is minimal, twenty to thirty a day. If at the end of every seafood special's life the last two orders of lemon sole, swordfish steak or sea scallops were thrown away, the effect would be disastrous. The food pc would be destroyed by this one shortsighted procedure. To highlight the importance of this problem, consider the thrown-away goods at their sale price, not their purchase price, because Chef Connie's pc is reduced by this larger amount. In one week, without her being aware of it, the night chef and other night cooks threw away two swordfish steaks, three orders of lamb chops, ten pounds of fresh pasta, three portions of bay scallops, one lobster, six chicken supremes, a halibut steak, two portions of pink salmon and three portions of cod fillet. The total value of these goods if they had been sold at market prices would have been a little over $400! During the 4.2 weeks in one month, that is an average loss of about $1800. Unbelievable, but it happens in thousands of restaurants every night at closing time. What does Chef Connie do? Unfortunately, the solution involves clerical work, and most chefs do not have a secretary at their disposal. The only way to stop this loss is by using a three-step process. First, find out how many portions came into the restaurant by counting the prepared portions. Second, make a count through the dupes to total the number of portions sold. And third, find the remaining portions and turn them into profit by revamping them with a new look and selling them at lunch. During slower shifts, two or three specials are enough to last throughout the major portion of the rush period. Fantastically creative chefs will have a repertoire of specials which can meet the challenge of their customers' needs. They can make the sale, the extra profit, and the customer happy, all with an inventive dish.

Chef Connie's preparation cooks must be trained to report the number of portions for specialty goods and high-priced goods as well. When there is a discrepancy between the number bought and sold, she must investigate — not in an accusatory fashion, at first, but to educate the staff about her new concern. This process is part of a chef's ongoing responsibilities; to stop using it, even for a month, has the effect of reversing the entire policy. Chef Connie solved her problem by establishing a new policy for the kitchen staff: No one throws anything away; that's the chef's job. If there are spoiled goods, put them aside and bring them to the chef's attention. It will never be necessary to loosen this regulation. The cooks and dishwashers will go through phases when they seem to forget that the policy even existed. Chef Connie will be required to reiterate her desires often.

Ma Petite Chou is a relatively small restaurant. Still, its losses caused by waste are proportionally great. What are the effects of this slipup on a large-volume or chain restaurant? The dollar loss would be enormous. The control techniques for large-volume stores should be include the three directives set forth earlier in this section but may also involve more sophisticated computer data retrieval systems. The chef of a computerized restaurant should be asking for daily food counts followed by weekly and monthly summaries. Higher management will expect it.

Computerized Inventory Systems

A chef doesn't really need a computer to handle the work effectively. Yet he or she may be working in a large restaurant chain which requires standardization or has an owner who insists on computerizing the inventory. For managers who prepare financial papers, the balance sheet, or profit and loss statements, a computer will save hours of work. Therefore, a chef should be expected to comply with computer procedures.

The food inventory itself will not be changed; fish will still be put on the same shelves in the walk-in; canned pimentos will be stacked where they've always been. The only change will be in the way the inventory is shown on paper. This outline of the food inventory should not interfere with the chef's ordering system. It has nothing to do with the way a chef orders. Computerized inventory sheets are lists in an outline format which standardize the way in which inventories are recorded. The computer list is an additional form used by management. The only time a chef would use it is as a list of goods to be inventoried; the sequence is important only when doing a dollar inventory for financial papers.

A chef may be asked to prepare an inventory list for computerization. Perhaps there is an existing computer program which is written with no concept of the precepts set forth in Chapter 4. As a result, the chef may waste time doing clerical work which the computer could easily do. Ask to design the inventory list for computerization around the system which is already in use for ordering and analysis. Use the same categories; meat, fish, dairy, pasta, fowl, vegetables, frozen goods, dry goods, desserts and baked goods.

Study the following example excerpts from a computerized inventory list. Note that each category will be assigned a code number, and each inventory item will have a number as well. The five- or six-digit numbers will hold the key to classification. The accountant will assign these numbers, but the chef will supply the listing in their proper categories.

EXAMPLE COMPUTERIZED INVENTORY LIST

01000	Meat
01001	Chopped Meat
01002	Ham Hocks
01003	Canadian Bacon
01004	Etc.
02000	Fish
02001	Sea Scallops
02002	Mussels
02003	Swordfish
02004	Etc.

Staff Food Consumption

Another potentially devastating problem with inventory control is the staff's consumption. They can hurt the food pc dramatically in any of three ways, and not necessarily maliciously:

1. By giving away food to customers.
2. By stealing food for home use.
3. By overeating or by eating high-priced entrees at staff meals.

Each restaurant's policies differ in these areas of concern, depending upon the tradition and attitudes of the hiring and firing team—the owner-manager and chef. Enforcement of these policies may involve several staff members, but it is essential. The chef of a restaurant with a large food pc must consider every small leak in the profitability of the operation as a significant part of the larger problem and approach it seriously. Usually when a kitchen is inefficient in a profit sense, there will be several little solutions, not one big one.

1. *Giving Away Food to Customers.* At times, it seems as though some regular customers are in collusion with the wait staff and bar staff against the house. The employees, either in their desire for tips or because they think it's the right thing to do, begin to give complimentary drinks, desserts and side dishes at will. In the normal course of business, the only reason to give free food to customers is if the service or quality has been terrible. Some manager-owners will allow a meal to be complimentary if the customer says that he or she didn't like it, even after eating the entire dish. That policy seems extremely generous. The only sure way to stop the flow of free food is to limit the wait staff's access. Make it a policy that they give a dupe, noting the table and check number for each item of food taken out of the kitchen. The cooking staff must be trained to operate according to this strict policy. They should never give out food without a dupe—never. With this procedure, the chef can do spot checks on individual items which are suspected losers—desserts, for example. Specific waitpersons can be checked, too, if they are rumored to be the culprits. Random checks of menu items and/or waitpersons are an excellent way to keep the policies effective. Again, the staff will see management's concern and respond accordingly. If particular waitpersons or bartenders flagrantly disregards management's policy, they should know that their job is in jeopardy. Firing someone for giving away food is the best way to set an example; doing this once a year is usually sufficient to make the point.

The cross-checking process is much like the quality control analysis described in Chapter 4. For example, consider how Chef Luis handled his problem. One day he came to work and discovered that the staff had gone on a pumpkin pie rampage. Four pies had been delivered, the first of the Thanksgiving season, for a total of twenty-four pieces. Luis had taken out twelve pieces at the beginning of the dinner hour, but when he returned the next morning, there were none left. Good seller, he thought. Then he checked the walk-in. The other two pies were gone too. By noon he had counted the checks and called the night chef. Sixteen had been sold. The night chef confirmed that the floor staff had run out of pumpkin pie early and asked for more to be cut. They had cut the remaining two pies. The desserts were kept in the waitress station, where the staff could help themselves, and they had. Luis wondered if all special desserts were being eaten so freely by the staff. He held no illusions about the cooks, dishwashers and porters, either. The entire staff was binging on the best. The pies had cost $36 and brought in $44—a remarkable eighty-two percent food cost. That afternoon, Luis cleared a shelf in one of the reach-ins behind the line. He instituted a dupe for dessert policy which took access away from the floor staff and gave the responsibility for control to the night cooks. His instructions were that no desserts were to be given out until a written order was placed in the kitchen. Even kitchen staff members were required to put in an employee dupe if they ate one. Of course, the manager was involved in this change in dessert policy from the beginning, and the staff members were informed accordingly.

Chef Luis reconciled dessert dupes and inventory totals every night for a week and then eased back into a routine of spot checking once or twice a week. The policy was effective. He also discovered an interesting fact. Though the desserts were selling well, the food pc for them was a high fifty percent. He analyzed his buying procedures and found that the pc could be lowered a little by buying more pies and fewer cakes. They sold equally well. Further investigation showed that dessert prices were due for an increase.

2. *Stealing Food.* One disgruntled or dishonest dishwasher can reverse the good effects of a week's worth of diligent, hard work. The food pc is, of course, directly affected. To combat this problem, there must be a working environment which helps to keep the honest workers honest. This means that owners must pay fairly and on time. The better liked the boss is, the less likely it is that the workers will steal. The owner's policies should be fair, and strict only when substantial money is involved. For example, allow workers to take home sandwiches or a beer, but anyone who is caught with a steak or lobster should be dismissed immediately.

Don't expect a worker who has been caught stealing to be rehabilitated by a pep talk. Dishonest workers must be removed. If a worker is a suspected thief, bait a trap to catch this person. For example, consider Chef Sam's problem of the disappearing shrimp.

The DOCKSIDE is a busy seafood restaurant in which shrimp is one of the key menu items. Chef Sam is using four or five cases a week of 51-60's and thirty to forty pounds of under-15's. That necessitates buying in bulk because the savings are tremendous. The frozen cases and boxes are used so quickly that it is impossible to lock up the goods during the night shift when the owner and Sam are off duty. Sam's first impression that something was wrong started with a thought about the amount of large shrimp (under-15's) that were being used. Usually the staff used about one box per night, sometimes only one-half, occasionally one and a half. But Sam thought that there had been five boxes of under-15's when he had left the day before, and this morning he finds only three. The restaurant could have used that much shrimp, but at $50 per box, it behooved Sam to check. The previous night's dupes show that less than one box should have been used. Now Sam tries to remember whether he saw four or five boxes the day before. He asks the other people who are just as involved with the shrimp as he is—the cooks who peel it. The day preparation cook is certain that five boxes were left. Sam checks the schedule to make a list of yesterday's crew. The total is five cooks, three dishwashers, two porters and fourteen floor staff. Obviously the kitchen workers have the best opportunity to steal. But a rogue busboy, someone slick and devious, a thief, could slip into the kitchen and steal a box of shrimp in any number of ways. The other telling factor is motive. Perhaps the dishwasher's family is living on hamburger helper, and he wants to give them a treat. Or the night chef is giving a little dinner party, and jumbo shrimp will be the entree. Hunger, greed, or any other emotion could spur the larceny. How does the chef eliminate suspects?

Chef Sam must consider the box of shrimp gone. He will never recoup that loss. What he has to do now is to proceed with the idea of dissuading the culprit from doing it again. The first step is to put up notices on the refrigerator and freezer doors in all necessary languages which explain the situation. "Food has been missing. Anyone caught stealing will be fired immediately!" Perhaps the owner's signature will help strengthen the chef's position. The same day the signs go up—which should be the day the theft is discovered—Sam makes it a point to talk to every kitchen worker present on the fateful day, even if he has to call them at home. He must ask them the pertinent questions, not to accuse or elicit a confession but to gain information. It is possible that someone saw the theft and will report it when asked. The chef can narrow down the time of the theft by asking, "How many boxes of shrimp did you use last night? Who got shrimp out of the freezer last night? How many boxes of under-15's did you see in the freezer last night?" A confidential opinion may be offered by one of the cooks at this point. Listen carefully because there may be some evidence or fact to back it up. Personal opinion isn't enough to convict anyone, however. With the staff on notice, they will be watching each other and the thief will stop, at least for a while. If the thief's motives are strong enough, however, when the time seems right, he or she will try again.

When the second box of shrimp is stolen, the problem becomes critical—something must be done. A larger restaurant corporation may rely on lie detector tests in order to point a finger at a likely suspect. These tests are not perfect; the results may be misleading. Should the worker still be fired? If the chef is reasonably certain of the person's guilt, the answer is yes. But the Dockside has no intention of spending money on polygraphs. It is up to Chef Sam to plug the leak. The manager-owner wants action. He totals the sales return on one box of shrimp, $150, and multiplies by fifty weeks. A year's worth of sales loss equals over $7550! The pressure is on. Sam begins to feel personally insulted. Again he gathers the facts. The new investigation narrows the suspects list to three, but Sam really thinks it's Bobby, one of the night cooks, who has a history of drug abuse. There is no hard evidence, just a feeling that Sam has—he doesn't trust Bobby. What if it isn't Bobby? Perhaps it's one of the dishwashers, and Sam just thinks it's Bobby. The solution can't be dictated by rules; there are too many variables involved. For instance, is Bobby the best cook on the night line? Same decides that someone has to go. He fires Bobby for poor attitude and the reflection of it in his presentation. Bobby is surprised but not shocked. He has obviously been fired before. Sam tells the staff that he didn't trust Bobby.

Chances are that Sam has fired the thief. If not, he has cleaned house a little. This may be one of the hardest jobs a chef must do, but in such a serious situation, business becomes a test of strength. In the case of a union house of minority group involvement, firing Bobby may cause a lot of problems. Other solutions, such as extensive security arrangements, will be necessary.

3. *Overeating at Staff Meals.* In Europe the tradition is set: Employees eat family style at noon and evening meals. The food is prepared by one of the younger chefs, who takes great pride in presenting a meal of distinction, even if the chef provided lamb kidneys that night. European chefs decide on staff meals; therefore, they have total control over costs. A few restaurants in the United States have adopted this tradition. Depending upon

whether the owner and chef desire to offer a good meal to the employees, the practice is success or a failure. In those restaurants where the chef gets rid of old food at staff meals, there is resentment.

Most restaurants serve their employees a la carte, to individual order. In this case strict policies defining the staff's allowed price range or the entrees available are necessary. The owner-manager and the chef need to decide on the rules together. Because the successful enforcement of this policy will depend upon discipline, both the kitchen and floor staffs need to know that the edict has come from the highest authority. One of two ways can be used to delineate staff and nonstaff meals: (1) a dollar dividing line, i.e., a menu price above which the staff may not order—$7.95 for example; (2) a hands-off list of entrees or items, such as no shrimp, lobster, steak or lamb chops. The management should post a list of staff meal rules where it can be seen by all personnel. Infractions of these rules can and should be cause for termination. Occasionally, the owner-manager will find it necessary to use harsh tactics in order to reinstill discipline. Without it the staff can quite literally eat up the profit.

Special dishes which are offered to the customers on a one-time basis in limited amounts should be forbidden to the staff. However, the staff members may want something different. Management can modify its policy by offering those items forbidden under the staff meal rules at an employee discount—half price, for instance. This has the effect of strengthening the policy by offering a satisfactory solution for everyone.

The kitchen staff often feels exempt from staff meal rules even though the manager may want them to be included. The cooks and dishwashers have such ready access to the food stocks that a more realistic approach is wise. Instead of specifying no steaks, no specials, and no lobster, for example, the chef should set an example of modest taste. Another effective control is to ask for a dupe on the spindle whenever a kitchen worker eats something expensive.

Chef Gene came to work one morning to discover that the shell steak stock was dangerously low. His restaurant, THE BLUE MIDNIGHT, wasn't even in its busy season. It bothered him that he had been so far off in ordering, so he investigated. A quick dupe count and reconciliation with the purchase records showed almost an entire shell missing. He confirmed with the preparation cook that fifteen small shell steaks had been cut and wrapped at the beginning of the previous night's service. Seven had been sold. Six were missing. Chef Gene began to ask the morning staff, individually and without pressure or threat: "Did you have a steak today?" Two porters, two dishwashers and two preparation cooks all answered yes—steak for breakfast. Chef Gene called an impromptu kitchen meeting. The foolishness of six cooks eating steak for breakfast was so blatant that the offenders themselves had to laugh. It was easy for them to see that the situation had to change. Gene asked for their cooperation. Whenever they wanted a special piece of meat or fish, they were to ask him. Nine times out of ten he would agree, provided that the requests were reasonable, but he had to be the clearing house. The staff agreed, and the rule worked so well that he extended it in various forms to all the kitchen workers. At night and on weekends, on any shift when Gene wasn't available, the chef in charge had the authority to approve special meals. That policy, coupled with the employee dupes which notified Chef Gene that a special had gone to staff, allowed him to control food costs in a potentially expensive area.

Highlights

The two major components of successful inventory control are implementation of the handling techniques peculiar to each item and the organization of foodstuffs within the allotted space.

Invoices should be checked for correct prices to ensure that they are consistent with the original quotes and have been computed correctly.

A chef must do a follow-up inspection of the storage facilities to ensure that goods were put in the correct place and, as is the case with most perishable goods, that they were stored properly.

If storage space is poorly lit, cramped, damp and dirty, some of the product being stored will be lost or spoiled.

The basic idea of the rotation system is to put the oldest goods in the place where they are most likely to be taken first.

The storage/rotation system must be patterned after the preparation/cooking routine.

After implementation, a chef's role in the rotation process should be one of overseer—checking the shelves to ensure that the system is being followed.

Vegetables, meats, fowl and fish which have stored well for two to seven days have a radically reduced shelf life after the preparation staff begins to carve, chop and cook.

To highlight the importance of thrown-away goods, consider these goods at their sale price, not their purchase price, because the food pc is increased by this larger amount.

The only way to stop this loss is by using a three-step process. First, find out how many portions came into the restaurant by counting the prepared portions. Second, make a count through the dupes to total the number of portions sold. Third, find the remaining portions and turn them into profitable items by revamping them with a new look and selling them at the slowest shifts.

Another potentially devastating problem with inventory control is the staff's consumption.

The chef of a restaurant with a large food pc must consider every small leak in the profitability of the operation as a significant part of the larger problem and approach it seriously.

To control staff eating costs, strict policies defining the employee's allowed price range or the entrees available are necessary.

Chapter 10

PRICING

Introduction

Menu and specials prices are one of the controls which management can use with precision to ensure the popularity and profitability of their restaurant. The pricing decisions are the least arbitrary of any facing them because all of the information about costs is available. There should be no guesswork. In many cases, the owner-manager will initiate price changes. But more often than not, the chef must supply pricing at the two crucial stages: when the menu is originally designed and when the need for price adjustments occurs. A chef with an effective pricing strategy will be able to make everyone's job easier by understanding the ways to allow for profit.

Pricing New Menus

Each menu item makes an impression of affordability to the customer, just as the entire menu's prices tend to create a body of affordability. Customers examine various categories, such as appetizers, salads, entrees and desserts, to understand the restaurant's offerings and prices. In designing the menu, these categories are placed in their logical position, based on the time when the course is eaten, and in the order of their importance based on the owner's desire to sell a particular kind of product. For example, if an owner wants to develop a reputation for grilled chicken, he or she will not list the hamburgers on top, but rather tuck them in at the bottom.

Pricing individual menu items is the beginning of menu pricing, but this must be approached holistically, with the end product firmly in sight. The factors which influence individual prices are the cost of goods sold, salaries, operating costs, competitors' prices, the history of the new market, the projected niche within the market, and the menu category's high and low ranges.

Cost of Goods Sold

This is a significant indicator of how little may be charged for a specific dish. A per plate analysis of each dish is essential. Without it, pricing is at best a rough guess. Begin the pricing procedure by doing a detailed cost breakdown of the ingredients needed to make one plate. Don't forget to figure in a waste factor. There will be one.

Salaries

This will have to be strictly an estimate. But at this stage, it will be good enough to build in a cost factor for the projected expense. It is simply a way to ensure that the final menu is a money maker. Based on the number of seats in the restaurant, approximate a bad week's food sales volume (see Chapter 7). Next, calculate the cost of management, floor staff, chef and kitchen staff—all the salaries of a skeleton staff. This dollar amount is the flat salary total for the restaurant. Divide it by the poor food sales figure. The resulting percentage is the payroll pc or percent. Keep it at hand.

Operating Costs

The more precise the estimates for these costs can be, the better equipped the restaurant will be to run a profit from the onset. The types of expenses to consider, like rents, taxes and utilities, can be found in any accounting textbook. Include all possible expenses other than the salary or the cost of goods sold. Divide the total estimated operating costs by the poor food sales figure. This percentage is the operating cost pc or percentage. When estimating these costs, a dramatically low rent will have a wonderful effect on the pc, just as a restaurant with a larger number of seats will produce a better poor food sales figure. It will be estimated higher, but this is only a paper figure; the seats must still be filled. Nevertheless, the importance of several business-related factors will be obvious when the estimates and projections are compiled. A chef who is pricing a menu for owners with a projected salary pc of thirty and an operating cost pc of forty should be alarmed. That leaves no room for profit. Perhaps the concept, location or other vital factors are faulty. If so, the beginning is a good time to change course.   .

Competitors' Prices

The best way to determine how much customers are willing to pay for a dish is to find an established restaurant which sells a version of it. Their price may be so high that they never sell it, so this is not a firm measure for new prices; it is simply a guideline, a part of the whole picture. One of the chef's duties is to be aware of price trends, from specialized, upscale establishments to simple American eateries. Every style has a price limit. Know the neighborhood or market well before trying to jump in. Prices that are too low cause a needless waste of profit, assuming that there is a profit. And the reverse problem—prices that are too high—may be the kiss of death, a reputation for being too expensive. Chefs or owners who are new at the business should make an effort to get a copy of every competitor's menu. They will provide a mini education in themselves.

For any new restaurant there is a risk factor. The best way to overcome it is to figure out what the traffic will bear and then undercut that price by a shade. This is perhaps a sour note for someone who wishes to sell the best French Nouvelle cuisine that Upper Sandusky Falls has ever seen; he would like it to be the most expensive cuisine as well. Perhaps this is justified, but spring the trap slowly. First, let the customers become thrilled with the food; then, after the line begins to form, raise the prices. Instead of resenting the move, the regulars will wonder what took so long and the new customers will go along with the trend. Try to prime the market with as many attractive attributes as possible—especially the price.

History of the New Market

If Cajun, California Nouvelle, or Tex-Mex cuisine has been very successful in many parts of the United States, it is entirely possible that a trendy restaurant patterned after another already successful one will be accepted as a fad in a new market area. This will allow more flexibility in setting prices because there is a built-in demand. Still, it is important not to price the menu into a range of exclusivity that discourages trend setters. With any untried cuisine, there is a possibility of failure. What if the residents of Hilton Head, South Carolina, just don't want Tex-Mex food? Maybe they don't understand it or care that the rest of the country loves it. In this case, the prices should be low enough to bring in customers who are willing to experiment. Prices should have an appeal which will make the customers travel a little longer to get a good deal. Hopefully, the trendy cuisine will catch on meanwhile.

Individual menu items which are exotic for the area also deserve special consideration. The same principles hold true for these items on otherwise simple menus as they do for entire menus of trendy cuisines. Buffalo steaks, for example, are an oddity. They should bring in more money than a regular steak. But if no one has ever tasted one, will they pay an extra five dollars or more for it? Build the demand for individual exotic dishes by pricing them well within the reach of the general public.

Projected Niche or Market

Most restaurants have ready-made competition in the area. They don't have to worry about being the first pizza parlor, for instance. In that case, it is an excellent idea to analyze every restaurant which sells food similar to the new restaurant's. Obtain a copy of the neighborhood's menus, from the white tablecloth, chi-chi operations to the wooden table, family places — any level of restaurant which sells a similar product, whether the package is silk or a brown paper bag.

Arrange the menus in order from the highest priced to the lowest. Where will the new restaurant fit into this progression of price ranges? Which restaurants are closest in style of presentation? Consider all the external factors, like the formality of the dining areas, type of service, location and how the liquor is handled. If there is an existing restaurant which has an operation similar to that of the new one, the prices should be very close. Unless there is a reason to go higher, the prices of the new competitor should be a little lower. That gives the new place an immediate edge. It doesn't make any difference that the existing store is terrible, with no business and bad food. Too many owners charge a little more for their product because they are certain that their restaurant will turn out a fine product. Then, when the first year turns into a roller coaster ride of personnel and inventory problems, they're stuck with an empty restaurant.

The same problems will occur with the lower prices, but the customers will have another attraction—the good deal. Problems are easier to solve if there are customers generating a turnover of stock and dollars.

High and Low Ranges

Within the new menu are various categories of courses—appetizers, salads, entrees, pastas, etc. Before pricing individual plates, establish a high and a low range—not a median, but how much the most expensive and least expensive items in a category will cost. Make a list of the types of courses on the new restaurant's menu. Set a range of prices for each category. These prices aren't arbitrary. They are based on the data and knowledge accumulated by analyzing the cost of goods sold, salaries, operating costs, competitors' prices, history of the new market and projected niche of the new restaurant.

Ordering Menu Items

Where individual items fall within their respective categories is a decision which will affect a dish's popularity, sales strength and customer acceptance. (Generally, the first item on a list sells the best. The cheapest one also sells well, without the need to be at the top.) The order in which the menu items are listed depends upon two factors: first, the order in which the customers are expected to eat the various courses—appetizers, salads, main courses and desserts, and second, the desired response of the customer. If the owner-chef wishes to sell all the dishes in equal volume, the order will reflect that goal. Another management team may want to sell more of one item—their specialty. This item should be positioned high and priced to sell. Another concept in ordering individual items is the "leader principle." Accent the bargains by placing them on the menu where the customer will see them first. If their appeal is strong enough, they will bring customers in. It is usually a combination of these various purposes which generates the price of each item and, in turn, contributes to the overall pricing of the categories and ultimately of the menu. A menu in which every category begins with a leader will serve a very different restaurant than a menu consisting of equally important specialty items. The former may wish to deal more on a dollar basis; the latter will depend more on the cuisine.

A good example of the former tactic is the dinner menu from SOME-THING SIMPLE (see Fig. 10-1). The owner-chef is Andrea. She started a

SOMETHING SIMPLE

SNACKS & STARTERS

New England Clam Chowder   cup 1.25   bowl 2.50
Soup of the Day   cup .95   bowl 2.00
Baked Vermont Cheddar Fondue w/Apples & Almonds   2.50
Spicy "Omaha" Chicken Wings   2.50
Avocado Vinaigrette   1.95
Deep-Fried Fish Fingers w/2 Tartar Sauces   3.50

SALADS

Andrea's Special Salad Sm. 2.95   Lrg. 3.95
Curried Chicken Salad Platter   Sm. 4.50   Lrg. 5.50
Herbed Tuna Salad Supreme   Sm. 4.50   Lrg. 5.50
Tortellini Salad Italienne   Sm. 3.50   Lrg. 4.50

SANDWICHES

Grilled Chicken Club Sandwich   4.95
California Melt   4.25
Avocado, Bacon, Lettuce & Tomato   0.00
Hot Pot Roast Sandwich   4.95
Simple 7 oz. Hamburger   3.95
BBQ Onions .50 Extra
California Platter   4.95
Blue Cheese Melt   .50 extra

MAIN PLATES

Baked Chicken Maryland   5.95
Roast Chicken w/Herbs   5.95
Southern Fried Chicken   5.95
Grilled New York Strip Steak   9.95
Gulf Shrimp Boil   8.95
Sauteed Sea Scallops   8.95
Catch of the Day   Priced Accordingly

Dinners Include a House Salad and Choice of Vegetable

VEGETABLE SIDE DISHES

Green Beans Saute   1.25
Mashed Potatoes   1.25
House Salad   1.50
Steamed Mixed Vegetables   1.25
Hand-cut French Fries   .95

DESSERTS

Sour Cherry Pie   2.00
Hot Apple Spice Cake   2.00
Chocolate Rum Comfort   2.00
Dessert of the Day   2.50

Figure 10–1. Something Simple. Menu.

161

reasonably priced restaurant on the basis of her years of home cooking and the purchase of a great lease. Her location is an old coffee shop in urban Omaha, Nebraska. She was able to get a low rent because the neighborhood is changing. The old manufacturing base was being absorbed by an expanding downtown area of primarily office buildings. Weeks after Andrea began remodeling, high-rise condominiums went on the market. Other restaurants had a steady office/lunch trade but a weak dinner clientele.

Chef Andrea's idea was to offer the best of two worlds—the coffee shop's low prices and speedy service combined with the pleasant decor and stylized food of a full-service restaurant. She redecorated the coffee shop with banquettes and tables, but no booths. The counter and kitchen were left intact, but other finishing touches, such as lighting, carpeting and decor, changed the atmosphere completely. The dinner trade, Andrea felt, would pick up as more urbanites moved into the area. High-rises were under construction. Andrea wanted to have one of the first spots to develop a regular clientele. She decided to offer a dinner menu comparable to that of real coffee shops in price, thereby undercutting every other restaurant in the neighborhood. The menu items selected were like her lunch menu, mostly things which she liked and cooked well. Her only dollar goal for nights was to do enough volume to pay the extra utilities costs, the salaries for the night staff and the food costs. Any revenues over that amount she considered excess profit because the day shift would already be paying the bills and supplying a profit. The cost estimate figure was approximately $2000 per week, or about $300 per night. Andrea sat down with the rough menu and asked herself the questions, "How can I bring in forty to fifty customers every night? How low do I have to go?" The answer for her scarcely populated night area was bargain basement. Something Simple's night menu is a perfect example of a low-priced, leader-dominated menu.

On the other end of the spectrum was *L'ALOUETTE RESTAURANT,* a French restaurant serving both Classic and Nouvelle cuisine. Their location was a historic landmark house whose lower floor had been redesigned with a kitchen, greeting parlour, and small dining rooms. Every step was taken to provide the ultimate dining experience. There was no thought of competing with leader items. The prices were to be at the going rate for a deluxe dinner out, only with a French twist—a prix fixe (see Fig. 10-2).

The use of French words written in classical script helped to set the mode for the higher prices of the prix fixe menu. Still, the owner-chef, Josette, had to make some concessions to the area, a small town in northern Colorado. She felt that including the appetizer with the prix fixe dinner would raise the price beyond her customers' limit and would offer

Nos Menus

For your enjoyment we have designed two menus best suited for different dining experiences.

Light Cuisine

For diners wishing a pleasant but light menu at a moderate price.

Soup
Entrée
Assorted Vegetables
Rice or Potatoes
Salad

$12.50

Grand Classique

"The Art of Tasting"

For a complete French Dining Experience, may we suggest our perfectly balanced Menu Dégustation

Soup
Fish Entrée
Meat or Poultry Entrée
Assorted Vegetables
Rice or Potatoes
Salad
Dessert

$18.50

coffee .60, espresso 1.05, cappuccino 1.35

A la Carte

Hors d'oeuvres

melon glacé au porto (in season)	3.25
Paté or Terrine	3.25

Hot or Cold

Smoked Salmon & cream cheese on toasts	3.75
Shrimp cocktail with curry mayonnaise	4.25
Stuffed mushrooms	3.25
Escargots de Bourgogne with garlic butter	4.25
Moules farcies persillade (when available)	4.25

Desserts

Plateau de Fromages	2.50
Grand Marnier Cheesecake	2.50
Petits Délices au chocolat	2.50
Cappuccino glacé	2.50

Please call ahead for a Special Celebration cake of any size.

Nos Entrées

Entrées Classiques
— You will find them on our Menu everynight.

— Lotte en Brochettes
  marinated monk fish on shishkebabs
— Canard roti au Basilic
  roasted duckling with fresh basil
— Boeuf à l'orange
  beef slices simmered in a red wine
  & orange sauce

Les Spécialités du jour

our specials tonight

Figure 10–2. L'Alouette. Menu.

much more food than Americans are used to eating. Even in the *menu degustation,* which is a service of several small portions, the total amount of food served adds up to an average meal, but the thought of being served four or five courses is repulsive to most Americans.

The appetizers were priced individually and were listed in order, with the easiest to prepare and most profitable ones at the top. Desserts too were priced separately from the prix fixe menu, using a standard practice of charging the same price for each.

When pricing for the prix fixe or other deluxe dining menu, the basic cost factors, including the cost of the goods sold, salaries and operating costs, are less of an influence than the competitors' prices. At the top of the dollar scale, the principles of free enterprise rule. Supply and demand dictate prices. The owner-chef supplying the best product is in a position to demand the highest prices. And provided the market exists for a high-quality product (usually when the economic climate makes price considerations for dining out immaterial), he or she will get it. Of course, too much of a good thing may kill the concept. *THE PALACE,* for example, was a French restaurant in New York City serving excellent High Classic cuisine. They offered two prix fixe dinners, one for $350 and the other for $500. Their small rooms held fewer than fifty customers, and yet even in New York City, where thousands of people could afford to eat well, they went out of business. Newspaper reviews not only pointed out the marvelous quality of the food but also talked about the audacious opulence. Public opinion soured, however, and potential customers got the impression that it would be better not to eat there.

Planning Price Changes

Repricing existing menus can be as simple as raising everything five or ten percent or as difficult as a computerized cost-sales-profit analysis complete with charts, tables and projections. Chances are that the average chef's job will fall somewhere in the middle, with a mix of both management styles. But the more data that are available, the better equipped a chef is to adjust the restaurant's sales volume in specific areas.

Most chefs inherit a menu complete with its style and prices. What happens if there are certain dishes which the chef feels are faulty? Perhaps they are old-fashioned, ill-conceived or misplaced. The likelihood of the owner's allowing a newly hired chef to rearrange the menu is almost nil. Prices, however, are something which an owner can be convinced to change. Changes in the positions of various menu categories and items could easily accompany price changes. An owner may be more flexible in allowing these changes, too. A chef serious about making the restaurant a success should think in terms of the long-range effects of any menu changes desired.

At the same time, the chef should plan to make the operation more profitable and the restaurant's offerings more popular. That means deciding which dishes should be highlighted. Chicken versus fish and pasta versus steak are two examples of complementary but competing styles. The overall goal is to build sales volume, but the smart way to do it is to build sales with items which offer the highest profit margin.

As stated in Chapter 4, the best way for a chef to influence the owner-management team is with data-based facts. Take actual counts of what sells and what doesn't. Figure the cost of goods sold for each category of food: meat, fish, fowl, vegetables, dairy, etc. Review Chapter 4, which gives a complete record-keeping system and a cost analysis method.

Raising Prices

It's not enough to rely on a once-a-year menu analysis—not if the goal is to make the maximum profit. The markets which supply goods are seasonal; their prices go up and down with the changes in weather. Plan ahead, incorporating the projected costs of goods for every month of the year. Even with intelligent planning, a volatile market can ruin a busy restaurant's season, especially during times of double-digit inflation. The following example illustrates the kinds of hidden profit drains which can develop. A chef who keeps no records may not even know it's happening until the owner asks why the kitchen costs were so high last month.

A busy American-Continental restaurant was one month into its busiest season, April through September, when the price of one of its main food products went up over fifty percent. Chicken cutlets rose from $1.90 to $3.40 per pound. Chef Baxter checked around; the prices of all the suppliers had jumped, apparently because demand was so much higher than supply. Chicken was in fashion. Everyone was off red meat and watching their weight. The restaurant bought $10,000 worth of food a week. The per plate food cost of chicken items had gone from twenty-five percent to forty-five percent in one week. Chef Baxter expected the raise to be permanent, at least through the summer, when the restaurant did the major portion of its annual sales volume. The projections showed that an average four-week month would accumulate lost profits of $1600. New menus would take a month, so they were ordered immediately with raised prices. The point is that Chef Baxter could have lost his job if he hadn't been keeping daily records and doing weekly analyses of the purchases and sales. These systems are a must for any operation which does food sales totaling $15,000 or more per week.

Chef Baxter decided that he needed a temporary plan to offset the higher chicken costs until the new menus arrived. He developed a two-faceted approach. First, the cooking staff was advised of the problem; the chef stressed the importance of strict portion size control. Second, Chef Baxter set about to outsell the menu chicken items with specials which would appeal to chicken-buying customers. Most of the restaurant's chicken cutlet volume was in two areas, chicken saute dishes and chicken salads. These plates accounted for seventy percent of the chicken use. The hot chicken specials prices were immediately raised one dollar. Baxter took pains to ensure that his hot chicken specials were highly popular. Their sales volume became stronger than ever. Chicken salad specials prices were also raised one dollar, and again Baxter made a strong effort to outdo his already strong reputation for good specials. When preparing the chicken salad specials, he was able to use whole chickens instead of cutlets. He substituted other types of chicken whenever possible. This was a money-saving procedure which he adopted permanently. Chicken sales stayed proportionately the same in relation to the rest of the menu, but the chicken specials sold well enough to recoup half of the projected loss. At the end of one month, the new menus came in and the pressure was off. Chicken sold better than ever at the new higher prices; profits were up. At the end of September, chicken prices dropped at the market, but the restaurant had developed a strong chicken clientele, and their menu prices stayed the same. Chef Baxter realized that he had hit upon a method for raising prices within food groups. His next target group was pasta.

Which restaurants get to raise prices? Certainly, not every one. There are certain times and business conditions which would be devastating if they were combined with price hikes. A business could literally be delivered the coup de grace. It is poor planning to raise prices at the beginning of the bad season. It is foolish to raise them if the customers aren't coming in at all. There is no basis for price increases if the restaurant isn't popular. Successful, i.e., busy restaurants have earned the right to raise prices, but even they must be cautious.

The most common price changes are small raises which become necessary every six to twelve months to balance the profit erosion due to single-digit inflation. Since customers seem to have become accustomed to gentle hikes, take advantage of the precedent, provided the signs continue to be positive. There are various ways to effect these across-the-board raises. One way is to institute a flat percentage increase for specific menu categories, such as seven percent for all entrees or five percent for all desserts. Another practice is to raise all menu items using the same ingredients a set rate; for example, all items containing chicken breasts could be raised ten percent.

Lowering Prices

In some cases, it may be necessary to lower prices. It means swallowing your pride, but that beats losing the whole investment. The surest sign of a menu item which is priced too high is one which is delicious but loses money because the raw ingredients are going into the trash. So little of the item is being sold that the turnover rate doesn't match that of the prepared goods. Price the item low enough to be a leader item. If it still doesn't sell, take it off the menu. Regardless of how good it is, the customers have voted no. Smart owner-chefs will respect that vote or pay for it.

Prices may need to be lowered due to a drastic change in the market — the local competition. If a larger, a more prestigious, or simply a cheaper competitor begins to cut into your sales volume, adjustments must be made. It may not be enough to tighten management controls, expecting to win out with a superior product and a standing reputation. In order to remain competitive, a business leader must be flexible. It often falls upon the chef to apprise the owner of the new realities.

The following examples are case histories which show three restaurants whose only common factor is location. They are in the same part of a coastal resort town, sharing the same economic climate. They are responding to a rise in wholesale food prices. The food is the same in all three cases, November 18. In addition, vegetable and fish prices are beginning their annual rise due to the colder weather.

Example 1. CAPTAIN BENNY'S SEAFOOD started out as a fish shack and grew into a sprawling restaurant. It has been remodeled three times. Throughout the rise in business volume, prices have remained low enough to attract casual and middle-income customers. Recently, Chef Dominic has been fielding complaints from the manager about rising food costs, so he analyzes the menu and his records to assess the possibility of a price hike (see Fig. 10-3). During the past year, the dollar sales volume has increased eight percent. Dominic feels that this is a positive sign. The last time prices were raised was over a year ago. Captain Benny's business is steady, with a small peak in July and August, but for the most part it is even throughout the year.

Clams, oysters and shrimp are Chef Dominic's first concern. They constitute over half of the menu items. Dominic does some quick calculations with today's wholesale prices, and he estimates how high the prices will

CAPTAIN BENNY'S SEAFOOD

ON THE HALF SHELL & APPETIZERS

Clams ½ Dozen or 1 Dozen   4.50   8.95
Oysters ½ Dozen or 1 Dozen   3.95   7.95
Oyster Cocktail ½ Dozen or 1 Dozen   3.95   7.95
Shirmp Cocktail   4.50
Oysters Rockefeller   3.95
Shrimp Scampi   4.50
Baked Clams Casino   4.95
Soup du Jour   1.95   Mixed Green Salad   1.95

CAPTAIN'S PLATTERS

Fish Fry All You Can Eat   4.95
Seafood Platter   7.95
Super Seafood Platter   11.95
Fried Shrimp   8.95
Fried Oysters   8.95
Combination Platter   9.95

PORTS OF CALL

Filet Mignon   11.95
Chicken Piccatta   6.95
Galley Salad Platter   5.95
Hamburger Platter   4.50
Kiddies Platter   4.50

FROM THE STEAM ROOM

Peel Your Own Shrimp   8.95
Steamed Crab (6)   7.95
Clams ½ Dozen or Dozen   4.50 or 8.95
Oysters ½ Dozen or Dozen   3.95 or 7.95

THE FIRST MATE'S SPECIALS

Broiled Sole Ala Benny   8.95
Brook Trout Almondine   6.95
Surf & Turf   14.95
(Your Choice of Seafood)
Grilled Salmon Steak Marinated in Wine & Herbs   11.95

DESSERTS:

Black Bottom Pie   2.25   Key Lime Pie 2.25   Peach Cake 2.50
Ice Cream Sundae with Whiskey Sauce   3.25

BEVERAGES:

Coffee   .95   Tea   .95   Milk   .95
Colas   .95   Iced Tea   .95   Decaffinated Coffee   .95
Ask Your Server for Cocktail & Beer Prices

Figure 10-3. Captain Benny's Seafood. Menu.

go before warmer weather arrives. Even at the present annual inflation rate of eleven percent, he can't envision wholesale prices rising more than ten percent. Some items may rise twenty percent, but the dry goods will probably rise much less. Guesswork aside, one thing Dominic knows is that Captain Benny's is packed every night. The traffic can bear a price increase.

Dominic starts with the appetizers. All the $4.50 items go to $4.95, the $3.95 items go to $4.50 and the one dozen-size items are raised $1.

Before moving to another category, Dominic considers the high and low effect of the menu. The restaurant's high-priced plates are Surf and Turf, Salmon Steaks and Filet Mignon. These items sell moderately well but don't account for much of the sales volume. Their individual food costs are still low. Chef Dominic decides to leave them alone. At the lower end of the price range are the Hamburger Platter, Kiddies Platter, Fish Fry and Galley Salad Platter. Of these items, only the Fish Fry is a main line item, part of Captain Benny's appeal. The other items are convenience plates to add appeal for the whole family. The Hamburger and Kiddies Platters are raised to $4.95 because they're still a good deal at that price. All the prices within the Captain's Platters category seem high to Dominic. They are high. That's the nature of raising prices. Dominic gets out the sales records. The top six sellers on a per plate basis are (1) Fried Shrimp, (2) Peel Your Own Shrimp, (3) Fish Fry, (4) Chicken Piccatta, (5) Seafood Platter and (6) Broiled Sole. These items account for sixty-three percent of Captain Benny's per plate volume and fifty-two percent of the entree dollar volume. The chef raises each of them $1. He brings two of the other items up to par: clams and oysters from the Steam Room and Brook Trout Almandine. Desserts and beverages are raised $.25. Chef Dominic is unable to raise their prices enough to completely offset the accumulated rise in wholesale prices, but he wisely defers further price increases until June. A little now, a little then; he must play catch-up because Captain Benny's missed an opportunity to raise the prices the previous June. Too much of a jolt now may alienate the customers.

Example 2. THE ADOBE COYOTE opened nine months ago to a dazzling array of media coverage, glittery clientele and major dollar volume. It has shared center stage as one of the "hot" new restaurants in town (see Fig. 10-4). The owner and chef team of Mary and Sid have no idea what their seasonal sales will be; so far, it has been capacity seating every night. Even the lunch trade has been respectable. They use the same menu for each service. Mary notices a slight rise in the food costs but their profits have remained steady, undoubtedly due to their ability to control proce- dures better after the first six months of madness. Mary and Sid eat out often. They see other prices rising throughout the area. It is time for a meeting to plan their own price strategy.

THE ADOBE COYOTE

★★★ A SOUTHWESTERN BISTRO ★★★

COCKTAILS
★ ★ ★ ★

Selected Margueritas and Daiquiris 5.00 16.50 per Pitcher
Corona Beer 5.00 Imports 4.25 Domestic 3.50
Wine Punch 3.50 per Glass 9.50 per Pitcher

APPETIZERS
★ ★ ★ ★ ★

Deep Fried Raviolis Stuffed with Monterey Jack, Cilantro and Jalapeno 3.00
Sante Fe Chorizos Nachos 3.00
Roasted Red Pepper, Avocado and Green Leaf Salad 4.50
Jicama and Shrimp Ceviche 4.95
Chicken Anticucaos Marinated in Herbed Wine 3.95

ENTREES
★ ★ ★ ★

Shrimp Paella (The Coyote's Specialty) 14.75
Pan-Fried Sea Scallops in Garlic, Corn and Basil Salsa 12.75
Grilled Chicken Breasts w/Hot and Cold Salsas and Black Bean Refritos 13.50
Vegetarian Tamale Pie 10.25
Chili Con Ribeye Steak 12.75
"Soft" Beef or Chicken Tacos with Cojack Cheese Sauce 11.25
Baked Red Snapper in Tomato and Pinon Pesto 14.75
Roast Chicken with Spicy Chocolate Glaze 13.50

Entrees are Served with a Green Salad and Grilled Vegetables

DESSERTS
★ ★ ★ ★ ★

Banana and Almond Empanadas 4.50
Deep-Fried Ice Cream 4.50
Raspberry Flan with Mexican Vanilla Creme 5.50
Esspresso 2.50 Cappucino 3.00

Figure 10-4. The Adobe Coyote. Menu.

"Is price much of an issue with our customer?" Mary wonders. They don't believe so—not now, at least. But what about two years from now, when the glamor has faded and other restaurants have opened to steal the limelight? Sid argues that the food is just getting better, and that will ensure their future. Their job is to assess the present business and forecast the next year's sales curve. Even that is guesswork. Provided the food and service continue to improve, the Adobe Coyote should ride the opening wave of prosperity into the following period of steady, if seasonal, volume. The better the product is now, the larger the regular clientele will be when the fad fades. The significant issue is: What are the other chi-chi eateries up to? How much do they charge, and how busy are they? Mary and Sid know of at least four other places which charge much more for entrees than the Adobe Coyote. One of them is very busy, two do an average business and the last is slow.

Mary and Sid condense the various issues down to two procedures: continue at the same prices, hoping to build good will and a broader base of customers by doing so, or raise prices and put the Adobe Coyote in direct competition for the most affluent dinner customers in town.

Their final decision is to raise appetizers $.50 each, entrees $1 each, and domestic beers, other imports and nonalcoholic beverages $.50 each. They choose to take a modest increase immediately for two reasons. First, they have a lot of faith in their ability to cope with the future, whatever business problems develop. Second, the sales volume is taking place now. It is time to make money while they are on top. However, a raise in prices puts a lot of pressure on them to ensure perfect service and food. They are willing to accept the challenge. Their goal is to become an institution of fine dining.

Example 3.   KING ARTHUR'S PUB, coincidentally, was one of the places which Mary and Sid considered sophisticated dining. The owner, Mr. Bartolli, has been increasingly alarmed by the lack of profit from operations. The restaurant has gone into its usual winter slump but has never pulled out (see Fig. 10-5). The entire summer and most of the Fall have passed with Mr. Bartolli wondering where the customers are. The chef, Charlie, has been on the job three years. His performance has been regular; perhaps the sparkling presentation of the previous chef is gone, but the food is good. Mr. Bartolli asks Charlie to take a look at the menu prices, compare them with his costs, and suggest where prices can be raised. Bartolli hates to do it, but by his calculations, he is working for less than $500 a week in profits. That is too little.

Chef Charlie does the calculations for each plate, figuring the cost of the basic ingredients from the weekly invoice bills. On paper the individual costs of goods sold are low, between twenty-five and thirty percent.

KING ARTHUR'S PUB

SOUPS AND APPETIZERS

Soup of the Day 1.50

Cream of Mushroom 2.50
  The Chef's Speciality

Jumbo Shrimp Cocktail 5.95

Coquille St. Jacques 4.95

Baked Stuffed Mushrooms 3.95
  Stuffed with Crabmeat

Chicken Tenderloins Scampi 4.95

FROM THE SEA

Baked Jumbo Shrimp with Hollandaise 12.95
  Stuffed with Crabmeat 14.95

Broiled Flounder Fillets 11.95
  In Lemon-Butter Sauce Enhanced with Herbs

Scallops Newberg 14.95

Rainbow Trout Almondine 13.95

Maine Lobster Tail . . . . P.A.
  Served with Drawn Butter

FROM THE CHARBROILER

New York Strip
  Selected Choice Western Beef, Charbroiled to Perfection
                                    Queen Cut 10.95
                                    King Cut 14.95

Delmonico Steak 13.95

T-Bone Steak 19.95

Filet Mignon – The King of Steaks 16.95
  Served with a Delicate Bearnaise Sauce

Center Cut Pork Chops – 1¼ inches thick 11.95

Rib Eye Steak
  Served with our Special Onion Aujus
                                    Queen Cut 11.95
                                    King Cut 14.95

COMBINATION ENTREES

Surf and Turf – The Classic . . . . P.A.
  Lobster Tail and Filet Mignon

Jumbo Shrimp Scampi and New York Strip 14.95

*All entrees include oven fresh bread, all you can eat salad bar,
and a choice of vegetable*

FOR THE ROUNDTABLE

Ask your waitress about our homemade desserts

Figure 10–5. King Arthur's Pub. Menu.

Charlie agrees with these figures and feels that King Arthur's prices are too high even for a fancy place. But the boss wants to raise prices, so it is his job to make suggestions. Charlie determines which two plates from each of the entree categories have the highest food cost and raises them each $2. He submits his recommendations and backup data to Bartolli.

What should Bartolli do? His chef's suggestions are reasonable, and the data seem to back them up. But he is surprised to find that the percentage figures for goods sold are so low. According to Charlie's figures, the restaurant should still be making a large profit. Bartolli begins to see that the problem isn't the low prices, it's Charlie. Sales are down and waste is up. Probably all of the lost profit is due to poor kitchen management in the face of a boring business downturn. Everyone from Bartolli to the porter has been lulled into a complacency which many restaurant owners find fatal. The solution for King Arthur's dilemma is marked improvement in service and food product, including adding a lot of pizazz. The last thing Bartolli should do is to raise prices. That may scare off the last remaining faithful customers. Perhaps the first thing Bartolli should do is to put Charlie on notice. Another alternative is to redesign the entire menu, offering lower prices and different entrees.

Highlights

Menu and specials prices are one of the controls which management can use with precision to ensure the popularity and profitability of their restaurant.

Customers examine various categories, such as appetizers, salads, entrees and desserts, to understand the restaurant's offerings and prices.

Pricing individual menu items is the beginning of menu pricing, but this must be approached holistically, with the end product firmly in sight.

Begin the pricing procedure by doing a detailed cost breakdown of the ingredients needed to make one plate.

Add the estimated salary costs to the cost of goods sold in order to ensure that the final menu is a money maker.

Include all possible expenses other than the salary or the cost of goods sold.

Before pricing individual plates, establish a high and a low range—not a median, but how much the most expensive and least expensive items in a category will cost.

Menu prices are based on the data and knowledge accumulated by analyzing the cost of goods sold, salaries, operating costs, competitor's prices, history of the new market and projected niche of the new restaurant.

A chef who is serious about making the restaurant a success should think in terms of the long-range effects of any menu changes desired.

The overall goal is to build sales volume, but the smart way to do it is to build sales with items which achieve the highest profit margin.

There are certain times and business conditions which would be devastating if combined with price hikes.

Busy restaurants have earned the right to raise prices, but even they must be cautious.

The surest sign that a menu item is priced too high is a plate which is delicious but loses money because the raw ingredients are going into the trash.

If a larger, a more prestigious, or simply a cheaper competitor begins to cut into the sales volume, price adjustments must be made.

Chapter 11

PRODUCT DESIGN (TRICKS OF THE TRADE)

Introduction

The design of any product, from a pencil to a twelve-burner stove, begins and ends with the product's expected purpose. As a product for sale, food is no different. The reason a dish is put together will dominate its ingredients, style of cuisine and presentation. In the marriage between the two goals of high profit and culinary excellence, myriad combinations can confuse the customer and the unaware chef. The more effectively a chef realizes the purpose of a dish and controls the makeup or design of the product, the greater the popularity and profit will be.

To assist the chef, there are tricks of the trade—those little (and not so little) shortcuts which seem to serve the purpose of aesthetics, in that the dishes are creative, popular and expensively presented, but actually increase profits through substitution and optical trickery.

Basic Design Purposes

While a successfully executed dish will have a combination of purposes, there will usually be a particular one from which the dish evolves. Perhaps the origin is random, based on a subconscious thought by the creating chef, but it still exists. Effective dishes are created by incorporating the elements of design, because they enhance a chef's ability to create a diversity of dishes. Uniqueness doesn't come from the variety of ingredients alone. It can be an inherent quality stemming from an unusual blend of design purposes. Rather than letting these decisions be made subconsciously in every case, have the knowledge to manipulate them into new combinations. The chef of a large-turnover, profit-oriented chain restaurant needs to concentrate on the lighter side of the final dishes' presentation—the aesthetics. He or she may have little or no reason to do so except to provide broader customer appeal, a business knack which is elusive enough to be called a talent. That is more than sufficient cause. The reverse situation is equally affected by narrow execution of design purposes. Chefs who spend their day tasting and fussing must focus on the harder aspect of reality—profit margins. If they do not, the only customers they will have will be the few who think exclusively of taste and visual excellence. Unfortunately, such customers are few. A chef's repertoire is enhanced by using each of the followings elements of design.

Aesthetics

This includes all the senses except taste which affect a first and lasting impression—the sight, smell, color and arrangement of a dish. The most extreme example of a dish created strictly for aesthetics is the food designed for photography—the work of food stylists. These plates may taste like cardboard or vinegar, it doesn't make any difference. They entice the palate through visual presentation alone.

The pleasing symmetry of a colorful, well-balanced presentation begins with the selection of ingredients and cooking styles. Obviously a blond sauce poured over a scallopini of meat can never be garnished to provide the same visual excitement as a melange of grilled vegetables and quail, for instance (at least, not without using extravagant nonedible garnishes, a trick which most restaurants can't employ). But there are ways to sauce familiar dishes which create visual newness. Experiment with sauces on the side, across in patterns, sauces of multiple colors, sauces underneath and visual perks within the sauces. The end result of a chef's experimentation with various presentations should be a pattern—a style which is pleasing, fast and effective. Constant change for the sake of change may defeat its purpose by confusing regular customers. Learn good design tactics for your repertoire and then reuse them.

Smell is a quality which all food has, provided the product is fresh. Obviously this is a key factor in a customer's acceptance of the meal.

When the customer smells the garlic and onion emanating from the kitchen, the saliva glands begin to bathe the taste buds and the hunger process begins. But consider the difference in aroma between fresh garlic and prechopped, canned garlic. The fresh variety is sweet and piquant to smell, the other dull. Prefer freshness in all ingredients, especially herbs and spices.

Taste

How can this sense be categorized? Someone should do a marketing survey of all the people in the United States and define what the best liked tastes are, from tomatoes to liver, from Manhattan to Baja California. Tastes are flavors which are blended together, either cooked or raw. Because a taste is identified by its source (apples, for example, are a definite taste sensation), in order for a taste or trend to be a rage, it must originate from a popular food source. People know what they like by experience. If they know they hate liver, sauteing it with leeks, bacon and champagne will not change their minds. The taste popularity of a dish depends entirely upon the diner's preference, and the motivation is a purely personal decision. No one can convince through argument that a certain food tastes best.

Preparation or creation of dishes involves a lot of planning for the purpose of taste satisfaction. One aspect of a tasty dish is familiarity, like the meal Grandma makes for the Thanksgiving Day feast. All the old favorites done just the way you expect them. Someone once said, "The happiest memories of your childhood, are the remembrances of the good things you had to eat as a child." Familiar tastes can be vastly popular or not, but each item, with its corresponding taste, has a following—its own clientele. Of course, regional differences do a lot to dictate the popularity of certain foods. A solid understanding of the region's culinary history is important for the successful design of a restaurant dish.

Chefs designing for taste have to be able to create from memory through a process similar to visualization. They must have enough experience with foods to put three tastes together in their mouths and imagine the result, using only suggestion, without the physical presence of the items. For example, close your eyes and smack your lips together as if to savor a fine wine. Think of the red, luscious body of a Beaujolais nouveau. In your mind's eye, pour a glass slowly. Feel the coolness of the bottle. Catch a whiff of the bouquet. Take a sip, and hold the flavor on your tongue. Swallow slowly, and take a final taste. In the creation process, a chef may combine many such familiar tastes. Usually you'll be smacking your lips together, trying to imagine that last ingredient which will finish off a dish and make it a taste sensation.

To Embody a Style

The clearest example of this design imperative is the chef of an Italian restaurant who must complement but not confuse a menu of pastas. The created dish must be some form of Italian. Whether the dish's origin is Northern, Southern, Classic or Nouvelle, it has to be recognized as Italian. An Italian food dictionary will help to name it. This will do a lot to lend authenticity. Ingredients from the region or country, in this example Italy, are an important design element. The cooking techniques, especially knife work and sauce execution, are another significant design component. Finally, the presentation, which is completely at the chef's whim, will provide an immediate visual signature.

One of the best ways to add variety to a menu or a specials list is to use many different styles. The popularity of nouvelle cuisine makes it especially easy to present a difficult or obscure style with greater flexibility. Chinese, German, Caribbean—all styles which in the past demanded strict adherence to their traditional techniques—are now open to intepretation. The ingredients play a greater role in defining the taste when the style of cooking moves under the umbrella of nouvelle.

For Acceptance or Popularity

Restaurants which are motivated by high turnover or those with many seats must offer a selection of popular dishes. These don't necessarily have to be classic favorites, although that is one type. It is exciting to anticipate the customer's tastes, to be a trend setter and ride the crest of a new cuisine's introductory phase. In this situation, one or two chefs may be the keeper of the concept by their dramatic style. They have gained an innovative edge by creating within the new style, not to satisfy the precepts of newness in the obscure sense, but to use a new style to create food which tastes fantastic. Popularity depends on common appreciation of tastes or trends.

There is a huge market for popular food. The largest retail food sales come from the fast food, coffee shop, pub and neighborhood restaurants segment. For these establishments the dishes must be simple, with the names and ingredients recognizable by the vast majority of the population. And there can be no surprises, pretenses or even imagination, because these may hurt the sales figures. In this case, the trick is to create more of the same, either by giving a new name to a tested favorite or by using popular ingredients in a new combination and flavor. Of course, top quality is always an issue.

When the purpose is to sell food in order to reduce stock or to build dollar volume, popularity must be the prime design consideration. Then the proven reasons for popularity should dominate the makeup and presentation of a dish. These include price, style, classic favorite, novelty and position on the menu.

Ease of Preparation

The physical limitations of the kitchen's equipment or space and the cooking abilities of the kitchen staff may impede the design of certain dishes. The lack of a stove or broiler, for instance, can totally change the chef's creative possibilities. I once worked in a busy lunch spot which had no stove, broiler or even hot plates. The few hot dishes were steamed, and yet the volume was heavy. It is possible to adapt to any situation or limitation.

Even in a full kitchen with an experienced and capable staff, it may be desirable to complement a complicated specials list with one less time-consuming dish or one with fewer mis-en-place elements. A dish designed for ease of preparation would be an aid to the timing of the workload. It is surprising how customers given a full range of specials to choose from often select the simplest to prepare, while the complicated favorites of the chef sell poorly.

High-volume operations need quick two-step recipes to keep the food coming out fast and the tables turning over. Try to imagine the absurdity of a coffee shop trying to sell Haute Nouvelle or a burger and fast food outlet adding Roast Goose with Apple and Onion Stuffing to the menu. Sometimes simple is better.

Profitability

At the other end of the spectrum from aesthetics is profit. The majority of dishes are designed primarily with the cost margin in mind (see Chapter 5). The purest example of the food-for-dollars exchange is vendor items, which are simple enough to be mass produced. Restaurants also serve items which can potentially be mass produced—salads and sandwiches, for example. Mass production reduces overhead by saving on salaries and reducing the waste factor. Simple dishes are some of the most profitable to sell.

Ironically, the most difficult dishes to prepare may be equally as profitable or even more so, depending on the restaurant's style of cuisine.

A restaurant with fewer than fifty to seventy seats must offer something more unique than food for dollars. Skill and talent must be lifted to the level of a show business presentation. It is after all, a sales game.

Chefs must know their ability to charge for the extras—service, ambiance, location, etc. Then in another calculation, they must figure the cost of goods sold per plate. If there is a ceiling price, as there usually is, some items will never be sold at particular restaurants; for instance, those which never top the $9 limit will never sell lobster. The general pricing format of a menu tells a chef what he or she may or may not sell at a profit. Therefore, as profitability is a key element of design, it determines what ingredients are available within the chef's price range.

Tricks of the Trade

Tricks of the trade are simply ways which allow a chef to accomplish any one of the other design purposes (aesthetics, taste, to embody a style, popularity, or ease of preparation) while making the dishes profitable.

One method of lowering food costs is to reduce the portion size of the main ingredient by ten to fifteen percent. This will increase the yield, thereby adding to the profit. Next, a cheaper ingredient can be added to compensate for the loss of weight. The substitutes can be put over, under, around or inside the main ingredient.

The following five recipes embody each of these approaches.

POACHED SALMON WITH GREEN PEPPERCORN CREAM
SERVED OVER A BED OF SPINACH

(Substitute Under)

10 lb. Salmon Fillet	2 qt. Heavy Cream
½ bushel Fresh Spinach	1 qt. Fish Stock
6 Shallots	4 cups White Wine
2 Lemons	2 T Butter
½ cup Salt	½ cup Cornstarch
	½-¼ cup Green Peppercorns

Remove all skin and bones from the salmon. Cut into six- or seven-ounce portions. Cover with a wet towel and refrigerate until service.

Clean, destem and steam the spinach. For the steamer, use three minced shallots, one cup of white wine, one-quarter cup of salt and one quart of water. Cool and refrigerate the spinach. Prepare the sauce ahead of time.

Mince three shallots; then saute them until brown, using one tablespoon of butter in a large sauce pan. Deglaze the pan with two cups of white wine. Reduce the wine at a high boil until no liquid remains. Add one quart of a clear fish stock. Boil and slowly reduce by half. Add the two quarts of heavy cream. Bring to a boil, and then reduce for thirty minutes. Salt to taste. Thicken with the cornstarch. Crush the soft green peppercorns, and then add them to the boiling cream. Stir in well. The sauce should be slightly thickened. Remove and cool until service.

On the Line. Prepare a poaching pan with one cup of white wine, four cups of water, sliced lemons and salt. Place one portion of salmon into the poacher. Ladle eight ounces of peppercorn cream into a small saucepan. As the fish nears doneness, heat the sauce, reducing it slowly. If necessary, use more thickening agents. Saute one-half cup of spinach in whole butter. Plate the spinach slightly off center. Plate the fish slightly on and off the spinach bed. Pour sauce over the fish where it lays on the spinach. Garnish with red pepper pearls and serve. Makes nineteen to twenty-two orders. Using regularly sized portions of salmon, the yield would be four to six fewer portions.

DEEP-FRIED CATFISH FINGERS WITH HONEY-MUSTARD SAUCE
AND HAND-CUT FRENCH FRIES

(Substitute Around)

5 lb. Catfish	1 lb. Honey
1 dozen Eggs Beaten	3 cups Dijon Mustard
2 lb. Flour	½ T Cayenne Pepper
4 T Tabasco	3 Minced Shallots
3 lb. Seasoned Bread Crumbs	1 T Olive Oil
10 Potatoes	

For the best portion control, use eight-ounce fillets of farm-fed catfish. Their size is standard, and the fillets are thick. Cut the fillets in half lengthwise. Still lengthwise but at a slight angle, cut three fingers from each side. Make them as uniform in size as possible.

Prepare a three-tray breading station: one tray of flour, one tray of seasoned bread crumbs (salt, thyme, mace and basil) and one tray of the whipped eggs with one cup of water and the tabasco added.

Bread the catfish fingers through the flour tray, egg wash, and then seasoned bread crumbs. Cover and refrigerate until service. Wash, peel and cut the potatoes, Retain in cold, salted water. To prepare the sauce, slightly brown the minced shallots in one tablespoon of olive oil. Add the mustard and honey. Heat slowly while stirring the elements together. Add the cayenne. Pot the sauce and place it on the steam table.

On the Line. Deep fry the french fries at 350°F until they float. Drain. Refry single portions to order. Deep fry four catfish fingers at 350°F until they float. Plate the catfish and french fries. Serve the sauce on the side in a ramekin or monkey dish. Garnish with a leaf lettuce bed and lemon wedges. Makes fifteen orders, five more than the portion control size from the fish farm dictates.

SAUTEED LOIN OF VEAL PAYSANNE

(Substitute Over)

5 lb. Loin of Veal	2 lb. Flour
5 lb. Button Mushrooms	2 cups Olive Oil
2 lb. Fresh Peas	½ cup Salt
1 cup Chopped Shallots	¼ cup White Pepper
1 qt. Marsala Wine	1 qt. Heavy Cream

Trim, cut and pound the veal into three-ounce medallions. Cover and refrigerate until service.

Wash the peas. Blanch them in salty water. Then cool, cover and refrigerate until service.

Clean and destem the mushrooms.

On the Line. Heat three ounces of olive oil in a saute pan over a medium high flame. Flour, salt and pepper two medallions. Place one tablespoon of shallots and the veal in the hot oil. Fry slowly. Add one-half cup of mushrooms. Turn the veal. When the meat is cooked, plate it and keep it warm. Pour off excess oil from the pan. Turn the flame to high. Deglaze the pan with two ounces of marsala wine. Add four ounces of heavy cream and reduce to sauce thickness. Add one-quarter of a cup of peas and two more ounces of marsala wine. Salt and pepper to taste. Pour over veal. Garnish with pimentoes and chives. Makes twelve servings. The colorful country style presented by whole mushrooms caps and green peas also adds mass to the plate. Six ounces of veal, a smallish portion, becomes a substantial plate.

ROTI DE CANARD SAUVAGE AUX FIGUES

(Substitute Around)

6 Wild Ducks	1 qt. Fond de Canard
24 Figs	½ cup Salt
1½ cups Olive Oil	½ cup Pepper
3 cups Cognac	

Remove the twelve individual duck breasts from their carriages. Cover and refrigerate until service. Use the remaining duck bones and cuisses in other recipes.

On the Line. Heat one ounce of olive oil in a saute pan. Season one duck breast with salt and pepper. Place it in the hot oil, skin side down. Brown the skin, turn the breast and put the pan and breast in a hot oven. Remove when rare. Put the duck on the cutting board. Pour away the oil. Place the pan on a medium flame and add three to four ounces of fond de canard, a rich duck stock, and reduce. Hold a washed fig bulb side up and cut an X halfway down to the stem. Prepare two figs this way. When two ounces of fond remain, add the figs. Add two ounces of cognac and flambe. Toss gently. The figs should remain whole, opening like a flower with four petals. Slice the duck breast thinly, and fan it across the plate. Pour the sauce over the duck. Arrange the figs on either side. Garnish with strawberry mountains and serve. Makes twelve orders. Wild duck breasts in the United States tend to be small and are usually served two per portion. By using a large, showy accompaniment, the figs, one breast fanned is sufficient for a Nouvelle serving.

GRILLED PORK CHOP STUFFED WITH CURRIED RAISINS AND ALMONDS

(Substitute Inside)

1 Loin of Pork	1 cup Seasoned Bread Crumbs
1 box Black Raisins	8 Egg Yolks
1 box Gold Raisins	1 T Almond Extract
2 cups Almonds	4 oz. Cognac
4 Minced Shallots	½ cup Salt
2 T Chopped Garlic	½ cup Pepper
½ cup Minced Celery	2 T Butter
½ cup Curry Powder	1 cup Olive Oil

Butcher the loin of pork. The yield should be sixteen to eighteen chops. Cut a pocket into each chop. For the stuffing, heat the butter in a large saute pan, and then brown the shallots, garlic and celery. Place them in a large mixing bowl. Toast the almonds, and add them to the bowl. Add the raisins, almond extract, bread crumbs and curry powder. Salt and pepper to taste. Mix in the egg yolks. Add the cognac. Stir well. Adjust the seasonings. Stuff the pork chops, cover and refrigerate until service.

On the Line. Rub the chop with olive oil, and season with salt and pepper. Place on the grill over a moderate flame. Cook until done. Plate and garnish with grilled apple wheels which are honey glazed and a green leafy sprig. Makes sixteen to eighteen orders, double the yield if two chops are used unstuffed.

Bait and Switch

No restaurant can build a regular clientele by selling inferior product. Most do just the opposite: They sell high-quality goods that are consistently well prepared. They charge reasonable to high prices so that they can stay in business at a profit while the demand remains strong. But what about the off season? During these periods, it is advisable for the chef to change the specials somewhat by substituting cheaper ingredients to camouflage a smaller portion size. The chef can even go further by substituting cheaper cuts of meat, fish and fowl. Some profit-making tactics, however, can compromise quality. It is up to the chef to decide what is within the restaurant's standards. Certainly some substitutions are worse than others. But a schedule on which cheaper goods are sold once a week or bimonthly seems allowable for any restaurant. The trick is to spend more time in planning and preparation so that the dish not only meets the prevailing standards but sells well, too.

Occasionally, the fish purveyor will try to deliver a batch of fish which is acceptable today but will have a much shorter shelf life because it has already been at the warehouse too long. Under normal circumstances, such substandard goods would be rejected. But what if the purveyor gives a cut in price? Then the goods may become attractive. Offer to keep the poor-quality fish, but for half price.

Using another approach, ask the butcher, fish wholesaler and dry goods salesperson to give some suggestions for cheap substitutes, such as swordfish chunks, sea legs, tongul tuna, veal ribs, or organ meats. Freshness, quality, good portion size, and originality are all the factors which translate into a steady clientele—this is the bait. A switch to a cheap substitute doesn't have to be obvious, should not be for a menu item, and should not be out of style with the regular menu. The best way to affect a switch is with a weekly special using a product similar to one of the menu items. The following five recipes show how easy it can be.

TOMATO PASTA ROULADE DIMARE IN ROAST GARLIC CREAM

2 Sheets Tomato Pasta	½ cup Garlic Kernels
8 lb. Seafood	3 qt. Heavy Cream
4 cups Fresh Basil	1 qt. White Wine
½ cup Chopped Garlic	1 T Shallots
3 lb. Ricotta	1 T Butter
4 cups Mushrooms	½ cup Salt
½ cup Shallots	¼ cup White Pepper
½ cup Olive Oil	½ cup Grated Parmesan
21 Egg Yolks	

A roulade is one form of pasta which Americans may not be familiar with but will accept quickly. For the stuffing, use the cheapest seafood available: sea legs, the imitation crab; swordfish chunks, the stomach flap scraps; small shrimp; canned lobster tails; and mussels. Wash everything well. In two or three large saute pans, heat the olive oil, using just enough to cover the bottom of the pan. Brown all the chopped garlic and shallots over a moderate flame. Turn the flame up to high, and then add the seafood, basil and mushrooms. Saute until cooked evenly. Remove from the pans, drain and cool. Add the parmesan, salt and pepper to taste. Grind the entire mixture into a large mixing bowl. Add the ricotta. Mix well. Season. Spread, roll, tie and cook the pasta.

For the cream, roast in a high oven about two dozen kernels of garlic until browned. In a sauce pan, heat the butter and brown the shallots. Add the white wine to the shallots. Reduce it at a high boil until all the liquid has evaporated. Add the heavy cream and the roasted garlic. Boil moderately for one hour. Strain and return the cream to a low boil. Puree the garlic and shallots, and return them to the cream. Salt and pepper to taste. Whip the sauce often to allow it to cool evenly, and then add the whipped egg yolks.

On the Line. Cut a serving of pasta—two or three slices—and place them on a plate. Cover with plastic wrap. Put in the microwave at moderate heat for two minutes. Heat one-half cup of the roast garlic cream. Pour onto a round plate. Place the hot roulade slices on the sauce. Garnish with a watercress sprig. Makes fourteen servings. The beauty of this recipe is that it can be priced according to its most expensive ingredient—lobster, swordfish or crab. The seafood must have a strong flavor to be right for the flavor of the dish. The poor texture of the miscellaneous seafood is masked by ricotta and pulverization.

GRILLED HALIBUT STEAK WITH FRESH OREGANO, CAYENNE AND MUSTARD CRUST

10 lb. Halibut Steaks	½ cup Olive Oil
2 bunches Fresh Oregano	½ cup Salt
1 T Cayenne	10 Lemons
24 oz. Poupon Mustard	

Buy eight-ounce portion-controlled halibut steaks. They should be very inexpensive. If not, substitute another frozen fish steak which is lower in cost. Prepare the mustard by adding fresh chopped oregano leaves and cayenne to it. Mix well.

On the Line. Rub olive oil and salt on the steak. Place on the grill. Squeeze the juice of one-half lemon on the fish. Turn. When the fish is nearly cooked, spread a layer of the mustard over the entire fish. Crust the layer by putting the fish underneath the broiler or in a high oven. Plate and garnish with a lemon swan and greenery. Makes twenty portions. Grilling with the piquant mustard masks the halibut's freezer origin. Even in restaurants where fresh fish is sold regularly, this dish can be used without a problem.

GRILLED LAMB STEAK ROSEMARY

2 large Legs of Lamb	8 Lemons
3 bunches Fresh Rosemary	½ cup Salt
1 qt. Olive Oil	¼ cup Pepper
¼ cup Meat Tenderizer	¼ cup Garlic Powder

Using a band saw or knife and meat saw, cut fourteen-ounce steaks. Trim the outer rim of fat and sinew. Pierce each steak with a paring knife to tenderize. Rub each steak with olive oil, garlic powder, salt and pepper. Place in a square pan in layers with rosemary leaves. Cover and leave overnight in the refrigerator.

On the Line. Remove most of the rosemary leaves and put aside. Sprinkle the steak with meat tenderizer and grill it. After turning, squeeze one-half of a lemon over the steak. Cook to the desired doneness. Plate the steak and garnish with rosemary leaves and lemon. Makes twelve to sixteen servings. Lamb steak is unique to the American palate. Though it is cheaper than red meat steaks, with a little tenderizing it can be sold more expensively.

HONEY-CINNAMON BARBEQUE RIBS

20 lb. Veal Ribs	¼ cup Bacon Fat
2 # 10 Cans Ketchup	½ cup Red Wine
4 Spanish Onions	2 T Red Vinegar
2 Green Peppers	1 lb. Honey
3 Bay Leaf	½ cup Garlic
1 qt. Ale	¼ cup Basil, Oregano, Thyme
1 qt. Pineapple Juice	1 cup Yellow Mustard
½ cup Cinnamon	2 T Salt
	2 T Black Pepper

Veal ribs are wide-boned, like spare ribs, with a layer of fat running the length of the rack between two layers of meat. Cut the racks down into individual ribs. Place them in deep hotel pans. Mix four cups of ketchup with two quarts of warm water and pour over the ribs evenly. Cover with aluminum foil. Roast in a hot oven (500°F) until the meat is tender. Remove from the hotel pans and place on sheet pans, meat side up. Sear the meat and fat under the broiler. Put ribs aside to cool, cover and refrigerate until service.

For the sauce, chop a mirepoix of the onions, peppers and garlic. Heat the bacon fat in a heavy stock pot. Add the mirepoix, bay leaf, basil, thyme and oregano. Stir to keep from sticking. When the onions begin to release liquid, add the red vinegar. Stir. Add the red wine. Saute for a few minutes, and then add the ale, pineapple juice, ketchup, mustard, one-half pound of honey, one-quarter cup of cinnamon, and one tablespoon each of salt and pepper. Cook for about forty-five minutes at a low boil until the sauce is heavy. Add the remaining cinnamon and honey. Adjust the seasonings. Cool evenly.

On the Line. Put five ribs on a sizzle platter and in a high oven. After the ribs are reheated, sauce them and finish them off under the broiler to brown the sauce. Plate and garnish with chopped parsley and lemon cartwheels. Serve. Makes twenty orders. Veal ribs are a little-used item. In some butcher shops, they may be a scrap item destined for the garbage. As a result, the per pound price is low. All that needs to be done is to sear the fat out, revealing the delicious meat inside.

BAKED CHICKEN LEGS STUFFED WITH MUSHROOMS, PIMENTO AND WILD RICE

1 Case 3 lb. Chickens	1 Spanish Onion
2 lb. Wild Rice	¼ cup Garlic
3 lb. Mushrooms	½ cup Celery
1 #303 Can Pimentos	¼ cup Salt
2 T Butter	¼ cup Pepper
12 oz. Cognac	2 T Thyme
2 qt. Chicken Stock	2 Bay Leaf
2 cups Olive Oil	1 cup Flour
3 cups Heavy Cream	

Remove the chicken cuisses from twenty-four chickens. Be sure to keep as much skin as possible with the leg and thigh. The chicken breast and carriage may be put aside for another recipe. Peel the meat away from the thigh bone. Do not cut the skin. Continue exposing the leg bone up to the ankle joint. Cut the leg bone, leaving the ankle joint and half an inch of bone. Do all forty-eight legs.

Chop a mirepoix of the onion, garlic and celery. Heat the butter in a saucepan, and brown the mirepoix. Add the bay leaves, thyme, and some salt and pepper. Clean and slice the mushrooms, which are added to the sauteing mirepoix. Wash and then add the wild rice. Add one quart of chicken stock. Keep at a low boil. Cook until the rice starts to open up and become tender. Add a little water if necessary. Mix in the chopped pimento, cover and steam for thirty minutes. Allow to cool. Place a chicken cuisse, skin side down. Stuff the cavity made by the absent bone and excess skin. Hold the skin together with toothpicks. Cover and refrigerate until service.

On the Line. Heat a little olive oil in a saute pan. Salt and pepper two cuisses. Sear the skin and turn. Place the pan in a high oven. The chickens should cook in ten to fifteen minutes. Plate them and keep them warm while the sauce is prepared.

Add one tablespoon of flour to the pan juices. Use a whip to cook it evenly. Add four ounces of chicken stock. Blend well. Add one-quarter cup of heavy cream. Reduce to sauce consistency, and then add one ounce of cognac. Add salt and thyme to taste. Pour sauce on a plate. Slice the chicken legs crossways to one inch from the ankle. Fan or lay the slices on the sauce in two arcs. Place the ankle stubs upright. Put on paper feet. Garnish with chive sprigs and pimento squares. Serve. Makes twelve orders. Chicken legs may not have much elegance, but as a once-in-a-while special, this recipe will be popular. The cost of the chicken legs is practically nil, as it is absorbed by the more fashionable remaining supremes.

Highlights

The more precisely a chef realizes the purpose of a dish, and controls the makeup or design of the product, the greater the popularity and profit will be.

While a successfully executed dish will have a combination of purposes, there will usually be a particular one from which the dish evolves.

The most extreme example of a dish created strictly for aesthetics is the food designed for photography—the work of food stylists.

The pleasing symmetry of a colorful, well-balanced presentation begins with the selection of ingredients and cooking styles.

Because a taste is identified by its source (apples, for example, are a definite taste sensation), in order for a taste or trend to be a rage, it must originate from a popular food source.

A solid understanding of the region's culinary history is important for the successful design of a restaurant dish.

A chef designing for taste has to be able to create from memory through a process similar to visualization.

Popularity depends on common appreciation of tastes or trends.

When the purpose is to sell food in order to reduce stock or to build dollar volume, popularity must be the prime design consideration.

High-volume operations need quick two-step recipes to keep the food coming out fast and the tables turning over.

Dishes which are simple in design are some of the most profitable to sell.

Profitability is a key element of design; it determines what ingredients are available within the chef's price range.

One method of lowering food costs is to reduce the portion size of the main ingredient by ten to fifteen percent.

Substitutes can be put over, under, around or inside the main ingredient to compensate for the smaller portion weight.

No restaurant can build a regular clientele by selling inferior product.

The trick is to spend more time in planning and preparation so that the dish not only meets the prevailing standards but sells well, too.

Chapter 12

THE WASTE FACTOR

Introduction

Waste should not be such an important issue except that it is too often overlooked. Any food product has an inherent waste factor, somewhere between two and fifty percent. This figure doesn't include mistakes in handling. All the raw food products that go into the garbage can every day were purchased; their impact on the profit margin can be significant. If waste figures are not factored into menu prices, the effects of these hidden costs are doubly devastating. Not only are they unscheduled losses, but they are usually mistakenly considered as salable weights. Head chefs must educate themselves about the types and amounts of waste and make plans to counter their effects.

Hidden Costs

Waste may be as obvious as an overcooked steak or as elusive as an unrotated case of broccoli. The solution is to pinpoint the areas where waste can and will occur, and make regular efforts to minimize and allow for the costs. Chapter 9 covered the procedures necessary to ensure that the staff is handling the food correctly. For the sake of discussion, let's assume that they are doing an excellent job; stocks are being rotated, prepared wisely, and cooked on the line without mistake. Still, there must be a waste factor, and this is the hidden cost which can cripple the profit margin. The purpose of this chapter is to identify those hidden costs and, whenever possible, to determine percentages of waste. These waste percentages are not to be interpreted as set yields for recipes; the variables with foods are strongly affected by size. They are vital, however, when pricing menus and calculating the costs of categories of ingredients. First, consider the individual categories of food product; then analyze the overall operation.

Meat and Fowl

Each cut of red meat or kind of fowl has its idiosyncracies—ways in which they must be deboned and trimmed. Here the waste is inevitable. For instance, domestic ducklings are so fatty that in order to get two reasonably sized portions from one duck, a four-pound bird is necessary. Using chicken, a three-pound bird is necessary. The extra pound of duck is lost during the roasting process as grease. Duck therefore is more wisely priced on a per bird basis, with twelve portions per case. The automatic assumption that four pounds of duck yield three or four servings, as chicken or turkey would, is the sort of hidden cost factor which waste produces. But this type of waste is easy to pinpoint. Other products need a hands-on approach, including weighing and counting of the finished portions.

Complicated cuts have a predictable amount of waste. For instance, cryovaced filet mignon, which is a readily available product, has a normal waste amount of approximately fifty percent. (Some extremely large filets may have a better yield.) Other untrimmed strips of filet include even more fat in the per pound price. Their waste factor is sixty percent or more. No matter how good you are with a knife, filet mignon costs twice as much as it seems to on paper. That is a high waste cost, especially considering the price of the cut. But any type of meat consists of at least twenty percent fat and sinew. Other examples may be less dramatic, but their cumulative effect is just as significant.

Hamburger has a ten percent weight loss for 80–20 blend after cooking and a higher weight loss for fattier blends.

Top round, if it is cooked rare and untrimmed, has a top yield of ninety-five percent. When cut and trimmed, the waste is twenty percent.

Beef triangles lose twenty-five percent in the trimming.

Sirloin butt loses thirty percent to trim, some of which may be salvageable for the soup pot.

Prime rib of beef has a fat flap and bones which cannot be sold, but, as with ducks, this cut has portions rather than pounds as its basic unit. A prime rib can yield seventeen cuts if it is large (fifteen to eighteen pounds), provided the carver is experienced. A normal yield, however, is fourteen cuts.

Shell steak has a waste factor of twenty-five to thirty percent.

Ribeye steak's loss is lower, only five to twenty percent.

Flank steak has ten percent fat and sinew loss.

Corned beef can vary in quality, price and fat content. An average piece will lose thirty percent after being cooked and trimmed.

Beef and pork ribs vary so much in size and weight that a firm estimate isn't possible. However, for the lean imported ribs, figure on fourteen ounces per serving, a small rack. For large spare ribs, sixteen to twenty ounces per serving is average.

Lamb shoulder should be cheap because waste runs up to seventy-five percent.

Leg of lamb, with the bone in, has a loss of twenty-five percent.

Lamb steaks have a waste factor of fifteen percent.

Fresh ham or pork roast loses thirty percent when trimmed, boned and tied.

Smoked ham loses thirty percent to bone and fat.

Loin of pork chops loses only five percent when sold on the bone.

Organ meats generally lose about twenty percent to veins and skin.

Veal chops have a waste factor of forty percent.

Loin of veal in the cryovaced bags already greatly trimmed has a waste factor of ten percent. Other untrimmed loins may have a waste factor of twenty-five to thirty percent.

Veal shank is fifty to eighty percent bone, depending on the length of the bone.

Turkey, goose and large capon are fifty to sixty percent bone, giblets and grease.

Turkey breasts on the bone have thirty percent waste.

Turkey legs are sixty-five percent bone.

Chicken cutlets vary from producer to producer, but generally you get what you pay for. The higher-priced cutlets have less fat, a waste factor of ten percent.

French chicken breasts have fifteen percent waste unless they are removed from the bone to make supremes; then the loss rises to thirty percent.

Chicken wings lose five percent.

Whole chickens weighing two pounds each are sixty percent bone and fat. At three pounds, they are fifty percent waste.

A one-pound game hen is seventy percent bone.

Fish

Wholesalers today are in such strong competition with each other that they will clean a whole fish down to the skin and eye bones for a nominal cost. Unless there is a skilled fish fileter on your preparation staff, fillet weight purchases is the method to use. They take the guesswork out of cost analysis, and, more importantly, eliminate hidden costs. The bone and head weight of a whole fish without guts can vary from forty to eighty percent of the total, depending on the variety of fish and even the size within that variety. Asking the wholesaler what the bone loss will be doesn't always ensure a successful portioning. Often the wholesaler is guessing, too. Buy fillets or portioned steaks. There is still plenty of waste. Clarify the waste quickly, before cleaning and portioning, using the following guidelines:

Large fillets (five to eight pounds each) have a common waste factor of fifteen percent.

Medium-sized fillets (three to five pounds each) have twenty percent bone, skin and stomach loss.

Smaller fillets have a greater range of loss factors, depending upon the shape of the fillet and the species of fish. Ten percent is a low figure, but twenty-five percent is possible, too. This is quite a range, something which experience with local varieties will make a chef better able to estimate.

Swordfish represents a unique example. Skin and bones account for twenty-five percent of the total unless it is a pinwheel cut; then the waste drops to twenty percent.

Shrimp shells are thin, but their weight adds up. The best way to control this waste is to portion by count rather than by pound. Scallops, oysters, mussels and clams should be portioned by count rather than weight. Of course, the chef makes the reconciliation between weight and count to decide how many shrimp should be in a portion. For example, ten to fifteen size shrimp yield approximately sixty-five pieces per five-pound box. Suppose that the shrimp costs $10 per pound. By dividing $50 by sixty-five shrimp, the per shrimp cost of $.77 has the waste factor built in.

Vegetables

Poor handling and preparation techniques account for most of the waste in vegetable purchases. But consider the ideal situation again: a restaurant where the vegetables arrive in perfect condition, are cared for properly and are cooked without extraordinary waste. Should chefs assume that their efforts have paid off? That there is no loss at all? Absolutely not. Every product purchased has a waste factor. And the fragility of vegetables indicates that they are subject to ruin. One night, the late waitress leaves the sliding glass door open on the salad station; three bus pans of salad are lost. The next night, the preparation team washes and cuts too many garnishes; they are mushy by the next service. This is waste—an actual dollar loss which must be factored into the menu prices. The following estimates of loss are for normal operations with above-average performance by the preparation cooks. They take into account the usual problems which result in waste. These percentages are additional losses after trimming and/or cooking.

Romaine, iceberg, greenleaf, redleaf, and bib lettuces and spinach have a five percent loss in the best circumstances. This loss could easily double due to downturns in volume.

Potatoes, in their many sizes and uses, are cheap. They are overprepared often. Some arrive broken or scarred. Ten percent waste occurs.

Fresh corn also has a ten percent loss factor.

Broccoli has only twenty percent waste unless there is an extraordinary downturn in business; then the loss may triple.

Zucchini and summer squashes have thin skins which are easily scarred. The result is five percent loss.

Onions, scallions and leeks may have almost no waste for weeks. Then twenty percent may be lost without the chef's being notified. Assume a ten percent loss.

Mushrooms have a five percent waste.

Green, red and other peppers average a ten percent loss.

Tomatoes of all sizes are lost at a rate of ten percent. This figure does not include those which never ripen or are too mushy to be used.

Avocados are lost at a rate of fifteen percent after preparation.

Carrots have a waste factor of five percent.

Cucumbers are lost, after cutting, up to fifteen percent of the total yield.

Watercress and parsley lose about five percent.

Eggplants go quickly before and after cutting; assume a fifteen percent loss.

Cabbages, cauliflower and brussel sprouts lose five percent.

Asparagus lose fifteen percent.

Peas may have only ten percent waste after preparation, but the waste during and before preparation is high.

Garlic is tough. Figure a three percent loss.

Celery loses ten percent.

Sprouts have the potential to lose twenty percent if not used within one or two days. Add a normal handling waste of five percent.

Fresh fruit, herbs and nuts after preparation will lose approximately ten percent as miscellaneous waste.

Even with strict inventory controls in place, as discussed in Chapter 9, waste is inevitable. Vegetables tend to be abused because they are cheap and plentiful. Always include the preceding waste factors in any per plate cost calculations.

Pasta

Fresh and dried pastas are handled and prepared in different ways; therefore, their waste factors differ.

Fresh pasta, in the best circumstances, loses fifteen percent.

Dried pasta loses ten percent through breakage before it is even cooked. After cooking, the normal loss is fifteen percent.

Frozen Goods

Fish, chicken, potatoes, vegetables—anything can and may be frozen today. The quality can be very good, provided the product has not been frozen for too long. Yet freezer burn is inevitable. Frozen goods, once thawed, tend to deteriorate faster than fresh goods. If the thawed food is not normally used immediately, as fryolater items are, this form of waste must be considered, too. In general for frozen foods, consider the waste factor to be twenty percent. That seems high, but the normal uses and abuses of food are greatly compounded by the freezing process.

Dairy Goods

The waste of dairy goods fluctuates radically due to the seasons, especially if the restaurant's refrigeration is slow to recover or insufficient for inventories. Milk and heavy cream seem to be the worst offenders, probably because these are the two items used in the highest volume. Any milk-based product, like cheeses and butter, will mold within one or two weeks, depending on the outside temperature and humidity. Strict rotation systems can reduce most of the waste during the cooler months. Estimate the waste factor to be five to ten percent during those times. The hotter months will push the loss to ten to twenty percent, provided the dairy products are arriving cold or at least cool. The products must be refrigerated immediately, and their storage spot within the unit must be away from the door, where the constant exposure to warm air retards the cooling process. Any time the amount of milk and heavy cream being lost approaches thirty percent, a change is indicated. Perhaps the inventory system needs rethinking or the refrigeration unit is faulty. Check all aspects immediately. Regular maintenance of the unit is one area where it may not be wise to delegate the responsibility to a manager. The manager is usually responsible for maintenance of any equipment, but if this person's response time is too slow, the chef must assume the responsibility or be prepared to lose on the food pc.

Dry Goods

This category of foodstuffs is immense, including oils, canned goods, herbs and spices, dried and processed grains, sugars, packaged goods and soft beverages. For any of these items, waste may be caused by man, animal or nature, but it is always a result of the stock's location. With dry goods, a well thought out plan of shelving and rotation will reduce the abuse by man (see Chapter 9). Waste caused by rodents and other animals may be occasional and slight or an ongoing battle for territory. This is another area of responsibility which is usually delegated to a manager. Be certain that the problem is handled efficiently and thoroughly; that is the best way to keep the food pc at its lowest.

Rarely do restaurants have modern, deluxe storage facilities. In the worst circumstances, cases of goods are left stacked on the floor or in the walk-in, where they invite disaster. Water damage from burst or leaking pipes is a recurring danger; goods left on the floor are susceptible to this and other abuses. Do not place goods beneath rows of coupled pipes or in any area which has a history of leaks. At the finish hint of moisture, relocate all goods to a dry spot. If the plumber needs to be called, don't wait for the manager in charge of maintenance to show up later.

Dry goods in a clean, dry environment last well on the shelf. All it takes is a little rotation to ensure optimum quality and minimum waste—on the average, ten percent. But that low figure assumes the presence of myriad containers with lids and shelves for order. Even in the best of arrangements, bottles will break.

Desserts

How devastating it is for a customer to finish an exciting, delicious entree, and then to follow it with a dessert which appears stunning but has a slight

refrigerator tinge. Either it goes into the garbage or the restaurant's reputation is tarnished. The best desserts come fresh, never frozen—that is,
when their flavors are vivid and unpolluted by the taste of the box they
were stored in. It is helpful if the refrigerator used to store desserts has only
desserts in it. At least, heavily scented vegetables, meats and sauces
should never share air space with pastries, pies, cakes and mousses.

The waste factor or losses with desserts can be enormous (see Chapter
9). An uncontrolled staff can easily eat over half of a superior dessert
(leaving the less spectacular ones for the customers!). Normal handling of
the fragile layers and fillings can result in a five to ten percent loss before
one dessert is served. That is provided an entire cake is cut, plated and
covered with plastic wrap all at once. If the desserts are being portioned to
order, there is a chance of serving optimum quality; that reduces one
type of waste—old age. But it increases the handling waste when pieces
are cut too large or are broken, or even when a certain amount of a dessert
sticks to the many serving utensils. The best approach for a chef to adopt
will depend upon the style of presentation desired and the space available.
One way to reduce waste is to reduce the number of persons who perform
the task. Waste will be lessened as the cook's skill increases.

Baked Goods

Breads, rolls, muffins, bagels, etc. have such a short shelf life that normal
changes in sales volume may be enough to cause waste. Assuming that
tight controls for ordering and rotation are in place, the next feasible loss
reducer is to find ways to use day-old breads, as in bread crumbs or
croutons.

Refrigerating breads in airtight containers will extend their life somewhat,
especialy if they will be warmed before serving. Including the use of
conservation techniques and old bread uses, waste occurs at a rate of
twenty percent. If there are no possible ways to recycle the stale bread and
it must be trashed, the waste factor jumps to twenty-five percent.

General Tips

Poor handling procedures due to inexperience, laziness or sloppiness
are the source of most waste problems. Each person on the kitchen team
must be an exacting professional; that's the ideal, but obviously not the
norm. Poor preparation and line cooking techniques, left uncorrected,

will cause a steady erosion of profit. The chef's role is one of overseer—
the supervisor who continues to point out waste as it occurs. The training
and retraining process is never ending. Just as one problem is discovered
and solved, another one occurs.

For example, Chef JJ of PASTA, PASTA...PASTA! had a simple preparation schedule for a few sauces, blanched pastas and cooked vegetables.
But because the kitchen's payroll budget was so low and the available staff
was unskilled, even these simple tasks became monumental. The linguini,
fettucini and tagliatelli left at the end of the evening service constantly
had to be thrown out the next morning. It was mushy after less than
twenty-four hours. JJ showed the three cooks who cooked pasta during the
week how to stop the preboiling process just before the pasta turned al
dente while it was still very firm. When he observed them, the pasta was
cooked perfectly, drained, oiled and wrapped in an airtight tray. Because
of the heavy volume in pasta, JJ's rotation system was well established.
Still, he double-checked it to make certain that the oldest pasta was used
first. Monday through Friday, while JJ was there, the pasta was beautiful;
then the weekend came, and JJ was off. When he returned on Monday, the
night chefs had more horror stories about two and three trays of pasta
having to be dumped every night. It was mushy again. The weekend was
the busiest period, so all three of the cooks whom he had been retraining
were working. Each had cooked some pasta. JJ could not isolate the problem
or place blame. JJ called a preparation meeting. His staff spoke little
English and had never eaten pasta before joining the restaurant's staff, but
a few of them were quick learners and loyal. JJ rearranged duties so that
the number two preparation cook did all the pastas every day. Since he
worked seven days a week, this was a perfect start. JJ went over the
procedures again. He also made a point of stressing the importance of al
dente pasta to the quality of the plates served and the sheer foolishness of
the repeated waste. Every day JJ checked the pasta and let the second
cook know he was checking. The quality improved and the pasta waste
stopped. But during the checking process, JJ discovered a similar problem
with trays of blanched broccoli. It too was going into the garbage daily.
The retraining efforts continued.

Common sources of waste are overproduction and overuse. One simple
way to curtail these losses is by having just enough in inventory to do the
job. This solution has limited effectiveness, however, because there should
be a cushion of supplies to ensure that all menu items are stocked. But the
tightly controlled inventory is effective in stopping gross overuse, which
occasionally occurs in every restaurant. This method is easy to incorporate into a regular procedure because the chef does the ordering in most
restaurants.

One of the principal sources of waste is the kitchen staff's throwing away of leftovers (see the section "Specific Problems" in Chapter 9 for a complete discussion of the "no throwaway law").

Another important way to reduce waste also includes staff retraining, but in a subtle way. The chef's own way of handling and saving food will do the most to set the standard for the staff. Verbal instructions will only go so far in incorporating a superior technique into the staff's daily routine. When the chef does the work better often enough, the kitchen staff will take notice, and eventually it will be noticed where it matters the most — by the customers. At that point, there will be no turning back even for the lazy or vindictive cook, at least not without causing attention to be drawn to this person's poor quality.

Highlights

If waste figures are not factored into menu prices, the effects of these hidden costs are doubly devasating.

The solution is to pinpoint the areas where waste can and will occur, and make regular efforts to minimize and allow for the costs.

Poor handling and preparation techniques account for most of the waste in vegetable purchases.

Every product purchased has a waste factor.

Frozen goods, once thawed, tend to deteriorate faster than fresh goods.

Poor handling procedures due to inexperience, laziness or sloppiness are the source of most waste problems.

The training and retraining process is never ending. Just as one problem is discovered and solved, another one occurs.

Common sources of waste are overproduction and overuse.

A tightly controlled inventory is effective in stopping gross overuse.

The chef's own handling and saving of food will do the most to set the standard for the staff.

Chapter 13

HOW TO CALCULATE FOOD PERCENTAGES

Introduction
Business Applications
Food PC Calculations
Average Estimates
Highlights

Introduction

The expenses of a restaurant's kitchen are divided into three types: food costs, labor costs and operating costs. These costs are also called *percentages* or *pc's*. Under normal operating circumstances, the food pc is the largest of these expenses, and therefore the most significant indicator of a restaurant's profitability and a chef's performance. Calculation of these costs isn't simply a numbers game better left to managers. Their importance can range from a good idea to stay on top of the job to an absolute must for job survival. In either case, food pc's are an important tool for assertive chefs.

Business Applications

As a part of the chef's duties, food pc's are essential in a numbers of ways. The gatering of data necessary to calculate a food pc is a regular discipline which keeps the chef in touch with the entire purchase/receiving system, especially at the end of the chain, where it is easy for the chef to ignore the invoices.

Making an educated guess about the current month's food pc is a chef's equivalent of secret intelligence gathering. The chef may have advance knowledge of a good month or bad month at least a week before the owner-manager can compute the facts. This advance information is invaluable in stopping a severe slide. With the facts mounting in the form of hard statistics as they happen, week to week, rather than a week or two after the period has closed, a chef may adjust buying and marketing practices. When problems occur, usually one item or a class of items are priced way above their normal market price and are causing a severe profit loss. Keeping tabs on the pc will show how disastrous the loss is. While it is true that doing the paperwork doesn't create any more profit for the period if it has just finished, clear knowledge of a kitchen's past operating costs is one element a chef can use to plan for the immediate future.

A chef's ability to survive the ups and downs of a volatile food pc may be the key to his or her own longevity on the job. Being informed by the owner-manager that the food pc was disastrous and being asked to explain why immediately is a common scenario. The unprepared chef will be left sputtering and concentrating while the owner-manager proceeds to give direction. Too many instances when management has to take control of kitchen operations will leave them wondering why they hired you! Stay ahead of management by forecasting the food pc on the basis of precise records. The chef of a large operation must have financial skills in addition to culinary skills. That means being comfortable when discussing finance and being able to make sense out of the computer readouts and financial papers prepared by the accountant. There will be combative moments when lines are drawn and sides are taken. At those times, the big weapons will be pc's and their spinoff numbers. Don't be left defenseless.

It is also advisable for chefs to know when they are doing a fantastic job. Since the food pc constitutes the major portion of gross sales, it is a prime indicator. If the food pc is low for the year while sales have stayed constant or risen, then profits are certainly up. That means that it is past time to ask for a raise. Provided your salary is still within market limits and you haven't gotten a raise since the turnaround, the owner-manager will be hard pressed to find a good reason to say no. If he or she does, pay close attention to Chapter 19.

Food PC Calculations

The actual arithmetic involved in calculating food pc's is elementary. Divide the total sales of the period into the total purchases for the period. The following examples show the basic process for three separate levels of restaurant operations. For a complete explanation of how to compile the data used in the division, see the section "Forms and Procedures" in Chapter 8.

Example A. *THE PICNIC GAZEBO* is a new restaurant both in location and in style. Its success hinges on the customers' acceptance of a countrified menu in sophisticated surroundings. After seven months of operation, sales have risen to a steady but low volume. Here are the figures for the current month, October.

PERIOD	DATE	SALES	PURCHASES		FOOD PC'S
Week 1	10/10	10,456	5,279	=	50.5
Week 2	10/17	10,711	5,216	=	48.7
Week 3	10/24	9,232	4,542	=	49.2
Week 4	10/31	11,062	4,823	=	43.6
October totals		$41,461	$19,860	=	47.9%

Example B. *THE PRIME MINISTER* is an established supper club with medium sales volume when compared to national figures, but is actually one of the most expensive and successful in its area. The chef is a part owner, which may help to explain the excellent profit margin. Here are July's figures.

PERIOD	DATE	SALES	PURCHASES		FOOD PC'S
Week 1	7/3	21,334	9,276	=	43.5
Week 2	7/10	24,792	8,603	=	34.7
Week 3	7/17	25,543	9,221	=	36.1
Week 4	7/24	28,191	9,162	=	32.5
Week 5	7/31	27,687	10,548	=	38.1
July totals		$127,547	$46,810	=	36.7%

Example C. *THE LEFT BANK EXPRESS* is a two hundred fifty-seat gold mine located across the street from a major university. The volume is heavy. Part of the reason for the Express' success is its low prices. It relies on high volume and rapid turnover to yield a high dollar profit. Therefore, the food pc is average. The figures below are from the peak month, April.

PERIOD	DATE	SALES	PURCHASES		FOOD PC'S
Week 1	4/10	64,271	30,336	=	47.2
Week 2	4/17	68,990	30,149	=	43.7
Week 3	4/24	66,734	28,095	=	42.1
Week 4	5/1	67,255	24,467	=	36.4
April totals		$267,250	$113,047	=	42.3%

Average Estimates

The three preceding examples show food pc's ranging from the high forties to the mid-thirties, a spread of about eleven points. A food pc in the middle to upper forties is poor, regardless of the pricing or style of the menu. Likewise, a food pc in the middle to upper thirties is excellent for a mid-sized, medium-scale restaurant. Most operations are doing very well if they bring in a forty percent food cost. That is the rule of thumb which separates mediocre chefs from superior ones. Some professional chefs whom I interviewed feel that a pc of forty-one or even forty-two is average. They are quoting from their own experience in kitchens.

The National Restaurant Association in Washington, D.C., publishes statistics annually in a report entitled "Restaurant Industry Operations Report." Their 1987 report shows a considerably lower range of food pc's for all types of full-menu table service restaurants. Figures dip into the twenties and concentrate in the low and middle thirties. A few percentages read forty, but just barely. The variable used to establish different classifications of restaurants are years in business, region, location, affiliation, types of meals served (breakfast, lunch or dinner), menu theme and sales volume. The report does exactly what it sets out to do: compile industrywide figures based upon the restaurants which completed their questionnaire, a large portion of which appear to be concept chains. This is interesting material but it is not specific enough to provide a firm comparison for individual restaurants.

The best way to find out how the monthly food pc at your restaurant compares with that of other places is to call chefs in your area who run kitchen operations similar to yours. If you are able to solicit enough responses, an average pc should emerge.

Highlights

Under normal operating circumstances, the food pc is the largest expense, and therefore the most significant indicator of a restaurant's profitability and a chef's performance.

The gathering of data necessary to calculate a food pc is a regular discipline which keeps the chef in touch with the entire purchase/receiving system.

While it is true that doing the paperwork doesn't create more profit for the period if it has already finished, clear knowledge of a kitchen's past operating costs is one element a chef can use to plan for the future.

Divide the total sales of the period into the total purchases for the period.

A food pc in the middle to upper forties is poor, regardless of the pricing or style of the menu.

A food pc in the middle to upper thirties is excellent for mid-sized, medium-scale restaurants.

Figures dip into the twenties and concentrate in the low and middle thirties for coffee shops, fast food and concept restaurants.

The best way to find out how the monthly food pc at your restaurant compares with that of other places is to call other chefs in your area who run kitchen operations similar to yours.

PART 3

LABOR PERCENTAGES (HOW TO KEEP LABOR COSTS LOW)

Chapter 14

SCHEDULING

Introduction

A good schedule is one which supplies enough labor to get the job done without overstaffing. More simply defined, scheduling is deciding who works when. Computers, employee lists and schedule forms can needlessly complicate and confuse the task, however. Let's look at some of the basic requirements needed to schedule effectively, at low cost, and then use these principles in examples which showcase various types of restaurants.

Two elements are needed to keep labor costs at a minimum: a willingness to work and a method of forecasting labor needs. Both come into play when schedules are made.

Willingness to Work

A chef's willingness to work allows for needed flexibility in the schedule, especially in gray areas where adding another worker would be an unnecessary luxury. Hard-working chefs are supposed to pick up the slack by filling in. That's one of the reasons they get the biggest pay check. The diligent chef also sets an example. The way a chef works becomes the tempo of the kitchen—fast, moderate, or slow. Very few workers will pace themselves faster than they are expected to work. Of course, there are always ways for the aging, or lazy chef to create a cushy little niche. Delegating undesirable tasks to subordinates, thereby saving the most favorable work for themselves, is one way. It takes a while, but it is possible for a chef to train the staff into a nearly perfect machine that functions without manual assistance from the chef. Chefs do not have to do anything that they don't want to do. Yet superior chefs become involved at all levels of the operation, because they are willing to do so for the responsibility or enjoyment of the job (see Chapter 15).

Methods of Forecasting Labor Needs

Personal experience and dutiful record keeping will give a chef the knowledge needed to forecast correctly how many line cooks, preparation cooks and dishwashers a particular shift needs. Most chefs have either worked in all phases of a kitchen's operation or have an ability to judge the average time needed to do the complete range of cooking tasks. Still, scheduling remains a tricky business, especially during the first months of a new restaurant's operation, when there are no past records to consult. Further complicating matters, the chef's experience may be based on another region or another style of restaurant.

The greatest danger is to have too few staff available to meet customers' demands. It is much better to have a slightly over budget labor cost than to turn off clientele with slow, shoddy production. The first goal is to get the job done to the best of anyone's ability. If, temporarily, two cooks are needed to do the job of one real professional, so be it. Keep two on until that professional comes along. Never sacrifice quality for the pc. In the long run, that will strangle the business' sales volume.

But what about the financial restrictions? Schedules with too much waste can lead to bankruptcy. Waste in labor is just as harmful as food waste. In fact, it may be more costly. This is an area where a lazy or inexperienced chef can literally destroy a restaurant. By always opting for an additional cook, just to be on the safe side, chefs evade their responsbility, perhaps because of inexperience. They may be afraid to work on a frenetic line. Whatever their reason for such cautious scheduling, they ae hurting their restaurant and themselves in a number of ways: The staff never reaches their full potential; the chef appears incompetent; the food is produced in a lackadaisical atmosphere; the quality fluctuates; and profit is lost through waste.

The goal is to schedule just enough people to have delicious, colorful dishes produced by a hard-working and efficient crew.

There are blind spots, however, especially in the first year of a restaurant's operation, when no past sales records are available. In those cases, scheduling relies on other variables: the size of the kitchen and the number of work stations; the number of seats in the restaurant; the size of the menu; the immediate area's projected sales potential; the budget for kitchen labor; holiday and seasonal shifts in volume; and styles of service.

For example, consider Chef Lisa's predicament at the Skyline Grill, an upscale bar and supper club set to open December 1. There will be either one hundred fifty or one hundred seventy-five seats. (The owner hasn't decided whether to extend the dance floor around a certain pillar. That would reduce the number of seats by twenty-five.) The area is new, part of an old-town refurbishing, where ancient factory buildings are being turned into boutiques and restaurants. The Grill's location offers a view of the urban center's newest skyline. Parking is safe and plentiful. Chef Lisa has worked in the town throughout her professional career, but the old-town renovation is still a wild card. The area is a gamble, at least in its early stages.

The Grill's menus are large, offering fifteen appetizers and salads, twenty-five entrees and assorted other dishes. The cuisine has its origins in the continental style, though several of the dishes reflect the region's tastes. The presentation is flavored by modern American trends for expensive eateries—mostly stylized along the simple, colorful lines of Haute Nouvelle.

The kitchen budget has been lavish. All the newest equipment has been built into an efficient work space with stations for up to eight cooks and dishwashers. But as the months to completion drag on, the owner tightens the purse strings. Now Lisa is hearing cautionary mumblings. The owner is beginning to question how busy they'll be. She must plan her schedule carefully.

Lisa's experience tells her that December is a strong month, a holiday month with parties and family gatherings. Coupling that retail surge with an opening, the first week and month look good. Her challenge will be to build a clientele quickly. The lean months of January, February and March will see no tourist trade, and many of the boutiques aren't scheduled to open until spring. The food and service must be impeccable.

The Grill will be open seven days a week, from eleven to three and five to midnight. Appetizers and drinks are available between three and five. Lisa designs a simple form which will give her plenty of room to schedule the entire crew on one page (see Table 14-1). (This format can be used to schedule a restaurant crew of any size, even those servicing a twenty-four-hour operation.) Though she has specific duties in mind for the various line chefs, Lisa keeps the terminology general. Her main concern is to have enough cooking talent to handle the anticipated rushes. Not shown are her hours. She expects to work days, overseeing the preparation and then working the line if necessary. The first week, at least, Lisa's primary duties will be job assignment and quality control. She plans to be in the kitchen during every significant rush period of the week. Her cooks are more than capable, especially the night and day chefs, but it is the unexpected problems which destroy a restaurant's first week. As a matter of fact, the

Table 14-1. The Blank Schedule Form.

HOURS	POSITION	MONDAY	TUESDAY	WEDNESDAY	THURSDAY	FRIDAY	SATURDAY	SUNDAY

Table 14-2. The Skyline Grill. Opening week.

HOURS	POSITION	MONDAY	TUESDAY	WEDNESDAY	THURSDAY	FRIDAY	SATURDAY	SUNDAY
8–6	Dishwasher	X	X	X	X	X	X	X
8–6	Dishwasher							X
8–6	Cold Prep.	X	X	X	X	X	X	X
8–6	Prep. Chef	X	X	X	X	X	X	X
12–10	Prep./Line	X	X	X	X	X	X	X
8–4	Line Chef	X	X	X	X	X	X	
8–4	Line Chef							
9–5	Line Chef	X				X	X	X
9–5	Line Chef							
4–12	Night Chef	X	X	X	X	X	X	X
4–12	Line Chef	X	X	X	X	X	X	X
4–12	Line Chef	X	X	X	X	X	X	X
4–12	Line Chef							
4–12	Line Chef							
5–10	Expediter	X	X	X	X	X	X	X
4–12	Dishwasher	X	X	X	X	X	X	X
6–2	Dishwasher	X	X	X	X	X	X	X

213

first month can be a nightmare of snafus—too little preparation, line cooks misunderstanding recipes and sloppy presentation. Taking too long to prepare and serve orders is a common problem. For example, one month after the New York reopening of a world-famous restaurant, dinner customers had to wait more than two hours for the food! The worst part of the problem is that most customers don't complain about bad food or service; they just never come back.

The extra cooks assigned the first week of operation are Lisa's insurance against failure (see Table 14-2). She must be prepared for a full restaurant during lunch or dinner. There is no supposition that Mondays are slow, so that she can cut back. No one knows when the customers will come. Monday may be the day everybody decides to try the "new place." The difference between a skeleton staff and a full staff isn't great—in this case, about seven cook shifts and five dishwasher shifts, or approximately $700 for the week. That's pretty inexpensive insurance. Later there will be plenty of time to cut corners. Opening expenses should include extra kitchen payroll money. The first week is the one time not to scrimp.

The second week and subsequent weeks through the first month will be erratic, too. Hopefully, volume will be high and building. If the opening was bad (sorry, it happens), cut back immediately by laying off the least impressive workers.

Forecasting Labor Needs Through The First Year

Without the benefit of past records, how does a chef go about predicting the effects of holidays or seasonal changes? Perhaps the restaurant has been at the same location for years, but the chef is new and has no records to refer to. That situation can be just as boggling as The Skyline Grill's, where a completely new commercial area is being developed. Take an assertive, positive approach by estimating optimistic sales levels for all calendar events, whether they are holidays or seasonal changes. Apply the old adage that the best defense is a good offense by promoting specials which will encourage maximum sales volume.

Holidays may or may not be important. If the chef or owner-manager has no ability for marketing, most holidays will pass by at an average sales pace. In fact, certain holiday shifts may be lower in sales than usual if the public does not fit you into their plans. The holiday crowd of daters, families and business groups likes to plan ahead. If the Skyline Grill has an assertive marketing policy, Lisa will bring in business. Her goal will be to run a full house. That way, scheduling is easy; she'll need a full crew. Standing back and waiting for customers to come without planning for special treatment is foolish. Make specials attractive by the festive quality of the dishes offered and the reasonable price. Here is the way Lisa, as the ideal chef of the future, planned her first year's holiday schedules:

Christmas Eve: Normal schedule and specials list. Consider the volume medium to below average.

Christmas Day: Open two full shifts, day and night, with a regular line schedule, but one extra preparation cook and one additional dishwasher for lunch and dinner. Aggressive advertising for a champagne Christmas brunch and an evening Christmas buffet. Seasonal and expensive specials offered at a much lower markup.

New Year's Eve: Consider this a potentially busy shift. Schedule a full Friday night crew. The specials are romantic, with dinners for two at a reasonable price. If the first month has been a tremendous success, the Skyline Grill will be the hot spot in town. Consider a one-seating party with champagne, a band, dancing and a prix fixe menu. If the first month has been slow, keep the regular menu on and offer special romantic dinners at a shade below your competitors' prices.

New Year's Day: Advertise an unusually long and glamorous brunch list, perhaps at a special price, again depending on how well December's brunches have been doing. Promote hard with location and media announcements. Add an expeditor and a dishwasher to the normal Sunday brunch crew.

Martin Luther King Day: This is the newest of the Monday holidays. Don't underestimate its business potential. Plan for a busy lunch and a fairly busy evening shift. It could reap great sales volume, depending on the region's history and the chef's ingenuity.

Valentine's Day: A special dinner for two is a must to promote if the chef wants to be certain that young couples include the restaurant in their plans for that night. Schedule for a busy Friday night's volume.

President's Day: Promote a special brunch and expect a good response. Put on a regular Sunday brunch crew for this day. The evening volume will be that of a busy Monday, but nothing staggering. A regular Monday night schedule will suffice.

Saint Patrick's Day: Traditional specials are an expected must on this day. The larger your area's celebration of this holiday, the greater your lunch volume will be. Plan for a busy day and night shift with one extra lunch cook, an additional preparation cook and an expeditor at night.

Easter Sunday, Mother's Day and *Father's Day:*   These are three important Sunday holidays which can be sales record busters if they are well promoted and staffed. It goes without saying that the food quality and service have to be impeccable. A new restaurant or one with a questionable chef cannot run big promotions if it alienates the customers who do come. Word of mouth is the best form of promotion. Advertising is only a help. Promote all three Sundays with a long specials list, including brunch and light dinner dishes. The schedule will reflect the chef's confidence, with a full brunch crew.

Memorial Day, the *Fourth of July* and *Labor Day:*   Picnic days deserve a traditional outdoorsy flair. Promotions can be patriotic. Specials are effective if they are casual and in the style of Americana. These are play days. If your restaurant is in a recreation or tourist area, plan for an onslaught. For example, The Skyline Grill is something new, something to see. By spring and summer, the shops and other restaurants will be operating. The converted area has a governing council which will promote a carnival atmosphere. Lisa's specials and schedule should reflect the Grill's past few months of success. She beefs up the crew to its full level for a very busy day and plans for volume on the level of a busy Friday night.

Columbus Day, Veteran's Day and *Election Day:*   These holidays will not be big sales days no matter what kind of promotion is planned. The lunch volume is above average but not tremendous. Schedule one extra day line cook on these holidays.

Halloween Night: This is a fun night for children and adults. Work with the owner-manager to plan decorations, costumes and specials price ranges. Promote a party atmosphere. Plan a schedule which will handle a busy Friday night's volume.

Thanksgiving Day and Night: Most restaurants simply close on this day rather than try to compete with Grandmother's cooking. Each area is different, but there is certainly enough clientele to warrant the opening of a few places. A full-service restaurant will be open Thanksgiving on both shifts. Plan a traditional turkey feast with a few untraditional options. The preparation list is the biggest of the year, involving one extra preparation person on Monday, one on Tuesday, two on Wednesday and two on Thursday. A full line crew is necessary for both day and night.

Seasonal shifts in business volume take place because of the weather's effect on the economic activity of a restaurant's local region. Each area is different. The best way to judge the effects of the weather on your restaurant is to analyze the physical attributes of the front of the house. How compatible are they with a pleasant dining atmosphere in spring, summer, fall or winter? It is the dining room's relationship to the outside which dictates how the restaurant will do in comparison to other restaurants in its area. If the dining room or rooms are dark, with few or no windows, the summer sun or winter chill will have no effect on the visual ambiance. But a cold winter day may send customers looking for a warm, cozy spot. Add a fireplace or a piano, and the cold season may be better than the warm season. Physical attributes which make the restaurant particularly attractive in one season will alter the usual pattern of high and low sales volume.

Bright, glassed-in dining rooms or outside cafes are an asset during the warm months. They can give one restaurant peak sales from April to September, while another spot on the same block slumps during the same period.

Summer vacations, sports schedules, school terms, or special events which are dictated by the changing seasons can cause business peaks if the restaurant is in a tourist area, has video screens, or is located near a college.

Add up the dining room's positive and negative characteristics, at least the ones which will affect business. Consider them when scheduling, especially during the first uncharted year. Many of the negative characteristics will seem unsurmountable. The only thing a chef can do to combat them is to pay strict attention to the quality and presentation of product. A restaurant which builds a reputation for good food will begin to even out the highs and lows by steadily improving the sales volume during all four seasons.

During the first year, expect to have incredibly busy days, weeks and months. But also plan to encounter weeks when sales are horrifying. Chef Lisa planned ahead for such eventualities. Study the examples of the Skyline Grill's trimmed-down staff (Table 14-3) and its full, busy, staff (Table 14-4).

Table 14-3. The Skyline Grill. Trimmed-down staff.

HOURS	POSITION	MONDAY	TUESDAY	WEDNESDAY	THURSDAY	FRIDAY	SATURDAY	SUNDAY
8–6	Dish Cold Prep.	X	X	X	X	X	X	X
8–6	Dishwasher							X
8–6	Prep. Chef	X	X	X	X	X	X	X
9–5	Line Chef	X	X	X	X	X	X	X
9–5	Line Chef						X	X
4–12	Night Chef	X	X	X	X	X	X	X
4–12	Line Chef	X	X	X	X	X	X	
4–12	Line Chef					X	X	
4–2	Dishwasher	X	X	X	X	X 4–12	X 4–12	X
6–2	Dishwasher					X	X	

218

Table 14-4. The Skyline Grill. Full, busy staff.

HOURS	POSITION	MONDAY	TUESDAY	WEDNESDAY	THURSDAY	FRIDAY	SATURDAY	SUNDAY
8–6	Dishwasher	X	X	X	X	X	X	X
8–6	Dishwasher			X		X	X	X
8–6	Cold Prep.	X	X	X	X	X	X	X
9–5	Prep. Chef	X	X	X	X	X	X	X
9–5	Pasta/Baker		X	X	X	X	X	
9–5	Prep. Cook				X		X	X
9–5	Prep./Line	X	X	X	X	X	X	X
8–4	Line Chef	X	X	X	X	X	X	X
8–4	Line Chef	X	X	X	X	X	X	X
9–5	Line Chef	X	X	X	X	X	X	X
9–5	Line Chef						X	X
12–3	Expediter						X	X
4–12	Night Chef	X	X	X	X	X	X	X
4–12	Line Chef	X	X	X	X	X	X	X
4–12	Line Chef	X	X	X	X	X	X	X
4–12	Line Chef	X	X	X	X	X	X	X
4–12	Line Chef					X	X	
5–10	Expediter	X	X	X	X	X	X	X
4–12	Prep. Cook			X	X	X	X	X
4–12	Dishwasher	X	X	X	X	X	X	X
6–12	Dishwasher	X	X	X	X	X	X	X

Planning for Fluctuating Sales

A trimmed-down staff represents the number of workers who must be present to handle the minimum number of customers. For the Skyline Grill, this number is higher than the total which would be needed for smaller restaurants. Restaurant owners may design their kitchens with five cooking stations, forgetting about the days when only thirteen lunch customers show up. On those days, even one cook is an expensive luxury. But if the lunch average has been twenty-five customers arriving all at once, and the kitchen is spread out, two cooks will be needed just to stay open for the minimum number of customers. Chefs must schedule to overcome the physical requirements of the kitchen. In the Skyline Grill's case, a large, expensive kitchen is an albatross during the slow season.

Special Labor Problems

The Skyline Grill's menu and style of presentation are another factor which require Chef Lisa to schedule more heavily than a restaurant with a short, simple menu executed in a casual style. In order for the quality to remain high, the Skyline Grill needs an extra line cook every night of the week, especially on Friday and Saturday night, when there is the possibility of becoming very busy. Even during a season when business is poor, the customers may surprise everyone and show up en masse one weekend night. The importance of that one night's service and food production is equal to an actress's only audition for a Broadway show. If they like you, they'll want to see you again. If not, it may be a year before you get another chance to prove your culinary prowess.

As the slow season passes, business begins to pick up and the work load gets heavier. Don't hire an extra dishwasher, preparation cook and line cook at the first sign of an upturn. Let the best workers pick up quarter or half shifts; they should be paid extra, of course. Rather than automatically opting for the rush schedule, hire hard workers. Cooks with experience know that output is part of their job. Favor your competent, fast workers with extra hours.

During the peak season, the schedule will be the fullest of the year, but the staff should also be the busiest of the year. All stations will have to be staffed ten to fourteen shifts a week. Most restaurants have enough kitchen work space to handle the number of dining room seats. However, some restaurants, even new ones, do not. There will be times when a full staff cannot effectively keep up with the turnover rate. A part-time expeditor can alleviate some of the stress by helping to speed food service. But beyond that, only a menu change will ease the production stress. A shorter menu means fewer cooking tasks. During a steady rush, a shorter menu, with its narrower field of requests, will be more time efficient to produce because more tasks will be shared and more time saved. For example, the Skyline Grill has twenty-five entrees. During a Friday night rush, they sell an average of three hundred eighty entrees. Seventy percent of those dishes are from the fifteen most popular plates. If the original menu had included only those fifteen entrees, the line cooks could combine most of their steps. A typical order coming in may have different entrees, but a full restaurant would be repeating dishes more often. The time saved between making ten of one dish and one each of ten different dishes is the advantage of a short menu. That is the type of time saving that could take place on a busy night at the Skyline Grill. Some kitchens simply are not designed to handle the menu.

A new chef or a new restaurant will need many personnel changes in their first year together. As the peak season begins to slow down, trim away those workers who refuse to work within the system. During the busy season mediocre workers may be needed, but as soon as an opportunity arises, they should be laid off.

Forecasting Labor Needs for Established Restaurants

The best way to estimate staffing needs is to consult the sales records for the particular day and week in the previous year or two. Many variables can alter the reliability of past records—events such as an upward sales trend, a downward sales trend, an economic calamity or bad weather— but they rarely have the power to throw the sales figures far from that of the previous year. A daily sales record is a must for any business-minded chef. Its importance to food purchasing has already been noted. It is tied to the scheduling process just as firmly, both as a forecast source and as a pc computator.

A daily record of sales is simple and straightforward—uncluttered by other information and easy to consult. A pocket diary or journal makes a perfect daily record. The basic data for one week is as follows:

DATE	DAY	DAY	NIGHT	TOTALS	COMMENTS
Mo/Day	Monday				
	Tuesday				
	Wednesday				
	Thursday				
	Friday				
	Saturday				
	Sunday				

Pertinent comments noting holidays or weather can help to explain highs and lows in the sales data. Usually business volume passes through its up and down cycles gradually. Just as it takes months of hard work to see an improvement in a restaurant which had been on the skids, so the rise in sales is slow and gradual. The average sales of a particular week's recorded daily totals will certainly be a reliable figure to use when filling your current schedule.

Complete records will show the year's sales volume and its relation to the seasons in a pattern of peaks and valleys. These records are important to interpret. They will help to project labor needs from month to month.

An established staff makes better wages, presumably because they produce more efficiently. There is also the American tradition of seniority. Just by staying on the same job, a worker may expect regular raises. This creates problems for a chef who is trying to maintain a twenty-five to thirty percent labor cost. Wasted hours by these high-paid professionals can cripple a labor pc. Use the previous year's records to forecast the current year's busy season. Then plan on using the regular crew until the upward swing has unmistakably started. Never overstaff. Be ready with a plan to increase the staff, and then wait for the sales volume to pick up. Let the business come to you. Inform the key staff members—sous chef, day chefs and night chefs—about the plan to make a nice profit. After the slow season, no cooks should complain about working to full potential, especially if they know the situation is controlled for a purpose. The staff must understand that their high wages are supported by the amount of work they do in relation to the total annual sales. During the slow season, labor costs may rise into the forty percent range. Since the core staff is being maintained to handle the regular season, little can be done to cut this cost besides encouraging long unpaid vacations.

A chef's annual plan for labor needs and costs must be mindful of the seasonal aspects of the restaurant's sales and the owner-manager's desired labor pc. The boss will begin to complain about kitchen costs when controls aren't maintained. Chefs who wait for the owner-manager to begin complaining about costs do not have full control of their responsibilities.

Use another interim technique which will supply enough labor and keep costs at a minimum. Instead of scheduling a full shift during the increasingly busy shifts, ask the best workers to stay an extra half shift. For a month into the beginning of the peak season, business will come in spurts until the volume evens out on the peak. Rather than making a dramatic schedule shift to the full busy staff mode, have a few workers whom you can depend on to pick up half shifts at short notice. Again, this procedure is facilitated if the workers understand your reasoning and the eventuality of the schedule.

For example, consdier *LONGO'S MARINA*, a two-hundred-seat American Continental bar-cafe-restaurant located across the street from the busiest marina in the state. Unfortunately, during the winter months, very few people visit the marina. By early spring, the boaters return as the weather warms. Then in April, the first weekend's sales volume goes up or down, depending on the temperature. Chef Jack still operates with a reduced winter staff. They do about three hundred covers per day in the off season. But Chef Jack uses some safeguards to handle the double volume which the first nice weekend brings (see Table 14-5). Their regular hours are Monday to Thursday, twelve to twelve, and Friday to Sunday, ten to two.

Jack has found that following the weather reports is sometimes helpful but often no indicator at all. If the temperature rises into the mid-sixties, predicted or not, the outside cafe, an additional forty seats, is set up. Then Longo's needs two extra line cooks and a preparation man per shift to cover the doubled trade of a spring weekend. Jack's preparation crew, Eligio and Arturo, are more than willing to work extra hours if the volume warrants. They work late Friday, Saturday and Sunday nights, per Jack's direction.

When the weather warrants, the chef calls in two line cooks at noon on Saturday and Sunday mornings. They are on notice for the six weekends of early spring and are scheduled from four to midnight on those days. If it appears that the night business will continue strong, Jack asks one or two day cooks to work an extra four hours, also by prearrangement. Jack's supplemental scheduling tactics save thousands of dollars in labor costs during the six weeks of early spring.

Usually, manpower should be added at the bottom of the pay scale, in the dishwasher and cold preparation slots. Other staff members can be

Table 14-5. Longo's Marina. Winter schedule.

HOURS	POSITION	MONDAY	TUESDAY	WEDNESDAY	THURSDAY	FRIDAY	SATURDAY	SUNDAY
7-4	Dishwasher	X	X	X	X	X	X	X
7-4	Dishwasher						X	X
8-6	Prep.	X	X	X	X	X	X	X
8-6	Prep.				X	X	X	X
8-6	Prep.							
8-4	Day Chef	X	X	X	X	X	X	X
8-4	Line Cook						X	X
8-4	Line Cook						X	X
8-4	Line Cook							
12-8	Chef		X	X	X	X	X	
Swing	Sous Chef	X			X	X	X	X
3-12	Night Chef	X	X	X	X	X	X	X
4-12	Line Chef	X	X	X	X	X	X	X
4-12	Line Chef			X	X	X	X	X
6-2	Line Chef							
6-2	Line Chef							
5-12	Line Chef							
4-12	Raw Bar			X	X	X	X	X
12-6	Raw Bar							
3-12	Dishwasher	X	X	X	X	X	X	X
4-2	Dishwasher					X	X	

224

temporarily pushed up one level to work in related jobs. This flexibility depends on having willing, well-trained workers, something most restaurants work for years to find. Training throughout the slow season pays off in higher profits when the peak season arrives.

Scheduling for Dollars

One of the wealthiest Japanese industrialists was asked about his personnel management theories. He said, "The top executive slots should be filled with highly capable individuals. But only pay for mediocre talent in the middle management levels." The idea is that one highly paid, exceptional executive can motivate or drive several poorly paid, mediocre managers. Many restaurant owners follow that principle without ever having heard this industrialist's thoughts. Perhaps this is one of the business tricks Americans exported to Japan just after World War II. At any rate, a chef should beware of an owner who classes chefs in the mediocre range. This will mean sixty to seventy hours of work per week and a mediocre salary. Talented chefs rarely stay in this atmosphere unless they themselves are workaholics. The pay is always relative. A salary of $700 a week for sixty hours may sound great at the time of hiring, but six months later, that chef will either be getting more money or looking for another job.

Like planned obsolescence, scheduling for profit entails regular replacement of items—in this case, workers. Each worker is brought in at the minimum wage and trained to do one job, usually the dishes. As other cooks up the chain of command quit or are fired, the dishwashers are retrained and moved up. They gain a raise of $.50 per hour or $5 per day each time they move up. The potential savings in labor costs are fantastic; that's the positive aspect. However, lost profits due to waste, stealing and poor sales offset the labor gain. It takes several months of quality preparation and handling by an entire kitchen staff before the customers register satisfaction. And several months are needed before a team effort begins to lower food costs dramatically. If the workers are constantly new, having to be taught the basics, the crew won't be experienced enough to produce at peak.

Widget A may look and perform like Widget B in every way until it breaks six months early. Food receives more immediate reviews. If it is not tasty and well presented, the customers know before they've purchased it that it was a waste of money. They probably will never say so, but they won't be back.

Part of a chef's responsibility in scheduling their workers is to understand individual limits. Some cooks and dishwashers work better in the day, others at night. Six shifts may be too much for one person and seven not enough for another. This will depend on what the workers want from their job and their life. If the owner-manager wants a crew of sixty-hour-a-week cooks, your prime concern in hiring will be to find responsible, hard workers. Cooking skills will take on secondary importance. Don't expect to get a staff together and keep it. A major portion of a chef's job will always consist of rehiring and retraining.

Highlights

Two elements are needed to keep labor costs at a minimum: a willingness to work and a method of forecasting labor needs.

The way a chef works becomes the tempo of the kitchen—fast, moderate, or slow.

Personal experience and dutiful record keeping will give a chef the knowledge needed to forecast correctly how many line cooks, preparation cooks and dishwashers a particular shift needs.

The greatest danger is to have too few staff available to meet customers' demands.

Waste in labor is just as harmful as food waste.

The goal is to schedule just enough people to have delicious, colorful dishes produced by a hard-working and efficient crew.

New restaurants' schedules rely on other variables: the size of the kitchen and the number of work stations; the number of seats in the restaurant; the size of the menu; the immediate area's projected sales potential; the budget for kitchen labor; holiday and seasonal shifts in volume; and styles of service.

The best way to judge the effects of the weather on your restaurant is to analyze the physical attributes of the front of the house.

A restaurant which builds a reputation for good food will begin to even out the highs and lows by steadily improving the sales volume during all four seasons.

A complicted menu and a difficult cuisine are other factors which require heavier scheduling than a restaurant with a short, simple menu.

During the peak season, the schedule will be the fullest of the year, but the staff should also be the busiest of the year.

A menu change will ease the production stress of an expertly staffed but slow kitchen.

The best way to estimate staffing needs is to consult the sales records for the particular day and week in the previous year or two.

Like planned obsolescence, scheduling for profit entails regular replacement of items—in this case, workers.

Lost profits due to waste, stealing and poor sales offset the labor expenses saved by using cheap, unskilled workers.

A major portion of a chef's job will always consist of rehiring and retraining.

Chapter 15

CHEFS AS TEAM LEADERS

Introduction

A congenial relationship between co-workers is desirable. It makes the work day pass more easily. Still, every chef has at least one horror story about a kitchen feud between line cooks who worked side by side without speaking for years. Often an excellent, busy restaurant will have cooks working in the same room, but not together. Oddly, production appears unaffected. Two seasoned pros at war will take pains to compensate for their attitude by maintaining strict adherence to quality standards. However, the majority of kitchen workers need a congenial atmosphere and take pains to find a job where they fit in.

The teamwork and pride addressed in this chapter aren't attitude rituals, like the male bonding seen in football. Instead, they refer to people working together to achieve efficiency, high quality and profit. There is a hard business edge to teamwork. It seems to be the best way to build productivity.

Attitude and Flexibility

The most important element of a team is its leader—in this case, the chef. Kitchen workers rarely compare the owner-manager's hours and duties with theirs, at least not as work models. However, the chef's hours, speed and quality are under constant casual and intense scrutiny. Cooks do what they see, not necessarily what they are told.

Chefs should be comfortable enough in their position to relax and be themselves. Strained, jerky efforts will puzzle the staff at best and turn

228

them into a carping, vindictive pack at worst. Understanding their attitudes' value to a restaurant is a secret weapon which chefs can use to build
their own reputation. The staff senses and responds well to confidence,
whether it is based on the chef's ability to turn out best-selling specials or
to achieve the lowest food pc's, or because the chef is the nephew of the
owner. Of course, chefs generally have worked around and have the
experience to back up their bossy demeanor.

A young star may encounter a different environment entirely. Expect
the staff to watch your output; at least one of them will be certain that he
or she can do your job better. Subconsciously, they may resent your fame,
hours or salary. Be careful to be part of the team. Don't leave any room for
doubt. Demonstrate your skills to every cook and dishwasher, not as a
sometime showoff but as a hard-working chef who regularly gets involved
in every aspect of production. Let them see you make sauces or work the
line during a rush period. Taste the food in process and then discuss the
final seasonings. Oversee the storage and handling of all products. And
lend a hand. When it gets so busy that the entire crew is pressured by
heavy volume, step in to make the difference. Keep your skills current,
and let the crew see your proficiency. While it is true that a chef's primary
responsibility is to manage the food business from a higher level than
peeling carrots, if you are perceived as aloof, that will disconnect you
from the rest of the team. Before long, you'll be sitting alone in the office
reading cooking magazines while the restaurant and its food flounder. Be
flexible enough to rinse out a pot once in a while. When it comes time to
ask workers to do a little more, they'll respond positively.

Working with the crew is a fine way to pick up advanced techniques,
successful recipes and timesaving tips. Every member of the staff knows
something valuable, whether they learned it from Andre Rene at the
Rainbow Room or their grandmother in Baja California. Standing apart
from the staff will cut you of from this excellent opportunity for adding to
your own experience.

When cooks fold their arms and say "That's not my job," labor dollars
are being lost and the customer's requests are almost certainly meeting
the same icy opposition. The chef who is willing to work at any station has
the edge because the staff understands the chef's position on flexibility.
This is one of the most important factors in keeping labor costs low. Of
course, food costs too are affected if the crew's efficiency drops. Inefficient workers are wasteful, and waste is a major source of lost profit. It's a
vicious cycle which can drag down sales and profits while everyone
wonders why the restaurant is dead. Customers often get the worst of this
poor service.

For example, Ben, the owner of an established American-Continental restaurant, was becoming alarmed by the recent months' poor sales. After twelve years of profits, he had to take a bank loan to get through a particularly poor winter season. He expected the spring volume to pick up dramatically, but it didn't. He was shocked because he knew that the food was good. He ate there often. Al, the chef, had been with him from the beginning, and the rest of the crew for over five years. What was different enough to cause the customers to run?

One afternoon Ben stopped for lunch. It happened to be Al's day off, and instead of a regular menu item, he wanted a chef's salad with plain poached shrimp on top. Ben entered the kitchen, voiced his request, and watched the cooks stare blankly at one another. It wasn't very busy, but the cooks spoke little English, so Ben made his request clear. However, no matter how hard he tried to explain, the cooks didn't get it. Finally, Ben yelled, "Where the hell is Al?" He gave up on his shrimp salad.

That night Ben tossed and turned. He imagined his restaurant going down the drain. If he was the owner and couldn't get what he asked for, how could the customers? Ben began to investigate. It turned out that Al was working about four hours a day, six days a week. The rest of the time, the kitchen staff were on their own. The manager and waitresses no longer spoke to anyone in the kitchen. All communication was by dupe slips with abbreviated food requests. Sandwiches came on white toast only. It wasn't even possible to get a sandwich on plain bread; they only came on toast.

This extreme example of inflexibility may sound absurd, but it is actually a true story. Al, the chef, had bought his own restaurant and couldn't be bothered with Ben's. Al's plan was to keep collecting his pay until Ben fired him. Ben not only obliged Al, but the entire kitchen crew as well. It took about two years for sales volume to return to its previous healthy level.

The restaurant business is a retail operation, but it is also a service-based enterprise. Customers expect to be served, to get what they want. That should be the ultimate purpose of a kitchen crew: to serve the customers. Whether the request is for a normal menu item or for peanut butter melted over Chicken Divan, do it.

Organization of Duties

Established restaurants have evolved work patterns and procedures which may or may not be completely effective. Remember, the existing way of doing things started out as the opening chef's concept, and was then revised by every chef and cook who came afterward. The chef's duties include deciding who does what and when. Take a long, hard look at the existing work process. Analyze it for time efficiency and quality output. There will be some tricks to the overall approach which you can learn and incorporate into your own style, as well as tasks to rearrange. Gauge the working system holistically at its root. Essentially, there are three types of kitchen duties: a chef's management tasks, the advance preparation of food, and line work including expediting. The chef's undelegated tasks may never need to be communicated. Therefore, lists or timetables are probably a waste of time for these easily remembered chores.

Preparation duties are another matter entirely. Many jobs must be completed by a volatile staff. Shift changes and employee turnover are some of the variables. The daily preparation job must be completed despite them. One way to mold the staff's efforts into a steady, productive process is to compile a master preparation list including every conceivable chore. Post this list under plastic so that it stays up for a year or two, and revise it if major changes in the menu make it obsolete. New preparation cooks and old employees will use it regularly to double-check their daily tasks.

A busy restaurant needs to make a preparation list of duties every morning. This is important as a guide which ensures that no job is forgotten. The head preparation man makes the list by comparing the master list with the actual inventory. Also, on a daily basis, the chef should discuss the preparation pars and list with the preparation staff. A short discussion about the weather and the sales expected that day will help to train the preparation cooks and make the list a precise instrument of direction. Becoming involved in early morning planning helps a chef to gauge the day's work load; perhaps an extra cook or dishwasher needs to be called in. The preparation list is a chef's safeguard against a lazy or preoccupied crew. It ensures that work doesn't stop at four o'clock, but only after the list has been finished. The preparation staff works as a team, dividing the tasks into manageable portions of responsibility which individuals specialize in. If there is a problem with quality or quantity, the chef deals with the responsible worker. If the problem persists, the chef may take specific remedies.

Figure 15-1 is a master preparation list for one of the largest menus in this book, that of *MUMBLES RESTAURANT* (see Fig. 7-12). In Chapter 7, the chef of Mumbles was concerned with the kitchen design and the opening week's production. For that new staff, the master preparation list simplifies the daily job of deciding what needs to be done.

HOT PREP	BREADING
Brown Sauce	Mozzarella Pizziola
Marinara Sauce	Chicken Fingers
Chili	Veal Parmigiana
French Onion	Chicken Parmigiana
Roast Turkey	Shrimp Parmigiana
Baked Potatoes	Onion Rings
Quiche	Zucchini Sticks

SALADS & DRESSINGS	MEAT & FISH BUTCHERING, ETC.
Tuna Salad	Burgers
Chicken Salad	Sliced Steaks
Creamy Dill Dressing	½ Chickens
Honey-Garlic Vinaigrette	16-Oz. Steaks
Russian Dressing	10-Oz. Steaks
Blue Cheese Dressing	Chicken Medallions
Tartar Sauce	Veal Medallions
	Scrod
GARDE MANGER	Swordfish Steaks
Broccoli	Mussels
House Salad	
Kitchen Salad	SLICING
Green Leaf	Mozzarella
Spinach	Swiss
Potato Skins	Ham
	Turkey
GARNISHES	Grate Cheddar
	Grate Parmesan
Red Onion Slices	
Cherry Tomato Halves	
Tomato Slices	
Cucumber Slices	
Carrot Slices	
Lemon Wedges	
Sliced Mushrooms	
Whole Cherry Tomatoes	

Figure 15-1. Master preparation list.

The Working Chef

A term used commonly by owner-managers and recruiters is "working chef." A redundant one, it seems; what other kind of chef is there? Chefs work. Even if they are sitting at a table discussing the menu degustation with a special customer, they are working. I believe some owners feel that a working chef may be seen peeling carrots or sweating on the line—not so. However, chefs who never cook are no longer chefs. They have moved into ownership or management, and their title should be changed. Even an executive chef cooks daily or at least creates specials. The executive chef may in fact be the head chef; the titles are synonymous, except in large operations where an executive chef oversees one or several head chefs. In that case, the executive chef is distinct from another chef in that he or she is never scheduled for a line slot. Executive chefs have enough manpower so that they never have to cook unless they want to, but the smart ones want to. They need to cook to do a superior job.

All chefs have their specialties. They must use their talents wisely, to the greatest benefit of the restaurant's owner. The two prime areas of expertise are high-quality cuisine and top profits. Obviously a master cook can't ignore the profit angle; nor can an ex-accountant turned chef leave the cooking to subordinates. Superb production is expected and demanded in both areas. Analyze your own strengths and weaknesses, likes and dislikes, in order to structure a workday schedule for yourself which will not only yield the greatest all-around success but also satisfy your career and basic needs. If you don't think in terms of organization and profit margins, hire a subordinate who does.

The following three examples are of chefs with different skills and desires. The way they constructed their daily schedules highlights the flexibility of a chef's role. When a chef works and what he or she does are decided in part by the owner-manager, but the basis for this decision must always be the goals mentioned—high-quality food and maximum profit margins.

Example 1. The Head Chef, Working Days. A typical schedule for the chef of a restaurant which does two-thirds of its volume at night:

9:00 A.M.   Arrive at work. Begin soup du jour. Go over last night's receipts. Locate leftovers. Make lunch specials list. Finish soup du jour. Do any lunch specials preparation, e.g., sauces, garde mange or butchering.

10:00 A.M.   Do the ordering. Check prices on the invoices received today. Physically check the newly arrived goods for brand, size and correct storage. Date items where feasible. Take care of any problems with the kitchen equipment.

11:00 A.M.   Go over the preparation list to note the work load and confirm the correct pars. Create the dinner specials list. Make a preparation list for the specials. Decide the division of specials preparation duties. Delegate some of them and retain the rest for the chef's preparation list.

12:00 NOON Double-check to be certain that the floor staff understands the lunch specials. Peruse the line setup. Check for freshness of products by tasting several. Begin working on the dinner specials preparation list. Be ready to assist or oversee line cooks if a lunch rush develops.

1:00 P.M. Continue specials preparation and line work as needed.

2:00 P.M. Continue specials preparation and line work as needed.

3:00 P.M. Check the progress on the daily preparation list. Make any adjustments necessary because of unusual lunch volume. Finish the specials preparation. Time for shopping around —get price quotes, arrange appointments. Do numbers work with food and/or labor pc's. Keep records up-to-date. Analyze the food cost, both projected and past. Check current sales volume with last year's.

4:00 P.M. Brief the night chef on the dinner specials list. Begin setting up for dinner service. Oversee the correct storage of leftover lunch items. Check the preparation crew's progress and the cleanup procedures. Arrange for workers to stay late or go home early. Confer with night chef one last time. Punch out.

Example 2. The Head Chef, Working Nights. A typical schedule for the chef of a restaurant who works the busy night line:

3:00 P.M. Arrive at work. Confer with the day chef regarding day sales. Adjust the specials raw goods list. Create the night specials list. Delegate some preparation duties. Make a list for personal preparation chores. Start any long projects.

4:00 P.M. Do the inventory/ordering. Check last night's receipts. Update records of sales and purchases. Check lunch receipts. Inspect goods which have arrived that day for correct brand, size and storage. Date any goods where possible. Oversee setup for night line.

5:00 P.M. Complete specials preparation. Be prepared to go on the line. Brief night cooks and floor staff on the evening's specials. Work on scheduling, menu planning and cost control systems until the dinner business picks up.

6:00–10:00 Work the line, doing only specials and expediting. Continue working the station from which most of the specials are prepared.

10:00 P.M. Call service people regarding any equipment problems. Leave messages on answering machines and notes for the day manger or day chef. Leave a note regarding any problems with the prepared food's pars or quality. Make a list of the items to be used for lunch specials. Punch out.

For a head chef with no inclination for numbers or, worse, no skill at purchasing or reorganization, working the line is a credible alternative, especially if years of habit have made this person a night person. This method assumes that the head chef is also a fantastic cook, at least the best in the restaurant.

This working chef trades off control over purchasing for better control over the food served. Since some may argue that quality food is paramount, there will be a good immediate response to the chef who announces a decision to work nights. The problem will be in delegation of purchasing and storage responsibilities. If the owner-manager doesn't see a firm profit line, he will insist that the chef work extra hours.

Example 3. The Executive Chef. A typical schedule for the chef of a large restaurant which has heavy lunch and dinner volume.

10:00 A.M.   Arrive at work. Review the previous night's sales. Confer with the day chef regarding the use of leftovers. Together create a lunch specials list. Delegate the daily preparation list and discuss its pars with the preparation chef.

11:00 A.M.   Inspect the goods received for correctness of brand, size and storage. Double-check invoice prices with the salesperson's quotes. Do the inventory/ordering for that day. Spend time considering the possibility of bulk purchases and other ways to get special prices, or coordinate all of the above with the purchasing agent.

12:00 NOON   Brings sales and purchase records up-to-date. Review the current year's trends and compare with those of the past years. Make decisions on adjustments of the staff's size during busier or slower shifts. Deal with equipment problems, especially maintenance and cleaning. Reorder lost or broken utensils, pots, pans, etc.

1:00 P.M.   Oversee the lunch rush, watching for quality in taste and presentation. Create the dinner specials list. Delegate preparation for specials. Plan to do one or two specials.

2:00 P.M.   Save time for meetings with owners, managers, union representatives, salespersons and staff members. Some time each day must be set aside for hiring, firing and rescheduling.

	Oversee preparation of dinner specials. Check on the quality and storage of all prepared foods. Oversee lunch business.
3:00 P.M.	Supervise the final stages of specials and regular preparation and the end of lunch business. Complete any projects for future specials or cost and profit analysis—office work. Study the trade magazines.
4:00 P.M.	Meet with the night chef about dinner specials. Discuss any problems of quality, speed or personnel. Include the night manager in those talks or seek this person out. Oversee the transition from lunch to dinner setup.
5:00 P.M.	Taste the completed dinner specials. Punch out. Sit down for dinner with one of the managers.

Executive chefs are not prima donnas. Their work is different—that of a troubleshooter and innovator. Their main responsibility is the same as that of every other chef: to produce a fresh, tasty and well-presented product at a profit. For the executive chef this can be done either with theatrical flair, by wearing a tall white hat and pitching the customers, or by strict management procedures which include a team of seasoned professionals. Probably a little of both is the norm, especially in upscale houses.

One of the key lessons to be learned by executive chefs is that their job is to create and delegate. Any manual labor they do is a waste of time. The owner will lose the valuable effects of that time more wisely spent. Executive chefs should not have to prove their manual dexterity to cooks.

Pride

One of the toughest positions for a chef is to be in charge of a restaurant's kitchen where the food is awful and everyone knows it. It is embarrassing, and always requires hard, consistent work to improve the quality. Ironically, the most difficult thing to change is public opinion, especially the staff's, and that has the effect of making matters worse. Bad attitudes make the food appear worse than it is even after the turnaround has begun. Here's one way the morale problem surfaces.

Bartenders will belittle the food if they have to feel embarrassed by poor quality. For example, Chef Louise finishes her day shift and stops at the bar for a glass of wine before heading home. She sits at the end of the bar by the waiters' stations because she's just taken over as chef and hasn't gotten to know anyone well. Business has been off; that's why she is new—the last chef was fired. The dinner customers are starting to come in slowly. A single man wearing a suit comes in, sits down two stools away from Chef Louise and orders a drink. He looks at the specials board and then asks for a menu. After a minute, he calls the bartender over and asks, "What's good tonight?" The bartender laughs. "Well, we all sent out for pizza." He looks at the waiters, and they all laugh. The customer glances nervously at the menu and then orders a hamburger. This is how bad it can get—the staff members work against themselves because they are too embarrassed to be associated with the food. Chef Louise not only has to make good food, she has to prove it, too.

The beginning is very difficult. There will be one or more kitchen workers at different levels who are lazy, stubborn or simply bad cooks. They can be fired or pressured to leave. This subject is covered completely in Chapter 17. Like the floor staff, there will be cooks who have no respect for the food they are serving. Bad attitudes cannot be tolerated. The new standard of excellence must begin with better work habits, a result of honest effort.

Pride is an attitude about life which carries over from personal life into the work place. Or the reverse may occur: it originates with a person's work and carries over into his or her personal life. Most people take pride in something; not everyone does, though. A new chef is in the perfect position to reinstill pride. The following program will assist in the challlenge: (1) be a hands-on professional; (2) listen carefully to complaints; (3) think carefully about changes; (4) upgrade the quality of the food and the work place; (5) build a team of loyal workers with raises and promotions.

1. Be a hands-on professional. If you wanted to be a chef in order to wear a white hat and sit in an air-conditioned office reading cooking magazines, you're in the wrong field. A chef cooks, teaches others to cook and tastes what others cook all day long. Cooks need to see their chef working. This is how workers learn what is expected of them and how they absorb the attitude of the kitchen. A chef who works pleasantly throughout the day has a staff which does the same. A chef's actions indicate what is right. Likewise, the chef must be on the scene in order to say, "That is wrong." Only by hard work will a chef have earned the right to criticize the cooks; then, hopefully, the result next time will be better. A chef must set the highest possible standard of quality by doing the work at least once, then remain involved enough to make sure that the standard is consistent.

2. Listen carefully to complaints. There will be a lot of problems to resolve—little ones, which start in the morning and end in the afternoon, and sour hatreds which will never be forgotten. It is not uncommon to find cooks working next to each other but never

speaking. Be diplomatic by listening carefully to personality problems and then taking one side or the other, the idea being to redirect energies toward cooking and work.

Legitimate complaints about recipes or presentations are an important source of ideas for change. The owners, bartenders, wait staff and regular customers all have their pet peeves about the menu. Don't wait for them to deluge you with complaints. A chef with a positive attitude can melt the defensiveness of others by sincerity. This attitude will mark the beginning of the change in morale in the front-of-the-house staff, too. They'll be watching for improvements and telling the chef when the quality is off.

3. Think carefully about changes. A chef may want to fire everybody from the sous-chef to the dishwasher, change the menu and get a new walk-in, but to advocate those things all at once would be a political mistake. A new chef or a chef fighting to correct personal mistakes must show many little improvements—successes, really— before he can request or affect anything dramatic. Think carefully, and then make a plan with detailed, step-by-step procedures and begin slowly with step one. Success will speed up the process. Remember, change means retraining, a time- and energy-consuming process.

4. Upgrade the quality of the food and the work place. As the changes start to happen, the cooks will begin to feel good about working again and the cumulative effect will work in the chef's favor. Change the basic recipes, preparation techniques and line procedures of those menu items which have come to your attention by working and listening. It is very important that the changes be correct because a reversal or an additional change will make it appear as if the chef is groping. The less often that occurs, the better. A chef generally has one or two superiors who must be consulted or informed. Don't ignore these powers. Neither should a chef listen to the wrong person, someone with no cooking background and a lot of idiosyncratic tastes. Changes are made to make the restaurant more popular —customerwise and dollarwise.

Nothing is more frustrating for a cook than to work with equipment that is falling apart. When something breaks, notify the proper person and tell the cooks that the service man has been called. Especially in a busy restaurant, the kitchen takes a pounding; it must be maintained through cleaning programs and fix-it campaigns. Work areas must be analyzed in terms of the present volume. There are probably ways to make the kitchen run more smoothly with additional shelves, refrigeration, racks, tools, pots, pans, and even stoves.

A chef must initiate these improvements and be ready to prove their cost effectiveness. The staff will appreciate the improved working conditions and will work more productively.

5. Build a team of loyal workers with raises and promotions. Very few cooks are working for the glory. They expect to be paid in direct proportion to the amount of work they do, the level of skills required, and their time on the job. If kitchen workers are being poorly paid, no amount of enthusiasm will get them to strive harder. A chef must know the salaries of each cook and talk frankly about them. What are the salary possibilities? Can the chef give raises or change jobs within the staff? Does the owner ever give bonuses? Perhaps nothing more can be done than is being done already. Create an opening at the top or middle by forcing out or firing a negative cook. Then promote down the line from among those who are following the new policies and new chef's direction.

Creative Initiative

With a positive attitude and direction established, a chef may further increase enthusiasm by allowing the more experienced and responsible cooks to exercise their creativity. Pride and creativity are main sources of reward for cooks. For workers who have been at the same restaurant for years, these may be their only outlets. A chef can encourage creativity and increase the restaurant's popularity at the same time by delegating the creation and preparation of specials.

Although the specific details of the plan depend upon job descriptions and the time available, the cooks in charge of the line while the chef is off should usually be made part of the creative process. They have the responsibility to execute the specials anyway. Why not get them involved in the total process? Their product will take on a crisp, personal flair. Line chefs can be further connected to the profit and popularity picture by keeping them apprised of the success or failure of their specials by doing individual counts to pinpoint the good and poor sellers. The total number of specials sold divided by the total number of dinners sold results in a percentage which offers a rule of thumb by which the various chefs specials sales can be judged for success against the menu. The specials do compete with menu items for popularity. Each chef's work should be monitored on a regular basis and the results of particularly good and bad shifts discussed. Pride in creative accomplishments is a good incentive for healthy competition between staff members. It brings out the best a cook has to offer. A motivated shift leader will inspire the other cooks to do their best as well. The whole atmosphere of the kitchen will be conducive to quality output.

False Illusions

Another important aspect of pride in the work place involves knowing where the restaurant falls within the spectrum from four-star to fast food establishments. It is a waste of time for a chef to indulge in false culinary illusions when the customers are on a completely different wavelength. Success is the best morale builder. And the best way to be successful is to gauge fairly what the customers want and give it to them. Don't try to jam regional Nouvelle down their throats if they want shepherd's pie. A chef must be professionally detached enough to make an honest appraisal of the ambiance, decor, service, clientele and existing menu. Here's a good example of how disastrous false illusions can be.

Chef Green received a fantastic offer to take over the kitchen of a newly purchased restaurant. It was an old established steakhouse with a four-decade reputation for success, but recently it had fallen on hard times. The new owners wanted to do some remodeling and breathe life into the staff. Chef Green was asked to design a new menu. No restrictions were mentioned about price or style; everything was left up to the chef. That was one of the attractions of the offer: a chance to create. The weak points of the new chefdom were the beginning salary and the kitchen itself. Both were a little below standard, but the promises were firm: After business picked up, the chef's salary would rise and new kitchen equipment would be ordered. The remodeling had cleaned up the old store but had not changed its appearance at all. The new owners had paid a large sum to retain the old name and logo, *BARNEY'S*. Chef Green was a top chef; his mechanics were letter perfect. He had several years' experience in chi-chi clubs which attracted young executives. He sat down and worked out a menu of American Continental-Nouvelle plates which had no theme or focus but were an eclectic mix of salads, pastas, seafood, duck, chicken and meats, all together about twenty items. The prices were reasonable compared to what had been charged for similar items at the last two places where he had worked. Barney's reopened. There was a little flurry the first three weeks, but then business leveled off at fifteen lunches and fifty dinners per day—a flop. Chef Green was fired after six months of excruciating boredom and infighting.

What went wrong? Barney's was not a chi-chi club. The gulf between the ambiance and menu was so dramatic that the customers were completely turned off by the contradiction. Chef Green created a menu for himself, not the clientele. His career was marred by a failure.

False pride works against a restaurant in another, perhaps more common, way—within line cooks or chefs who feel that their work is beneath them. They believe that their experience and expertise are being wasted because the restaurant's level of cuisine is too common for their sensibilities. Ironically, cooks with this attitude tend to do the worst work. They must be watched for carelessness.

Pride is a matter of concern in the kitchen because, low or high, it affects quality and reputation, either as a deterrent to sales or an aid.

Highlights

There is a hard business edge to teamwork. It seems to be the best way to build productivity.

The most important element of a team is its leader.

The chef's hours, speed and quality are under constant casual and intense scrutiny.

The chef who is willing to work at any station has the edge because the staff understands the chef's position on flexibility.

The ultimate purpose of a kitchen crew is to serve the customers.

Essentially there are three types of kitchen duties: a chef's management tasks, the advance preparation of food, and line work including expediting.

Executive chefs have enough manpower so that they never have to cook unless they want to, but the smart ones want to.

Executive chefs are not prima donnas. Their work is different—that of a troubleshooter and innovator.

A new chef is in the perfect position to reinstill pride.

Build a team of loyal workers with raises and promotions.

Pride and creativity are the main sources of reward for cooks.

The cooks in charge of the line while the chef is off should usually be made part of the creative process.

Success is the best morale builder.

It is a waste of time for a chef to indulge in false culinary illusions when the customers are on a completely different wavelength.

Pride is a matter of concern in the kitchen because, low or high, it affects quality and reputation, either as a deterrent to sales or as an aid.

Chapter 16

MOBILITY AND
THE SCHEDULE CRISIS

Introduction
Mobility and the Restaurant Business
How to Handle the Schedule Crisis
Highlights

Introduction

A kitchen staff which is short on cooks is in a weakened position and is less likely to accomplish its purpose: to produce high-quality food at the greatest possible profit. If once in a while a staff member wants to take off a day and makes arrangements with the chef to do so, there is no problem. With enough notice, even the most unorganized chef can find competent fill-ins. The crisis occurs because of the mobility of kitchen workers, from the first cook to the last dishwasher. The industry seems plagued with drifters. An assertive chef must be ready to handle regular upheavals in staff and schedule, changes which can cripple an unaware chef. Part of a chef's talents will be used to restaff the kitchen without letting the product suffer. Sometimes the effort borders on art.

Mobility and the Restaurant Business

For a number of reasons, people who work in restaurants feel free to move on with the frequency of the changing seasons. These jobs perhaps one of the most mobile of all types. For example, a restaurant in Greenwich Village, New York, once hired over three hundred waiters and waitresses in the course of one year to staff fewer than fifteen permanent positions. Sound absurd? It was.

The kitchen staff can be just as volatile. The reasons are both economic and social. Some people move to restaurant after restaurant because their work is substandard; they get fired. They have an absentee or alcohol or drug problem. A caustic temper causes them to quit over insignificant affronts, or the chef's temper causes others to quit. Many restaurants offer poor wages; cooks leave for better pay or hours. Advancement, more responsibility, a fancier menu, and a more prestigious house are other reasons which entice cooks to move. Migrant workers from all over the world come to the United States with the idea of getting a menial restaurant job; these workers are constantly traveling. Compounding these factors seems to be the nature of the restaurant business. How can a chef really know which worker is looking for a long-term position and which one will work for a week and then disappear? There is no way to know how long a staff will stay together or who is planning an unannounced exit. But be certain that the upheaval will come.

How to Handle the Schedule Crisis

Obviously, the occasional shifts caused by short-term illness or vacations do not constitute a crisis. A full-blown emergency develops when a significant number of the staff are out for any reason. If the number of shifts open becomes more than the remaining staff can handle, either comfortably or without hurting the quality, the chef may have to draw on outside resources to supply the necessary kitchen staff.

Even in the happiest working environments, where the staff is well paid and steady, problems occur often enough to converge into one or two major crisis per year. Take the example of THE PRIME MINISTER, an established, upscale steakhouse with a severe staff problem. It occurred at the end of their slow season, the second week of February. Usually this is a period of relative calm due to the sales, so Chef JR had two workers out on their annual vacations. Then a series of unforseen events left his staff in shreds. First, study the original schedule in Table 16-1. This gives the staff's normal hours before any vacations or absences began to necessitate the hiring of fill-in workers.

On February 7 the dishwasher, Galo, began a five-week vacation to his home country. His replacement, Walter, at first seemed good, but the night manager began to complain about dirty glasses and silverware.

February 14 was the beginning of Steve's one-month vacation, his first in two years. It was JR's policy to allow the staff any time off they requested, provided there was enough time to schedule replacements. Steve's vacation wasn't initially a problem; later it became a contributing factor.

Events began to coincide. On February 16 Victor didn't show up for his shift. His roommate called two days later to say that Victor had admitted himself to a cocaine rehabilitation program. That explained Victor's recent absenteeism. He wouldn't be back.

On Friday, February 19, Jose called from the doctor's office; he had a

Table 16-1. The Prime Minister. Original schedule.

HOURS	POSITION	MONDAY	TUESDAY	WEDNESDAY	THURSDAY	FRIDAY	SATURDAY	SUNDAY
7-3	Day Chef	Ron	Ron	Ron	Ron	Ron	Steve	Steve
7-3	Line Cook	Steve	Steve	Steve	Felipe	Felipe	Felipe	Felipe
7-3	Line Cook	Felipe	George	George	George	George	X	X
9-5	Line Cook	George	Victor	Victor	Victor	Victor	X	Victor
7-3	Prep. Cook	Jose	Jose	Jose	Jose	Jose	Jose	Jose
7-3	Prep. Cook	Benny	Benny	Benny	Arturo	Arturo	X	Benny
10-6	Prep. Cook	X	X	X	Benny	Benny	Arturo	Arturo
11-3	Expediter	John	John	Dave	Dave	Dave	X	Dave 12-4
6-3	Dishwasher	Mohammed	Rocky	Rocky	Mohammed	Mohammed	Mohammed	Mohammed
8-5	Dishwasher	Rocky	Arturo	Arturo	Rocky	Rocky	X	Rocky
4-12	Night Chef	John	John	Nick	Nick	Nick	Nick	Nick
4-12	Line Cook	Sue	Sue	Sue	Sue	Sue	John	John
4-12	Line Cook	X	X	X	Sue	Sue	Steve 3-10	X
6-10	Expediter	X	X	X	X	George	Dave	X
4-12	Dishwasher	X	X	Ray	Ray	Ray	Ray	X
5-1	Dishwasher	Galo	Ray	Galo	Galo	Galo	Galo	Galo

hernia and high blood pressure. He needed two days off, the 19th and 20th, on his doctor's orders. His regular schedule would also have to be adjusted; he could work only five days a week until his blood pressure dropped.

On February 21 Mohammed called JR at home to say that he had received a telephone call from his country; his mother was dying. Mohammed was leaving for Bengali in the morning. He didn't know how long he'd be gone. JR offered his condolences.

Four out of sixteen regular workers were now absent—twenty-five percent. If anyone else got a touch of the flu or even a hangover, the staff might not have enough cook power left to cope. Table 16-2 shows the interim schedule which JR had used to cover Steve's and Galo's vacations. It also includes the gaps created by the absences of Victor, Jose and Mohammed, a total of twelve open shifts. How could the chef have solved his scheduling dilemma? Is there anything he could have done to head off this disaster?

On the surface, as the problems occurred—Victor's leaving, Jose's illness and Mohammed's leaving—they appear to have been coincidental, with no common source. That is a false assumption, and part of the problem's long-term solution will be to identify the weaknesses.

During the week in which it happens, swift action is needed to lessen the impact of a weakened staff, i.e., poor quality, menu item shortages and unsafe/unsanitary conditions. A chef's primary responsibility is to the owner-manager, not to save jobs for the staff. If an opening pops up, fill it—quickly and perhaps resourcefully. Make a temporary schedule to cover the open shifts with any trained substitute or willing staff members. But don't stop there. Two buffers should separate the chef from staff exhaustion at all times: (1) the chef's own ability to work the shift and (2) the hiring of a cook or dishwasher on the spur of the moment. It is vital to try to maintain these two avenues of response, because even with great effort, they will be used, too.

The day Victor didn't show for his day shift, JR called in Sue four hours early, so the immediate problem was alleviated. But he wondered about the next day. Would Victor be back? Should JR wait for an explanatory telephone call? Yes and no. He should have waited for the call but begun retraining job candidates immediately—the same night. For a complete discussion of labor sources, see Chapter 17. How JR would have responded to Victor's call is significant in understanding how the staff became so stretched out in the first place. But Victor didn't call, so the point is moot. JR was proven correct by immediately trailing replacements. A mediocre cook may not be someone to hire for a long-term solution, but this person may supply the additional manpower necessary to help the regular staff

Table 16-2. The Prime Minister. Interim schedule.

HOURS	POSITION	MONDAY	TUESDAY	WEDNESDAY	THURSDAY	FRIDAY	SATURDAY	SUNDAY
7-3	Day Chef	Ron	Ron	Ron	John	Ron	Ron	Ron
7-3	Line Cook	Sue	John	Felipe	Felipe	Felipe	Felipe	Felipe
7-3	Line Cook	Felipe	George	George	George	George	/////	/////
9-5	Line Cook	George	X	X	X	X	/////	X
7-3	Prep. Cook	Jose	Jose	Jose	Jose	Jose	X	X
7-3	Prep. Cook	Benny	Benny	Benny	Arturo	Arturo	/////	Benny
10-6	Prep. Cook	/////	/////	/////	Benny	Benny	Arturo	Arturo
11-3	Expediter	Dave	Nick	Dave	Dave	Dave	/////	Dave 12-4
6-3	Dishwasher	X	Rocky	Rocky	X	X	X	X
8-5	Dishwasher	Rocky	Arturo	Arturo	Rocky	Rocky	/////	Rocky
4-12	Night Chef	John	Nick	Nick	Nick	Nick	Nick	Nick
4-12	Line Cook	Sue	Sue	Sue	John	John	John	John
4-12	Line Cook	/////	Sue	Sue	Sue	Sue	Felipe 3-10	/////
6-10	Expediter					George	Dave	
4-12	Dishwasher		Walter	Walter	Walter	Walter	Walter	/////
5-1	Dishwasher	Ray		Ray	Ray	Ray	Ray	Ray

get the job done. Fortunately, Victor was the lowest cook on the line. If Steve's absence hadn't already given the regular staffers six and seven shifts, JR could fill in with in-house talent. Now, in order to do that, each cook would have to work eight or nine shifts; the effects would be counter-productive. JR set up three job candidates with appointments to trail, each understanding that nothing was definite. One candidate didn't show up, another had too little experience, and the third didn't like being in Victor's line position—garde manger. JR had Sue and Nick coming in four hours early to help cover the lunch rush while he continued to schedule candidates for trailing shifts. Sunday he himself expected to work on his day off; he hated to do this, but there didn't seem to be any alternative. Then Friday morning, Jose called.

If Galo's replacement, Walter, had turned out to be both fast and clean, it would have been simple for JR to give Walter two more shifts and move Arturo into two more preparation shifts. But Walter's work was slow, his plates were dirty—he didn't accomplish the basics. JR would have been ill-advised to give him more days. JR asked Benny to work a seventh shift, Saturday preparation. Mohammed would change his Sunday shift to the seven-to-three preparation, and Ray would work a double as dishwasher from ten to one. Rocky would work from six to five. Then the very first Sunday of the new schedule, Mohammed called JR with the news of his leaving.

A job candidate for the line position, Sam, who trailed Friday night, worked out fine and wanted the position, so JR hired him, starting Saturday. Just as one crisis was averted, however, another cropped up. JR scrambled to get two new dishwashers into position. He kept bringing them in for trails. Sometimes they lasted an hour, sometimes a week. But by trailing two at a time, the job got done correctly. The extra cost was at a minimum wage, between $200 and $300 for the week. JR switched the fill-in dishwashers around to see how they could handle the various aspects of the job—dishes, cold preparation and cleanup. The person JR was looking for would have to do well in all areas, especially the person replacing Mohammed. The night shift was a little easier; still, Walter couldn't handle it. JR expected a second dishwasher to be Walter's replacement.

By the second week in March, there seemed to be a bit of a lull. An entire week passed without a schedule change. Table 16-3 shows how the schedule finally worked out. Of the ninety-one shifts on the one-week schedule, thirty-eight were changed—over forty percent. Imagine the potentially devastating impact of untrained and uncoordinated workers.

When a big shakeup occurs, there is little to be done except react quickly to changing schedule needs. Some reactions will be costly; others

Table 16-3. The Prime Minister. Final schedule.

HOURS	POSITION	MONDAY	TUESDAY	WEDNESDAY	THURSDAY	FRIDAY	SATURDAY	SUNDAY
7–3	Day Chef	Ron	Ron	Ron	John	Ron	Ron	Ron
7–3	Line Cook	Sue	John	Felipe	Felipe	Felipe	Felipe	Felipe
7–3	Line Cook	Felipe	George	George	George	George	▨	▨
9–5	Line Cook	George	Sam	Sam	Sam	Sam	▨	Sam
7–3	Prep. Cook	Jose	Jose	Jose	Jose	Jose	Benny	Benny
7–3	Prep. Cook	Benny	Arturo	Benny	Arturo	Arturo	▨	Phil
10–6	Prep. Cook	▨	▨	▨	Benny	Benny	Arturo	Arturo
11–3	Expediter	Dave	Nick	Dave	Dave	Dave	▨	Dave 12–4
6–3	Dishwasher	Phil	Phil	Rocky	Phil	Phil	Phil	Rocky
8–5	Dishwasher	Rocky	Rocky	Arturo	Rocky	Rocky	▨	Ray 10–5
4–12	Night Chef	John	Nick	Nick	Nick	Nick	Nick	Nick
4–12	Line Cook	Sue	Sue	Sue	John	John	John	John
4–12	Line Cook	▨	▨	▨	Sue	Sue	Felipe 3–10	▨
6–10	Expediter					George	Dave	
4–12	Dishwasher			Youssou	Youssou	Youssou	Youssou	▨
5–1	Dishwasher	Ray	Youssou	Ray	Ray	Ray	Ray	Ray

248

may even save money. Consider the following suggested procedures for covering shifts:

1. Match skills, but use a worker who is paid less than the normal rate for the shift being covered (if you are lucky enough to have workers training up).
2. Cut the shift hours from eight to six in order to pay the overtime rate without exceeding the budget.
3. Too many hours for some individuals may cause their quality to slip. Overwork is also a source of waste. Know the limits of your workers. Do not overuse them, even in emergencies.
4. Don't let the stress of the moment affect your guideline for starting wages. A worker hired at an above-average rate will cause pay scale problems with the rest of the staff.
5. When there is concern about the new staff's ability to get the job done, add another worker at the bottom of the pay scale.

The sporadic occurrence of small or large schedule gaps necessitates a constant awareness of this potential problem. Plans must be made which will alleviate the effect on quality and efficiency. If a chef is unprepared to deal with a significant loss in staff, he or she is not meeting one of the major challenges of the job. How to prepare for and lessen the occurrence of these schedule upheavals is covered at length in Chapter 17.

Highlights

An assertive chef must be ready to handle regular upheavals in staff and schedule, changes which can cripple an unaware chef.

Even in the happiest working environments, where the staff is well paid and steady, problems occur often enough to converge into one or two major crisis per year.

A chef's primary responsibility is to the owner-manager, not to save jobs for the staff.

Two buffers should protect the staff from exhaustion at all times: (1) the chef's own ability to work the shift and (2) the hiring of a cook or dishwasher on the spur of the moment.

When a big shakeup occurs, there is little to be done except react quickly to changing schedule needs.

If a chef is unprepared to deal with a significant loss in staff, he or she is not meeting one of the major challenges of the job.

Chapter 17

HIRING AND FIRING

Introduction

A significant part of a chef's responsibilities is the hiring and firing of kitchen workers. These sometimes difficult tasks are part of the personnel management duties. Firing is considered an especially distasteful chore and is usually one of the last skills learned because so many chefs shy away from being disciplinarians.

Certain hiring techniques will lessen the need to change cooks and reduce stress during the firing process. These techniques are the subject of this chapter. There are other personal factors which influence the hiring and firing process. A chef looks for a worker with specific skills *and* personal needs which match the job requirements. As the worker's skills and goals change, both the chef and the worker must be ready to reevaluate their relationship and even terminate it.

The Hiring Process

Beginning at the moment a position becomes open, a new set of options or job requirements is created. The first possibility is to find another worker with the same experience as the one who is leaving. Another option is to rearrange staff duties in order to accent a strength or correct a weakness in the menu or staff. For example, existing restaurants with poor sales and little profit are targets for staff reorganization. Hiring one new worker of higher quality may be the first step toward increasing sales and profitability. Kitchen workers aren't pegs to be pulled out and replaced by equal pegs. The object of a comprehensive hiring program is to build a team of responsible individuals. That demands some flexibility in the chef's concept of the ideal kitchen crew. Take every occasion of a rehiring to evaluate each team member's performance. Are the workers making their best contribution to the restaurant's food production cycle? If it were possible, what would be the ideal position for each worker? The ultimate purpose of any replacement is to create an improvement, not just fill a slot.

Hiring a staff for an unopened restaurant begins the same way, with an imaginative concept of how the ideal staff would work together.

Recruitment

Finding possible job candidates appears easy at first glance, especially for the bottom-scale jobs like dishwasher. But the problems of finding a good worker who is serious, sober and motivated may make the search seem endless. Before the slot is filled, every source of employees will have been exhausted. For that reason, it makes sense to start with the sources which have proven most reliable in the past. Develop a network of sources so that when the time comes, often during a last-minute emergency, new workers will begin to arrive within hours.

The sources which prove most successful are those which yield permanent workers of high quality, not just bodies. The following list should be part of any chef's employment network: promote from within the existing staff, ask the staff about friends who qualify, call chefs whom you share information with, call employment agencies, place an ad in the classified ads sections of local newspapers, or call the workers whose phone numbers you have collected.

Each method of recruitment has pluses and minuses, which make them stronger or weaker from region to region. In some areas, the want ads will yield the largest number of highly qualified candidates. The drawback is the time it takes for an ad to appear—from one day to one week. Often employment needs are immediate. In this situation, a network of business acquaintances will be the quickest source of workers. A few telephone calls will bring in the friend of a friend, who may turn out to be one of your best workers.

No matter what method of search has proven most reliable in the past for a specific area, a chef should try all possible avenues every time a permanent position opens up. The chances of finding a perfect candidate after the first telephone call are minute. Increase the likelihood of getting a highly qualified worker by seeing as many people as possible, quickly.

Checking References

No matter where you live or how good the job candidate looks, references must be checked. The only possible exceptions are when it is impractical, as with menial jobs, or where personal references have brought the candidate to you in the first place. All other applicants should be screened. Ninety percent of the time, a telephone call will reveal nothing unusual. In fact, former employers will give glowing appraisals of workers they have fired. This is an ironic twist which must be considered. Casual questions will not accomplish the reference check's goals. Ask tough questions to find out the truth about a worker's weaknesses. For instance: Can I ask why you fired Mr. Jones? How long did he work for you? What was his salary? Did he have any problems with drugs, alcohol or absentee-ism? Often an owner-manager or chef will be reluctant to tell the horrible truth about bad workers. If you feel that the answers are evasive rather than explicit, call another reference. Job candidates who have no refer-ences are poor risks.

The purpose of the reference check is twofold. The first is to find and disqualify that ten to fifteen percent of workers in the bad risk category—cooks who have personality disorders or are substance abusers or thieves. The second purpose is the real focus of the call—to discuss the job candidate's cooking skills. For this reason, recent employers will give the most current appraisal of a candidates cooking ability and experience. During the interview, cooks are likely to describe their skills at a level or two above what their actual experience has been. Many cooks think that by working next to a chef for a long time, they are as qualified as the chef. A few are, but most need practice in order to perfect the intricacies of their craft. Therefore, a description of their duties by their former employer is the best way to gauge their experience.

The Interview

Be very specific about the times for interviews. It is better to see twenty people in two hours than to spread the process out over a day or two. By reading a resume or job application, a chef can eliminate the bulk of candidates immediately. But asking candidates to leave their resumes alienates some of the best prospects. The most productive procedure is to read the resume or application at the beginning of the interview. If it shows a candidate who is over- or underqualified, say so. But also indicate that you would like to keep the resume in case another position closer to their level of experience opens up. Don't waste time chatting with workers who haven't got a chance. They will appreciate your honest approach, provided you are polite.

Since many cooks don't have resumes, the job application becomes a significant tool for the interview process. Any stationary store will sell an adequate one by the stack. Keep them handy. If necessary, make a one-sheet form, like the one in Figure 17-1. Notice that the information about high school, junior high school and grade school is missing. That may be the only problem with the stationary store's form—it is too complete. A hand-tailored job application tells a chef quickly what he or she needs to know. Design your own and copy it. As a cautionary note, be certain that any job application used has taken into full consideration the federal and state regulations concerning legally permissible questions. Another important development is the use of the I-9 Form, the questionnaire which asks about citizenship status. This form must be filled out. Be certain to check all pertinent documents.

Before describing the job, draw out the candidate with questions about past experience. For example: What exactly were your duties? Which do you prefer, day or night shifts? Why did you leave your last job? What styles of cuisine do you know best? Do you have any outside interests? All these questions may have been asked on the application; nevertheless, get the candidate to expound. This will be your first glimpse of the person's ability to deal with people. A candidate who speaks softly, with the head lowered, may make an excellent garde manger or saute cook but a terrible expeditor. Personality will be revealed in these few minutes, but the subject should be food. Get the candidate to reveal his or her interest, knowledge and experience with food, both as a preparer and a diner.

Cooking positions require a balance of technical skill and creativity, depending upon the scale of restaurant and the originality of the menu. For a job as hamburger flipper in a fast food store, ninety-nine percent of the effort is technical; in fact, originality would get in the way. A job candidate with a great interest in creative cuisine would not be happy. This person should be considered overqualified. In the opposite situation, a worker with top-notch technical experience but little interest in original cuisine would not be right for a position involving the creation of specials for upscale menus.

JOB APPLICATION

DATE_____

NAME_____

ADDRESS_____

PHONE NUMBER_____

WORK HISTORY

Date Employed From/To	Restaurant	Owner/Chef	Position	Salary	Reason for Leaving
1.					
2.					
3.					

EDUCATION, INCLUDING UNIVERSITY, TRADE SCHOOLS & SPECIAL COURSES

School	Location	Course Studied	Dates	Degree
1.				
2.				
3.				

What are your foreign language capabilities?_____

What position are you applying for?_____

What past experience qualifies you for this position?_____

_____

SIGNED_____

Figure 17-1. Job application.

A chef must understand the scale of the restaurant and the basic purpose of the business. In order to attract and keep a highly motivated staff, workers must be chosen for their practical contributions. That means matching skills and attitudes with the right job. State openly the position's hardest attributes, e.g., that the restaurant sells a lot of club sandwiches or that the person will be required to cut his or her own vegetables. If the candidate is a good possibility, begin to describe the restaurant's strong points: busy seasons, busy shifts, creative qualities, reputation, owners, the staff; whatever you deem a plus for the working environment, state it directly. Go on to describe realistically how the open position fits into the operation; don't build up false hopes. In some cases, a difficult job has other pluses. For instance, the cook who must stand in front of a busy broiler making steak sandwiches until two or three in the morning can expect to be paid the same as a saute chef in a less busy house. If you are buying technical skills, buy them. Don't confuse your efforts and end up with a creative chef who hates the job. Likewise, if you have a prestigious name, use it as a selling factor. You will be able to attract top-notch talent without offering any more than the going salary, and perhaps less. A chef with a clear and realistic understanding of the restaurant's creative and technical limits is in the best position to hire workers who will fit the job being offered.

Good talkers aren't necessarily good cooks. My favorite candidate will say something like "Let me come in and work one shift. I'll show what I can do, and if you like me, hire me. If you don't, it's on me—no charge." In every group of prospective workers, there will be one or two candidates with this offer. It certainly is attractive, but if the worker can't do the job, valuable time will have been lost. It is better to trail the ideal candidate, at least the one best suited for the open position, even if it costs a shift's pay.

From the interview process and any other source, select the best candidates for trailing. Bring in as many workers as necessary until the right one clicks. Just be clear about the ground rules. The hours, pay and competitive elements should be mentioned specifically. Usually the first four hours of a shift will cover at least one rush; for line cooks, this will be enough time for a trail shift. The working skills of a preparation cook or dishwasher will be evident much sooner. Whether or not to pay for a trail shift is a matter of policy; there is no set rule. Some restaurants do not pay; others pay at one-half the regular rate; still others pay the full amount. A set policy is too inflexible. Getting the right worker is the goal. In a job market with numerous candidates, it may not be necessary to pay for trail shifts. At another times of the year, there may be only three people to choose from, and the best one wants to be paid. Of course, you pay.

The Ideal Prospective Employee

Is there such a thing? Can a job candidate seem totally wrong for the job but in actuality turn out to be an ideal worker? About one time out of one thousand, this will happen. If the person is an excellent worker with perfect experience, the interview or reference check will indicate this.

Hiring the kitchen staff is not an intuitive process. One quirk in a candidate's presentation should not eliminate this person from consideration. There are too many factors of equal importance to disqualify a candidate abruptly for one oddity. Consider the following elements which go into the makeup of a perfect prospective employee:

1. At least two years' experience in the same position at a restaurant with an ambiance and menu similar to those of the restaurant at which they are applying.
2. Currently employed, but prefers the hours, position or salary you offer.
3. Flexible in schedule matters.
4. A work history including at least one stay at a restaurant for over three years.
5. The pay asked for is a notch below the regular pay for the position offered, or at least in the same range.
6. No offensive personal habits.
7. Communicates a desire to work hard.
8. Absolutely no hint of lateness, absenteeism, or drug or alcohol abuse.

The Moment of Hiring

A candidate has successfully passed the interview and trailing tests; now you are ready to hire. This is the best time to make known your personal goals for the restaurant's quality. The specific duties of the job should be outlined clearly so that the new employee understands them from the onset. Essentially, the purpose is to communicate the standard of performance expected and to put new workers on notice that their production will be checked. All personnel policies should be stated clearly at this time, especially those relating to lateness and missed shifts. All policies must conform to state and city laws. Make it clear that the employee is on probation and can be terminated for any infractions. If these matters are stated and understood before hiring takes place, the worker will be much more receptive and respectful of the restaurant's standards. The new worker's transformation into a fully seasoned team member will be shorter. Just as important, workers who do not measure up to these clearly stated goals are very easily dismissed. Stating the job duties will also prevent potential lawsuits, an increasing problem among employers. Consider any worker still in the first month of employment to be a junior partner. During this period, minor infractions take on greater significance than they would for employees with one or two years of solid performance behind them.

Employees generally are what they seem. For example, a new employee who shows up one or two hours late during his second week can be expected to repeat this behavior often. Don't saddle the restaurant with a liability. Experience shows that the best way to handle a worker who makes a serious mistake during the first few weeks is to replace him. That's one reason to make very clear the expectations or standards set by policy—your policy. There will be less whining at the firing.

Staffing Brand New Restaurants

The interview, reference check and hiring procedure take on added significance when a new restaurant is being staffed. With no employees at all on the payroll, the importance of matching one responsible, experienced worker with one opening is multiplied ten, twenty or thirty times. The tension produced can be extremely distracting. Safety valves must be installed to reduce the pressure. The first day and first week of a restaurant's life is not a normal period; consequently, the preparation must be extraordinarily good.

Begin the hiring process four weeks before the opening day. Sometimes it is possible to recruit key employees, such as the sous chef, night chef or head preparation cook, well in advance by using connections in the business. This is recommended. Another wise approach is to hire former associates, whose work you respect and who work well with you, for a temporary period, even if it's just for the opening week. They may be able to get time off from their current job or anxious to pick up extra shifts.

The hiring process doesn't stop with opening day; it continues, at a heavy turnover rate, for months. Be prepared to keep interviewing, hiring and firing until the staff achieves the expected level of quality and proficiency.

With a high turnover rate expected, hire one and one-half times the number of workers projected for a heavy sales volume week. Unknown factors will weed out the excess by day three after the opening. There will be a different story or excuse for each no-show, argumentative, slow, lazy, poorly experienced and sloppy worker. Keep the staff flush with new candidates, and prune dead weight as soon as a replacement can be trained.

Training should start two weeks before opening. Take as much time as the owner-manager will allow. This training period will be the only cushion between the mob of customers arriving for the opening week and the threat of bad food prepared at a snail's pace. Even cooks with the right experience will need several explanations for their job and the recipes to begin working. Then, with the head chef on site to answer occasional questions, the separate kitchen workers, from sous chef to pot scrubber, can begin to develop their team muscle. They will have to be able to work together as the head chef originally conceived the operation. A confusion of solo performances will cause inconsistent quality. The strong cooks will be needed to hold the line together by working a little into the stations around them. It is common for some overlap to occur even with an established staff, and it is even more crucial with a new team. The training session can consist of two parts or more, depending on the number of different menus. A breakfast, brunch, lunch or dinner menu will be the focus of each training session. For instance, serve a full dinner menu of appetizers through desserts to the floor staff, managers and owners. Do the same for the lunch menu and any other menus the restaurant will use. Preview performances by the staff are valuable for conveying the recipes and style of the head chef to all the cooks and workers. Questions which are answered during the training period represent problems already solved before opening night.

The first day of operation should be one of the busiest shifts of the first year. To complicate matters, many of the first day's customers will be connected personally with the restaurant's owners. This environment is a hotbed for premature criticism and ego flareups. The only defense a chef has is to deliver sheer perfection—high quality at reasonable speed. It is possible to have a nearly flawless opening. A calm staff made up of seasoned professionals working under the constant guidance of proven specialists will be able to get the job done nicely.

Hiring + Firing = Boss

The person who does the hiring must also do the firing. Workers expect it. They look to that person as the boss, because he or she has the ultimate power. Any head chef must at least retain final approval, if not actually interviewing, hiring and firing personally. Along with the power comes a responsibility. The chef is the kitchen staff's representative to the owner-manager. That means defending a worker's request for a raise or special benefit and mediating problems between the floor staff and the kitchen staff. It is essential for workers to have someone who speaks for them to management. Without it, their attitude and quality go down together. A chef who is a concerned boss earns the authority needed to manage during hectic periods.

Quality, Discipline and Termination

In addition to their own high-quality performance, chefs are required to use other methods to ensure that the standard remains high at all times— even when the chef is off. Making a sincere effort to hire responsible workers is the single most effective action a chef can take. But it is also important to rid the staff of any bad habits or irresponsible workers.

Bad habits begin with an insignificant action; for instance, late at night, someone takes a shortcut because he is tired. That action is repeated by the same cook from time to time until others decide that the new way is easier and no one seems to care. Any new procedure which lessens the quality of the taste or presentation must be stopped immediately. One of a chef's ongoing concerns is quality, especially in the way the cooks are following the guidelines originally set. Some evolution of technique is inevitable and can definitely be for the better, as in the case of a timesaving step. But lazy shortcuts must be stopped abruptly. This requires discipline.

A staff will be as disciplined as its head chef. If the chef doesn't have the conviction or experience to stop a slide in quality, no one else will. Sloppiness, poor technique, lazy shortcuts—all these problems have to be mentioned every time they are spotted. Other cooks take notice if a substandard plate goes out under the chef's observation without an objection. However, while these infractions are detrimental to the restaurant's business health, it isn't feasible for a chef to criticize indefinitely. A termination may be in order.

The ultimate solution, termination, is a tool like any other at the chef's disposal. Used wisely, it can lead to higher quality. Some workers will do things their way no matter how often the chef voices dissatisfaction. Sloppy, lazy workers have little regard for the chef's direction. Establish which of the offenders is the worst and then begin a short campaign to be rid of this criticism. Oral criticism on the line while the work is being done is the first step. When that fails to change the problem worker, have a personal conference with the cook in the office before or after this person's shift. Be explicit about how important quality is to you. Make certain that the worker understands that his or her job is in jeopardy. If there is any resentment, you can be certain that the worker will take the first opportunity to be slipshod, probably when you're off. Do what you have to do, but fire any cook who continues to produce below standard. At the time of firing, it is important that the kitchen workers understand the details. Half of the value of a firing is that it sends a signal to the staff. They realize your seriousness on the quality issue. Therefore, derive the full value of any firing by making the reasons clear. This also keeps the staff from building an image of you as a ruthless egomaniac. Unwarranted firings discourage other workers and weaken overall authority. Good cooks will begin to look for other jobs if they sense that the chef is too free with the ultimate solution.

When to Fire

Almost any worker's mistake can be handled by lighter discipline than firing. Sometimes it depends upon the chef's frame of mind. If the staff is generally lazy, late or absent, a firing will be necessary for the chef's own piece of mind. At times of relative calm, the chef may be inclined to be more lenient. When tempers flare in the kitchen, the results are usually disastrous. Chefs can best guard against blowups by dealing with staff deficiencies as they occur, rather than waiting for a buildup of resentment and an explosion of emotions.

There are some actions which demand immediate dismissal, regardless of the chef's frame of mind. Stealing, gross insubordination, or violent behavior are inappropriate for a working kitchen, regardless of the excuses. These infractions should not be allowed to happen a second time. That means giving no second chances.

Absenteeism is another regular problem, and one which is usually related to poor personal habits, especially drug and alcohol abuse. As a rule of thumb, a worker who doesn't show for the shift and doesn't call does not deserve a second chance. This is one of the rules which a chef needs to convey explicitly at the time of hiring. A good excuse may warrant a second chance, but don't fool yourself. It will happen again and again until the worker is fired.

Lateness is no great problem if it happens once. But if it occurs week after week, an hour here and thirty minutes there, before long the rest of the staff becomes disgruntled—with good reason. It will be only a matter of time before lateness becomes the norm. Even pampered cooks cannot be allowed to show up late. Counseling is the first step in rectifying the problem. Specific warnings must be given.

It is important to state your intention to fire a worker if the person is an otherwise good cook whom you would like to keep on. But whether the person has a variety of problems or only one—preparing mediocre food—

almost any infraction can be built into a case for firing. Sometimes it is necessary to use a roundabout route. For instance, a worker whom the owner-manager praises may in actuality be the worst cook on the staff. Ironically, being a poor cook is one of the poorest reasons for dismissal in many restaurants. It should be the one solid cause for dismissal, but usually it has to be coupled with another problem before the culprit can be expunged. Owner-managers love to say "But he comes every day on time. We never have a problem with him." Then, in the next breath, they ask you what you're going to do to make business better. Even if no one else agrees, a chef must fire workers who are consistently mediocre or incompetent. The head chef is the person best trained to make this decision. Furthermore, that's what this person is getting paid to do.

Good Ways to Fire

As discusssed earlier, how often a chef dismisses can become a concern for the owner-manager if the chef's control seems sporadic or too emotional. Similarly, *how* a chef fires will build an impression of either professionalism or emotionalism. Dismissals are a matter of business; at least, they must appear to be. Even at the firing of a hated nemesis, a chef must remain detached.

There are other things to be gained by a professional procedure besides enhancement of one's reputation. An employee may have been let go for a number of reasons which combined to make him a terrible full-time worker. But as a temporary worker for emergency fill-ins, an ex-employee might have a good attitude, arrive on time, and be better trained than other potential substitutes. A temporary shift offers ex-employees the opportunity to vindicate themselves in their own eyes. By contrast, an emotional firing will build a wall between the chef and outgoing personnel. Don't make enemies, and don't throw away their phone numbers.

An important aspect of the firing process is the employee's frame of mind. The person will be most receptive to the inevitable when made to feel comfortable in formal surroundings. A sit-down meeting in the office is preferable to speaking in the kitchen or dining room, where other staff members may hover close by. Allow the outgoing employee some dignity. If the quickest and gentlest way is to dismiss by phone, use this method. Start by stating your intention to fire. Then offer to speak personally, at length, whenever the ex-employee wants to meet.

The best time to fire is as soon as possible after the outgoing worker's last shift. Don't keep the person dangling because you are timid or "too busy." Casual or arrogant disregard for another person's source of livelihood is grist for the bad reputation mill. As a rule of thumb, the less humiliation an employee feels after a firing, the greater respect the other workers will have for their chef's management skills. Thinking that an emotional firing will cause fear and build discipline is wrong. It will cause fear, but it will also cause the smart workers to look for a calmer environment.

One of the reasons a chef must adopt an unemotional attitude is that this is the best way to counter the employee's pleading. Last-minute excuses should not be enough to change the chef's decision. If they are able to sway the chef, then the dismissal was not well thought out. Know exactly why someone is being fired because the subject may come up. Surprisingly, it usually doesn't—not if the dismissal is quick and to the point. But ethically and legally, a chef is required to discuss and justify any termination.

Begin the firing by clearly stating your decision to fire, lay off, let go, dismiss, give notice, or discharge the worker. Don't try to justify your decision with a planned argument or detailed list of faults. Let the news sink in. Nine times out of ten, employees will simply nod, knowing that it was inevitable. They'll be anxious to get their pay and leave. It is very important to have their pay ready. An ex-employee may be a disruptive influence. It is better to break clean, leaving no reason for them to return.

Occasionally, a worker will disagree with the decision to fire. Always be prepared to defend the dismissal. If the worker has a reputation as a hothead, have another manager present. Let the worker present his side, up to a point. This is only fair. But after the worker's defense has been presented once, the meeting is over. This is not a trial or hearing; the chef's purpose is to fire swiftly. Keep that in mind. Don't allow yourself to be cowed or threatened by loud emotionalism. While emergency situations may necessitate the temporary use of an ex-employee, never rehire anyone who has been fired. No matter how easy the rehiring solution seems, move on. Ex-employees will return with all of their old faults. Eventually they will have to be fired again. One of the reasons a worker is fired is so that a new one can be tried, presumably one who does the job better.

The New Chef versus the Established Staff

The staff of an existing restaurant has an established working relationship which includes good and bad techniques. The restaurant's record of failure will do a lot to make the owner-manager receptive to a new chef's approach. Naturally, a slow, unprofitable restaurant will be hoping for firm, new direction. An already busy and profitable one will be reluctant to change anything. Enter the new chef, full of enthusiasm, ideas and criticism. Resistance is everywhere. The first week is a trial by tasting. Little verbal contact occurs between the chef and the kitchen or floor staff. The problem is that, in the staff's opinion, a new chef is just the next chef. Whether or not this person will measure up and become permanent remains to be seen. A well-handled dismissal, for any cause, will be the signal to the staff that the new chef is in charge. Of course, it is especially important that the dismissal and replacement come off without a hitch. Special care to plan backups, should the first replacement fail, is part of the process.

The occurrence of the first firing after taking over a new chefdom depends on two variables: the new chef's relationship with the owner-manager and the reason for the targeted employee's dismissal.

Usually a new chef is getting to know the owners and managers for the first time. In that case, it is wise to use a cautious approach to understand the actual lines of power (some owners do not care about who is fired) and one's perceived role in the kitchen management. As always, a chef's power derives from the ability to increase sales and keep profits growing. Until the owner-managers see a monthly report on those statistics, they won't want a new chef tampering with the status quo.

Before those statistics come in, a number of things may happen which would normally be cause for dismissal. If there is insubordination or other challenges to the new chef's authority, the owner-managers should not be expected to support the chef. They may be very supportive; just don't expect it. More than likely, if the owner-managers believe that the new chef is creating friction with one or two trusted employees, the chef may be fired before he or she can start.

When taking a chef's job, always establish the ground rules, which will become vitally important in the first week. If an owner-manager has no more confidence in the new chef than to hem and haw evasively when asked directly to clarify hiring and firing policy, the chef candidate should consider the possible pitfalls. An uncooperative or even insubordinate staff will be measuring the chef's every move.

Any chef should have the power to fire under certain circumstances with the total support of superiors. Whether the chef is new or established, successful or failing, the circumstances of the chef's employment should not interfere with the discipline of the kitchen. Any owner-manager who is reluctant to give dismissal power in the following problems will probably be reserving much of the power for himself. This can be a workable situation, but it requires the new chef to put a lot of trust in the owner-manager. Still these infractions should be cause for dismissal, no matter who holds the power:

1. Stealing
2. Absenteeism
3. Chronic lateness
4. Gross insubordination
5. Violent behavior

Highlights

Certain hiring techniques will lessen the need to change cooks and reduce stress during the firing process.

Hiring one new worker of higher quality may be the first step toward increasing sales and profitability.

The ultimate purpose of hiring for an open position is to create an improvement, not just fill a slot.

Develop a network of sources so that when the time comes, often during a last-minute emergency, new workers will begin to arrive within hours.

No matter where you live or how good the job candidate looks, references must be checked.

Recent employers will give the most current appraisal of a candidate's cooking ability and experience.

Get the candidate to reveal his or her interest, knowledge and experience with food, both as a preparer and a diner.

In order to attract and keep a highly motivated staff, workers must be chosen for their practical contributions.

A chef with a clear and realistic understanding of the restaurant's creative and technical limits is in the best position to hire workers who will fit the job being offered.

The specific duties of the job should be outlined clearly so that the new employee understands them from the onset.

The first day and first week of a restaurant's life is not a normal period; consequently, the preparation must be extraordinarily good.

Training for new menus should start three or four weeks before the restaurant opens.

The first day of operation should be one of the busiest shifts of the first year.

The chef is the kitchen staff's representative to the owner-manager.

A chef who is a concerned boss earns the authority needed to manage during hectic periods.

Half of the value of a firing is that it sends a signal to the staff.

Chefs can best guard against blowups by dealing with staff deficiencies as they occur, rather than waiting for a buildup of resentment and an explosion of emotions.

Stealing, gross insubordination and violent behavior are inappropriate for a working kitchen, regardless of the excuses.

How often a chef dismisses can become a concern for the owner-manager if the chef's control seems sporadic or too emotional.

As a rule of thumb, the less humiliation an employee feels after a firing, the greater respect the other workers will have for their chef's management skills.

A chef's power derives from the ability to increase sales and keep profits growing.

If the owner-manager believes that the new chef is creating friction with one or two trusted employees, the chef may be fired before he or she can start.

Chapter 18

HOW TO CALCULATE LABOR PERCENTAGES

Introduction

Three types of expenses are generated by a kitchen operation: food purchases, labor costs and operating costs. They are commonly called percentages or pc's. Labor pc's usually rank as the second highest kitchen expense after food pc's. It is odd how much attention an owner-manager will give to the food pc but rarely discuss the labor costs, perhaps because labor costs are supposedly less within the control of the chef. However, the previous four chapters show how payroll costs can be controlled. A well-informed, assertive chef needs to calculate labor pc's as a regular part of the control system. An unchecked labor pc can grow greater than the food pc, especially during the off season when sales are down. That is when the labor pc will become a major issue. A high labor cost can become the only negative factor in a chef's otherwise good performance. If the expense is high enough, it may jeopardize the chef's present position and career moves.

The Chef as Manager

Head chefs are not simply glorified cooks. Their role includes the dual aspects of cuisine and management. Therefore, they must either accept the traditional responsibilities of a manager in addition to performing culinary tasks, or have a competent subordinate who takes care of business. Most operations cannot afford two head chefs; the owner-manager expects one person to supply adequate expertise in both areas. Some excellent chefs may create tantalizing, delicious dishes but have no organizational skills or business training. They are at a severe disadvantage and usually fail miserably as head chefs.

Knowledge is a tool. Keep weekly and monthly figures on the labor pc to gauge the kitchen's performance from month to month. One way to minimize this expense is through planning. Past records will help to predict future labor costs. Records are the beginning of the planning effort.

Knowledge can also be a defensive weapon. Know the business well enough to set the record straight when necessary. A talented night manager may call the owner-manager's attention to the last month's labor pc, 38.1 percent, a high cost that even exceeds the food costs. At that point, the head chef should point to the previous year's labor pc, the highs and lows for the individual months, and the exact comparison of corresponding months. If the annual labor pc is in line, this will be immediately obvious. If there is a problem, that will be clear too. At least the head chef will give the impression of being in control of the labor expenses. However, the night manager may ask, "If you knew the labor pc was so high, why didn't you do something about it?"

The calculation of pc's, labor included, is the best tool for monitoring profit gains and losses, but it is only a tool. To be valuable, it must be applied. Simply playing numbers games does not solve problems. Effective chef-managers should have this tool at their disposal just as readily as the utensils in the kitchen.

Labor PC's and Raises

One certain benefit of a labor pc is that it can indicate when to refuse to give raises. Even the most successful restaurants cannot continue to raise their employees' salaries indefinitely. One fact of business is that sometimes workers need to move on, if for no other reason than their desire to make more money. This means breaking up an efficient team and starting over again with new workers until the right replacement is found. As difficult as the hiring process can be, the chef and owner-manager must discuss the limits of labor costs and the individual salaries which make up the overall pc.

Ironically, chefs are caught in the middle of this controversy because their salary is calculated as part of the kitchen labor. Their willingness to set a lower ceiling for other cooks' salaries will ease the way for their own next raise. However, if an artificially low ceiling is set by a greedy chef or one ascribing to the philosophy of planned turnover discussed in Chapter 14, an extraordinarily high turnover rate can be expected. (Chefs, beware owner-managers who do not pay their cooks the going rate. They will expect their chef to hold things together by working fifty- to sixty-hour weeks and training dishwashers to be saute and broiler cooks. Later, when it's time for you to ask for a raise, they'll give your job to one of the people you've trained.)

The best way to deal with this dilemma is to know the salaries of cooks in corresponding positions at restaurants with similar sales records and apply that standard fairly. This will result in the least amount of turnover and a manageable labor pc.

Calculating Labor PC's

The actual arithmetic involved in the calculation of labor pc's is elementary. Divide the period's kitchen payroll by the corresponding period's food sales. The following examples show the basic process for three separate levels of restaurant operations. For a complete explanation of how the raw data is compiled, see the section on "Forms and Procedures" in Chapter 8. Payroll totals can be obtained from the payroll clerk or owner-manager.

Example A. *THE PICNIC GAZEBO* is a new restaurant both in location and in style. Its success depends on the customer's acceptance of a countrified menu in sophisticated surroundings. After seven months of operation, sales have risen to a steady but low volume. The staff has some periods of inactivity due to slow sales. Here are the figures for the current month, October.

PERIOD	DATE	SALES	KITCHEN PAYROLL		KITCHEN LABOR PC'S
Week 1	10/10	10,456	4,550	=	43.5
Week 2	10/17	10,711	4,496	=	41.9
Week 3	10/24	9,232	4,358	=	47.2
Week 4	10/31	11,062	4,508	=	40.7
October totals		$41,461	$17,912	=	43.2%

Example B. *THE PRIME MINISTER* is an established supper club with medium sales volume when compared to national figures, but is actually one of the most expensive and successful in its area. The chef is part owner, which may explain the restaurant's excellent profit margin. Here are the figures for July.

PERIOD	DATE	SALES	KITCHEN PAYROLL		KITCHEN LABOR PC'S
Week 1	7/3	21,334	7,817	=	36.6
Week 2	7/10	24,792	8,259	=	33.3
Week 3	7/17	25,543	8,473	=	33.2
Week 4	7/24	28,191	8,545	=	30.3
Week 5	7/31	27,687	8,614	=	31.1
July totals		$127,547	$41,708	=	32.7%

Example C. The *LEFT BANK EXPRESS* is a two hundred fifty-seat gold mine located across the street from a major university. The volume is heavy. Part of the reason for the Express' success is its low prices. It relies on high volume and heavy turnover to yield a high dollar profit. The staff consists of college students working for little more than the minimum wage, except for a few responsible positions. The following figures are from the peak month, April.

PERIOD	DATE	SALES	KITCHEN PAYROLL		KITCHEN LABOR PC'S
Week 1	4/10	64,271	16,683	=	25.9
Week 2	4/17	68,990	16,455	=	23.8
Week 3	4/24	66,734	16,471	=	24.7
Week 4	5/1	67,255	16,669	=	24.8
April totals		$267,250	$66,278	=	24.8%

Interpreting Labor PC's

Unlike food expenses, which can be regulated to match the sales volume, labor costs remain constant from one week to the next. Every restaurant has a minimum number of cooks and dishwashers who are needed to operate the business. If sales are too low to keep even the skeleton staff busy, a high labor pc is the result. This was the case for The Picnic Gazebo. Note that the dip in sales during Week 3 causes an astronomical pc of 47.2 percent.

A busy restaurant utilizes the staff to its fullest potential; that is an important factor in controlling labor pc's, but not the only factor. The Prime Minister has a steady, high sales record and a high labor pc. The staff is well paid and is perhaps a little too large. The glory days of the beginning, when the staff worked hard together as a team to build the restaurant's reputation and sales, have faded. Now the staff feels that it has earned the right to relax a little and to be paid well. The result is a labor pc two to five points above what it should be. That's a monthly wasted profit of between $2550 and $6375.

The most profitable operations have just enough staff turnover to keep salaries down, but not to affect the quality or the sales volume. The Left Bank Express has a fantastic labor pc for a full-service restaurant.

Depending on the type of restaurant, including menu prices, number of seats, turnover rate and preparation difficulties, labor pc's should range from twenty-five to thirty-three percent. This spread of almost ten points can represent thousands of dollars. How should chefs judge the level of performance of their own operation? Should their pc's be in the low thirties or high twenties?

An existing restaurant has a record of accomplishment which includes the owner-manger's estimates of what a reasonable kitchen payroll should be. If the restaurant is successful *and* profitable, that estimate is probably valid. But if the business is failing and no one seems to know where the money is going, all expenses should be considered too high, especially payroll. The absolute minimum a kitchen will cost to run is the entry-level salary rate for each position on the existing staff. For example, The Prime Minister has a staff of sixteen earning approximately $8300 per week. The chef made a list of the sixteen positions, estimated how much it would cost to replace each person with a new worker, and calculated the weekly payroll with the new rates. The difference was almost $1000 dollars per week. The estimated reduction in the monthly labor pc would be 3.7 percent. That must be considered a realistic, low target. The chef has a responsibility to bring these facts to the owner-manager's attention for discussion. Together they must decide the continued policies of the restaurant, largely based on the operation's policies of the restaurant, largely based on the operation's profit margin.

Highlights

Labor pc's usually rank as the second highest kitchen expense after food pc's.

A high labor cost can become the only negative factor in a chef's otherwise good performance.

Chefs must either accept the traditional responsibilities of a manager, in addition to performing culinary tasks, or have a competent subordinate who takes care of business.

Past records will help to predict future labor costs.

The calculation of pc's, labor included, is the best tool for monitoring profit gains and losses, but it is only a tool. To be valuable, it must be applied.

One certain benefit of a labor pc is that it indicates when to refuse to give raises.

As difficult as the hiring process can be, the chef and owner-manager must discuss the limits of labor costs and the individual salaries which make up the overall pc.

The actual arithmetic involved in the calculation of labor pc's is elementary. Divide the period's kitchen payroll by the corresponding period's food sales.

The most profitable operations have just enough staff turnover to keep salaries down, but not to affect the quality or the sales volume.

If the business is failing and no one seems to know where the money is going, all expenses should be considered too high, especially payroll.

PART 4

CAREER ADVANCEMENT (HOW TO GET RICH AND FAMOUS)

Chapter 19

REMUNERATION TO THE CHEF

Introduction

The rewards a chef gains by work aren't measured by wealth alone. As in any career, there are a host of other gratifications: prestige, security, environment, city or location, worker relations, learning opportunities and possibilities for advancement. The importance of each separate gain depends upon the value a chef places on it. Each individuals has unique needs.

Remuneration comes in many forms, but the most generally accepted is the tangible one—anything which can be converted into cash. This chapter deals with the monetary rewards of being a chef, what the top salaries are and how to get them.

Job Definition

The way chefs are rated by their peers reveals the most about their realistic net worth. After all, the job market is demand based, like every other negotiable market. A key factor in deciding the head chef's salary is what the owner-manager perceives as the going rate for excellent, mediocre or poor performance by chefs in the same type of restaurant. Chefs with an unrealistically high salary in mind will be disappointed to discover that chefs in their category never earn above a certain rate. The owner will more than likely be the first to tell them. Why should chefs expect to receive high payment for their services? A replacement may be hired for less. What is the chef's leverage?

275

Chefs must assess their performance by using the same two criteria which the owners use. First, the difficulty of the job is a prime consideration, especially the cooking and management skills required. From the owner's point of view, this involves the difficulty of finding a suitable replacement. The second criterion is the financial success of the chef, or how much money he or she earns for the boss by controlling food and labor costs. An owner will be especially reasonable with salary offers if the chef is the golden goose.

The difficulty of the job and the financial success of the chef are the two defining factors chefs should use to compare their net worth with that of other chefs. The following chart categorizes the level of chefs' responsibilities from large, four-star restaurants to small, take-out stores. This represents the difficulty factor only.

1. Upscale   250+   seats
2. Upscale   100–250 seats
3. Upscale   0–100 seats
4. Medium scale   250+   seats
5. Medium scale   100–250 seats
6. Medium scale   0–100 seats
7. Low scale   250+   seats
8. Low scale   100–250 seats
9. Low scale   0–100 seats

While the progression from level one to level nine marks a general decline in the difficulty of responsibilities, a restaurant at level four could conceivably involve a much harder job than one at level three. The purpose of the chart is not to compare restaurants at various levels. It is merely a guide for chefs who wish to determine how their salaries rank with those of others within their level. Where does your restaurant stand? More than likely at level five, where most of the nation's restaurants fall.

The second factor is the amount of extra money the chef earns for the owner. The owner knows exactly how good things are if the chef is filling the house and spending wisely. The chef of a low- to medium-scale restaurant with only one hundred fifty seats could end up earning more than the chef of an upscale restaurant of the same size with poor sales and profits. As always, it is the blend of culinary creativity and business acumen which rules a chefs' career, in this case by determining their net worth. The following chart delineates food sales by total dollar volume and levels of profitability.

FOOD SALES PER YEAR($)		LEVEL OF PROFITABILITY	
1. 2,000,000 and up	Poor	Average	Excellent
2. 1,500,000-2,000,000	Poor	Average	Excellent
3. 1,000,000-1,500,000	Poor	Average	Excellent
4. 750,000-1,000,000	Poor	Average	Excellent
5. 500,000- 750,000	Poor	Average	Excellent
6. 0- 500,000	Poor	Average	Excellent

Head chefs who expect to get top salaries for their services need to know the restaurant's total annual food sales. This is one good reason to keep a running total from day to day as part of the effort to control spending. The total sales volume tells the owner how the business compares with that of previous years. It also tells the chef how big the operation is. Fully half of a chef's job description consists of the dollar volume and the level of profitability. The more specific a chef's knowledge is concerning his or her own store and the figures of other restaurants, the greater the likelihood of achieving monetary success.

National Salary Levels

The best way to find out the salaries of head chefs in a local area is to contact individuals who are in a position to know. Employment agents, for instance, spend most of their day discussing salaries. They have a lot of information about the chefs in their area. Head chefs hear many rumors and conjectures regarding salaries among their peers, even without trying to find out. By asking around, it takes only an afternoon to get a reliable picture of salary levels. The following chart shows current salaries in New York City, one of the largest local areas.

TYPE OF RESTAURANT		AVERAGE SALARY ($)
Upscale	250+ seats	100-250,000+
Upscale	100-250 seats	60- 80,000
Upscale	0-100 seats	40- 50,000
Medium scale	250+ seats	50- 80,000+
Medium scale	100-250 seats	30- 60,000
Medium scale	0-100 seats	30- 40,000
Low scale	250+ seats	40- 60,000
Low scale	100-250 seats	20- 30,000
Low scale	0-100 seats	15- 20,000

While investigating the New York City salary levels, some interesting bits of information came to light.

A soon to be opened French restaurant on Manhattan's Upper East Side will pay the chef a starting salary of $150,000.

The executive chef of a recently opened upscale dance and dinner club received a contract for $250,000 per year plus one percent of the banquet sales, estimated at $10,000,000.

It is impossible to find a chef for an upscale or large medium-scale house who will start for less than $50,000 per year.

In comparison with the rest of the country, New York City is a constant. It is compared to so often that most people know automatically how prices, styles and a salaries differ between their local area and the New York market. As a rule of thumb, assume that salaries around the country will reach the same peaks as those shown on the chart for New York City but that the density will be different. Of course, other large cities have restaurant populations comparable to New York's. That will keep salaries higher, because the demand for qualified chefs is heavy, too. But other factors based on the local area's economy will move salaries to a regional level. Real estate prices and the unemployment rate do much to dictate regional salaries.

The chart of chefs' salaries indicates that each level has an average salary range. The poor profit makers will be at the bottom of the scale, while the excellent ones will be near the top. For example, the chef of a medium-scale restaurant with up to one hundred seats may take over a poorly run operation at a starting salary of $30,000, but may be earning $40,000 by the end of the first year and $50,000 two years later. Chefs' awareness of their net worth and a diligent effort to keep their salary commensurate with the profit line are the tactics that have proven most profitable.

Compensations Based on Productivity

Rather than getting paid by one check every week, head chefs accumulate a package of benefits and bonuses. These unique payments are meant to satisfy and to supply the fairest system of compensation. Since a chef's duties include bringing in the customers, it is fair that they be paid according to their success rate. A simple weekly check would not cover that factor, considering the seasonal peculiarities of the restaurant business.

An assertive chef should discuss the types of bonuses and salary additions which the owner has given in the past. Whenever raises are being discussed, be prepared with a flexible assortment of compensation options. A certain style which the chef favors may not fit into the owner-manager's plans. Then flexibility is in order. By having a good general knowledge of the types of payment possible, chefs enhance their chances of getting the most lucrative package. The following types of rewards are tied to the chef's productivity or profitability.

Seasonal Bonuses. Given at the busiest times of the year, these bonuses may be calculated at a percentage rate which the owner-manager has predetermined with the chef. They may also be a flat dollar payment based on the owner's profit picture.

Annual Bonuses. These bonuses are given at year's end to congratulate the chef and key workers on a job well done. The bonus usually grows a little with the chef's seniority, but the prime motivation is good sales and profits from the preceding year.

Per Customer Bonuses. Expensive, upscale or new restaurants will offer a bonus based on the number of customers, usually $1 per diner. This ties the chef to the immediate success of the restaurant and allows the owner-manager to pay a top professional's high salary in direct proportion to the sales volume.

Percentage of Sales or Profits. Usually a chef must have a solid reputation or a fine working relationship with the owner-manager before this plum is offered. Owners use this reward to tie top chefs to their operation. From a chef's point of view, it is an excellent arrangement which allows the chef to participate in the benefits of ownership, provided sales are good and there is a profit, without having to take any risks. The percentage points are small—one, two or three percent for sales volumes and two to five percent for profit numbers.

Percentage of the Business. In addition to money, some chefs have the goal of owning a restaurant some day. This perk is designed to keep excellent chefs tied to an owner's business. There are many stories of chefs who claimed to have gained a percentage of the business by opening the restaurant and working for a substandard salary. Unfortunately, most of these stories are false. If you are the type of chef who must have a percentage of the business, have the terms described in a firm legal contract. Be certain to include in the presigning discussion the terms of settlement. Since most restaurants do not sell stock publicly, the liquidity of a percentage of the business clouds the merit of the entire plan. While the chef is happily employed with the principal owner, the piece of the business is lucrative and substantial, an extremely attractive situation. But the day after the chef leaves the job, what does he or she have? At best, a piece of paper and the prospect of a lengthy, expensive court battle.

Stock Options. Large companies can offer their stock at attractive below-market prices. This is a wonderful way for chefs to increase their earnings and be loyal to the company at the same time. Of course, the stock market does come down. It is a good idea for the chef to have some experience with stock ownership or to get the assistance of a professional money manager with stock expertise.

The Basic Package

Bonuses are perks added to the salary packages of highly productive head chefs. They are different in form; therefore, they may be added to a chef's payment schedule without affecting the natural progression of the basic salary. A salary begins in it's simplest form—the gross pay check—and then rises by the addition of both dollars to the gross and perks or benefits. Generally, chefs can expect to build a salary and benefits package, piece by piece, until it is choice. The following types of payment are possible for any chef's package.

Salary Check. Higher chefs' salaries and the tax laws have somewhat modified this form or payment. Now it is usual for a chef to negotiate for higher net rather than gross payment. As this is the first salary component to be agreed upon, the amounts run from subsistence to lush.

Insurance. Medical and dental plans which cover either the individual or the family are common in the restaurant industry but are by no means a national standard. If a restaurant has any employee coverage, the chef should expect to receive this perk automatically.

Retirement Plans. IRA's, 401-K's and other plans are excellent saving systems which can benefit the chef in a number of ways, not the least of which is tax deductibility. Unfortunately, except for large restaurant groups, such plans are uncommon. An established chef may be able to initiate a retirement plan with the help of the company accountant.

Little Perks. There are some things which only successful chefs can do, at least with the owner-manager's consent. Signing checks for themselves, family members and friends, for instance, is one way in which chefs can increase their income. Another method is to take food home for private use. An owner who is told every time the chef takes an expensive portion of raw goods home will either accept the wholesale price or give the food to the chef for free, depending upon how successful the restaurant is.

Other income enhancers include cookbooks, magazines, knives, equipment and uniforms. Collected over the years, these items represent little cost to the owner but do supply necessary tools and education for a competitive chef.

Negotiating Raises

Chefs should begin preparing to ask for their next raise the day after receiving their last one. There is nothing more aggravating to an owner-manager than a chef whose marked improvement begins one month before asking for a raise and stops abruptly two weeks afterward. That sort of climate, one of distrust and usury, will work against you—and for good reason. Raises are given primarily for performance. Therefore, maintain the perfect raise posture year round by doing the best job possible and maintaining excellent rapport with the powers that be. Running battles with managers or owners are out. Any resentment they have built up toward the chef will be revealed with a vengeance at the mention of a raise. That doesn't mean that the raise isn't merited or forthcoming, but the process will certainly be hampered by angry finger pointing.

Another prepatory step which a chef should take is to thoroughly investigate the current job market. It is valuable to know how many positions are open for a chef of the right caliber. In other words, the market is one of supply and demand. If there is a great demand for chefs, owners may be aware of this and temper their response. The reverse situation may also affect some owners' willingness to give a raise. The market will also dictate specific rates for various types of chefs. Be aware of the range of salaries and where you are already positioned—low, medium or high.

The timing of a request for a raise can cause immediate failure of the attempt or help to achieve it. When chefs are first hired, they should make it clear to the owner-manager when they expect a salary review. In some circumstances, annual or semi-annual reviews will be agreed upon. Special circumstances may be cause for immediate salary discussion, so leave the door open for early progress if the business has the potential to build rapidly.

Ask for a raise whenever more responsibility is given to you.

Ask for a raise if sudden information makes you realize how underpaid you are.

Anytime from six months to one year since the last raise is a good time to ask, provided the restaurant is in its busy season.

When you receive an outside offer of employment, you should ask for a raise.

Never broach the subject of a salary increase during bad times or low-profit periods. But beware the owners who make it a point to plead poverty. Occasionally, owners will try to argue their chefs out of earned raises. Chefs who are not receiving a rate of pay comparable to that of contemporaries should make this fact clear to the owner and stress their dissatisfaction. They should not work for promises. Owner-managers who pay below scale will rarely be swayed by the reasoning or threats of their chef. Learn to spot these types of bosses early, and move on to more lucrative environments. Some owners prefer to pay low salaries and take whatever chef fate hands them.

Under normal circumstances, raises are a subject of negotiation. The chef, of course, wants to earn as much as possible, while the owner-manager team is judging the raise by the standards of performance and longevity. Owners need to feel that a chef is staying on. They won't be inspired to offer a percentage of the net profit to a meteoric chef simply passing by on the way up. These two qualities of chefs, performance and time on the job, are the active reasons for which an owner will confer raises. Sometimes they can be discussed concurrently; at other times, only one will merit consideration and therefore mention.

At the beginning of a chef–owner relationship, the chef is generally hired with a lower salary and a promise. The idea from the start is that after the chef's worth has been proven, the raises will come quickly. Perhaps a chef with an excellent track record has been hired at an average or above-average starting wage, but there is always room for growth. The owner's first salary arrangements always reflect the down side, the worst possible sales and profits picture. A chef who has a good performance record for any amount of time has earned the right to ask for an increase. Again, market rates dictate the limits, but if a chef's work has created the busiest, most profitable restaurant in the area, the chef should be paid accordingly. That is the basis of the chef's performance argument. During the first two years before the seniority element can be used effectively, a chef must rely on performance to gain the big raises.

Although a raise is welcome, no matter what its form, it may be easier to get a reasonable amount of asking for the appropriate kind. Make your case for certain types of compensation for a productivity-based raise and other types for a longevity-based raise. For instance, the chef who has shown the owner a long period of sales increases and high profits has earned the unique privilege of asking for a percentage of the profits. The chef may not get it (few owners will confer such lofty raises), but at least the effort can be made. The owner will be prepared to counter with a fine offer. A chef with an excellent performance record would be wasting time by asking for something mundane like health insurance or a week's paid vacation. Those basic perks should be given automatically with the passage of months or years. The most salable attribute is the chef's record of sales and profits. It must be used when it has the strongest effect, and only for the richest prizes.

Standard negotiating tactics apply to the raise discussion between chef and owner, just as they would to any employer and boss. A chef with little or no experience in asking for raises would do well to read a book or two on the subject. The trick is to leave the owner-manager with an impression that you are ambitious and competitive, but never greedy.

The Ideal Moneymaking Career

Often the salary ceiling of a chef is set by the owners based on a previous salary history. Owners feel that a gradual progression through the ranks is the norm; therefore, radical increases in pay are unmerited. In that restrictive way, a chef's entire career is established. A chef who has a history of low wages will more than likely continue in the same rut.

Assertive chefs can think about money as it affects their present and future jobs without disturbing their culinary education and work responsibilities. Some types of jobs pay better than others, as do some owners and companies. The skills required vary, as do the working environments. But the odd thing is that a high-paying job is often no more difficult or demanding than a medium- to low-paying one. Career chefs are wise to let pay levels dictate the direction of their rise. They will eventually be in a position to work in the exact style of restaurant they prefer and at their desired pay level. The important aspects of a chef's moneymaking career are training credentials, upscale restaurant experience, mastery of at least three cuisines, heavy sales volume control and reliability. Consider the following career progression. It is an ideal picture of a chef whose primary goal is a large salary.

1. *The Beginning.* Graduates from a large culinary program, or attended a European culinary school, or worked under a recognized master in Europe, preferably France. No salary requirements for the first position.
2. *The First Job.* Starts as the night chef or day chef of a moderate-volume, medium- to high-scale restaurant. Stays for at least one year. Salary is in the high first cook or low night chef range to start, but rises to an average night chef level.
3. *The Volume Job.* Hired as the sous chef of a low- to medium-scale, heavy-volume restaurant. Stays for at least three months and then decides whether the head chef is vulnerable. By six months, the

careerist has either moved on or has become the chef. Now earning at least a high sous chef's salary due to the volume.

4. *The Upscale Job.* Works as the sous chef or night chef of a fashionable, upscale restaurant. Had to take a pay cut to graduate to the upscale level, but quickly proves worth to the chef and owner. Stays for at least six months in the job before assessing advancement or salary potential.

5. *The First Chefdom.* Takes over as head chef of an ailing upscale restaurant. The size is unimportant, but the location should be excellent. Initial pay is equal to the high sous chef's pay of the previous position. Works until the volume is heavy and the profits are good, or until the major faults are judged irreparable. Must repeat this step until success is achieved.

6. *Looking for Mr. Goodowner.* Now in a position to earn top pay, the chef searches for the perfect position. The restaurant must have the size and scale preferred. The owner will have personal or business reasons for spending little time at the restaurant and, as result, the pay will include a high base salary and a profit-sharing program.

Approximately two years after finishing their education period, assertives chef can be in their prime. This schedule assumes sober, hard work and an aptitude for fast learning, but it is entirely feasible. As a matter of fact, cooks may be given an opportunity to take over as head chef long before they are ready. It is common for individuals to get their first chefdom offer after less than six months in the kitchen. Such chances appear often. Their ability to control the production process will probably be lacking and the job will be short-lived, but not necessarily. Some individuals seem to be natural chefs. With awareness of acceptable pay rates, chefs can achieve their full financial potential.

Highlights

Remuneration comes in many forms, but the most generally accepted is the tangible one—anything which can be converted into cash.

A key factor in the head chef's salary is what the owner-manager perceives as the going rate for excellent, mediocre or poor performance by chefs in the same type of restaurant.

The difficulty of the job and the financial success of the chef are the two defining factors chefs should use to compare their net worth with that of other chefs.

Real estate prices and the unemployment rate do much to dictate regional salaries.

Chefs' awareness of their net worth and a diligent effort to keep their salary commensurate with the profit line are the tactics that have proven most profitable.

Whenever raises are being discussed, be prepared with a flexible assortment of compensation options.

Maintain the perfect raise posture year round by doing the best job possible and maintaining excellent rapport with the powers that be.

When chefs are first hired, they should make it clear to the owner-manager when they expect a salary review.

The two qualities of chefs, performance and time on the job, are the active reasons for which an owner will confer raises.

The important aspects of a chef's moneymaking career are training credentials, upscale restaurant experience, mastery of at least three cuisines, heavy sales volume control and reliability.

It is common for individuals to get their first chefdom offer after less than six months in the kitchen.

With awareness of acceptable pay rates, chefs can achieve their full financial potential.

Chapter 20

RESTAURANT RELATIONS

Introduction

The executive chef and head chef are part of the restaurant's management team. As such, they are responsible for the culinary tasks and profit lines; those are their primary duties. But without a solid relationship with bosses, peers, subordinates and customers, chefs will not be able to achieve their highest potential. Personal isolation will occur. The time when chefs were allowed to indulge in extravagant mood swings is past or quickly passing. Today's chefs are finding that outbursts are a luxury afforded only a few eccentrics—culinary stars whose reputations eventually fade away.

A Chef Without a Friend

Chefs who are completely isolated from the kitchen staff are in a crisis situation; their job is in jeopardy. Unfortunately, many chefs don't realize what is happening. They have set themselves up to be hit when they aren't looking. Even though the chef has the power to fire any one or all of the staff, if the chef's behavior has become harsh or emotional—in other words, if this person has not used good personnel management techniques —the boss may not allow firing to take place. A backlash occurs. The kitchen staff may complain about abusive treatment to the owner or managers. They will certainly complain to each other and the floor staff. It will be only a matter of time before everyone's opinion is that the chef is hot-tempered and irrational. As this reputation builds among the kitchen and floor staffs, it spreads to the chef's peers and bosses. They may not want to believe it, especially if the chef's culinary and profit-making duties are well handled, but a trickle may become a stream and then a river of protest.

A good example of how this can happen to even the most invincible of chefs is illustrated by the "Doctor Death" story. Alan was the successful chef of a Manhattan restaurant. He had been at the helm for over two years. The food was excellent; sales and profits were high. The owner was a real estate mogul who lived in another part of town and rarely ate at the restaurant. The chef, one manager and the bookkeeper reported to the owner by phone once a month. This triumvirate was completely in charge. The owner hoped to sell the restaurant and didn't want to change anything until then.

Alan had been a stern disciplinarian, but fair and unemotional about it, at least until the change occurred. He began to have noticeable mood swings caused by substance abuse. His verbal tirades led to abrupt firings. Other cooks quit because of the poor working climate. Before long, two-thirds of the staff had been replaced, and it was still changing. Alan remained civil to two or three of his top cooks. But on the others, a reign of terror fell. Cooks and dishwashers came and went regularly. At the end of six months, Alan's twenty-position kitchen staff had gone through over sixty people. The staff began to joke about it behind Alan's back.

One day, the bookkeeper became the object of Alan's verbal abuse. The chef had been snappy with the floor staff, but this was the first time he had attacked one of his peers. The bookkeeper was incensed. She plotted to have Alan fired. Using her good relations with the staff, she began a campaign to discredit Alan in any way she could. She and the sous chef coined the nickname "Doctor Death," referring to the termination rate, and then used it repeatedly until everyone had adopted it.

Alan kept his food quality at a decent level by working eighty-hour weeks. But the verbal tirades and turnover of personnel continued. Finally, the manager and bookkeeper made a joint complaint to the owner. Still, nothing was done. In a normal situation, Alan would have been fired long ago because most owners work at least part-time at their restaurants. The bookkeeper was blocked, but she continued to build her case. A breakthrough came when the owner sold the restaurant. The new owners were deluged with talk of Alan's problems. They had no reason to believe or disbelieve the stories. On the one hand, there was Alan's sales and profit record, which was fairly good. (The new owners felt that there was room for improvement, though.) Then the bookkeeper presented facts which negated Alan's profitability picture. The high turnover rate in the kitchen staff was causing extra unemployment taxes, over $15,000 worth in the past nine months of terror. The new owners watched Alan closely. Within one month, he was fired.

Alan's problem began as substance abuse, but it is just as easy for chefs to work themselves into a no-win situation through arrogance, ignorance or poor technique. Personnel management is a skill, in part, but it is also a reflection of a person's philosophy of life. Chefs with a negative or caustic view will have to work hard to smooth their relations with fellow workers.

Assessing a Chef's Image

Since image is defined as a concept held by others, a chef's image is mostly created by the major elements of his or her relationships with owners, peers, subordinates and customers.

The owner likes quality food delivered at a profit. Accomplishing those tasks gives any owner a wonderful impression of the chef. Assess the owner's opinion of your performance by looking at the sales record. Are sales up or down? Does the owner expect sales to go up? If you don't know the answer to these questions, your relationship is weak with both the owners and their representatives, the managers. Open lines of communication. Not only will discussion clarify your position in the owner's eyes, it will help to overcome any negative impression the owner has. Simply by expressing interest, a chef signals the desire to do better. Perhaps the owner and managers have decided that you don't care or are lazy. Discussion will air any negative points and put you in a position to overcome them. Profitability, food quality, personnel management, or any other of the chef's duties should be discussed openly before bad impressions can harden into permanent opinions.

Lines of communication should be kept open always, as a matter of policy. There are situations which can signal the urgent need to spruce up not only the image, but the job performance as well. For example, owners or co-workers may stop talking to you. It sounds odd, but often an owner will decide to fire an employee, tell one or two others of the planned dismissal, and then be curt or silent until a replacement is found. Silence from any quarter—owners, peers, subordinates or customers—signals a bad image. That is a reflection of poor job performance and a cause for alarm.

Owners can also signal dissatisfaction by trying to cut your salary, reverse bonuses and cancel days off. They may voice a series of complaints over a period of weeks and then either become strangely silent or erupt with an argument. As long as there is still some discussion, do your best to satisfy their wishes. If the owners refuse to discuss quality and profits, beware. They may have given up on you. Acknowledge the uncomfortable feelings you are experiencing. They may be the only indication you get that others find your work unsatisfactory.

Petty personality disputes, unfounded rumors and malicious gossip are not the same problem, however. They should be gauged differently. A chef's image is directly dependent upon job performance, not personality quirks. Image and popularity shouldn't be considered as equals. A chef may be extremely unpopular with the floor staff because of curtness, for example, but if the restaurant is busy, i.e., tips are good, the staff will forgive officious behavior.

Another way for chefs to measure their image is to watch the regular customers' reactions. They may want to speak to the chef, either to compliment or to complain. Some customers are like groupies at a rock concert; they like to be acknowledged by the inner circle of their favorite watering hole. Others expect special treatment and will go to the chef to get it. Then there are the complainers, customers who never seem satisfied but return every night for dinner. Assertive chefs will make themselves available to customers and listen carefully to their special requests and opinions.

Working Relationships

Each restaurant's working atmosphere is different, depending on several factors, including the chef's demeanor. However, the major contributor to the variety of styles, from autocratic to laid back, is the owner, especially his or her method of working with the staff. A strict, authoritarian boss will expect prompt responses and officious behavior; clowning around will not be tolerated. The owner's style has to be understood clearly before chefs can adjust their own style to complement it. Some adjustment is bound to be necessary, but not too much. If a chef works in an authoritarian atmosphere and is the laid-back type, almost certainly the job will not work out. Look for a working climate in which you can thrive or at least survive.

After making concessions to the method or madness of the existing staff, consider the elements of the chef's relationships with others. These are key aspects indicating whether a job is being successfully executed or not. There are certain qualities, which chefs can display in their style, that will clarify and strengthen the working relationships between the various levels of personnel.

Owners

Their main concern is job performance, so strengthen their opinion of you by doing everything possible to do a great job. That translates into responsiveness. Do what you are told to do with a positive attitude. Don't be afraid to offer your opinions, of course, but be sensitive to the situation by soliciting the owner's ideas and direction.

Solid, consistent effort is the best way to achieve positive results. It is also the best way to assure the boss that the kitchen is in reliable hands.

Maintain an excellent working relationship with the owners through fine job performance, responsiveness, respect and reliability.

Peers

The pressures of working in a fast-paced restaurant will try the patience of all professionals, whether they have a temperamental nature or not. Quality and service problems often develop because of personality clashes between the kitchen and floor staffs. The one sure way to keep minor skirmishes from becoming major wars is for chefs and their peers, usually the managers, to maintain a friendly working relationship. A cooperative attitude on both sides is necessary. The chef can display this attitude by soliciting comments from peers about food quality and staff performance, and then following up on any negative feedback. Not only is a potentially bad situation diffused by reversing a manager's bad impression, but the chef's primary responsibility to perform well is enhanced. While it isn't necessary to become chummy (remember, this is work, not a clubhouse), cover your peers' areas of responsibility to ensure the smooth running of the business. Never overstep your authority, however. Newly hired chefs can make tactical mistakes by pushing too far too fast. Gauge your peers' reaction to your authority; compare their judgment to the owner's voiced directions; and obtain confirmation about any overlapping or confusing responsibilities.

Staff

The kitchen workers aren't the chef's personal property; they should be treated the same way as the floor and bar staffs. The best way to maintain good relations with the staff is to be businesslike in your demeanor. The malingerers—and every staff has some—will complain that you are humorless, but in general, workers will respond in a businesslike fashion. State directions and procedures clearly in an organized, respectful and level-headed fashion. Inappropriate responses from a particular staff member will not become part of their job performance, provided you don't allow them to bait you into giving a harsh or caustic retort. If you do, it will become part of your work record. Personalities, and the occasional conflicts they cause, are common in any business. An assertive chef quickly learns to counter a worker's negative attitude by using management techniques rather than bullying tantrums. Subordinates like to imagine that their bosses have problems with power abuse. Fairness is always an issue, then, but never to the extent that it supersedes the quality and profit concerns of the business. In other words, don't allow the staff to cow you into adopting a lax attitude. In the long run, the business will suffer. When the owner starts to get nervous, the people you thought were your friends will turn on you with complaints of ineptness.

Customers

One of the ways a dining experience can be made special is if the chef gives special attention to the customers. While you are in the kitchen, be responsive to the particular cooking instructions, often completely off the menu's original plan, which the wait staff delivers from the customers. The restaurant business is part of the service industry. This means that the chef has a responsibility to serve in any way possible, including complying with bizarre requests.

Some customers require an appearance by the head chef. It's part of the show. After the major portion of the afternoon or evening service is completed, remove your apron, don your toque and venture into the main dining room for a chat with the customers. This hands-on public relations work can go far to develop a regular clientele. Don't push yourself on people by sitting down uninvited or pausing too long at one table. Express your concern over the quality and tastiness of their meal. Listen to special requests. Some master chefs will take a drink if it is offered, but this changes the customer–chef relationship dramatically by infusing the element of familiarity. Perhaps the customer offers to buy a drink out of politeness but feels awkward after it arrives. The chef may feel obligated to sit or stand until the drink is finished. It is far better for the chef to offer an after-dinner drink to regulars; that's good customer relations because it builds word-of-mouth popularity.

Image Makers and Breakers

It is amazing how fickle public opinion can be. Politicians who have a record of years of faithful service can be suddenly disgraced and deposed by one foolish incident. The same holds true for chefs; they are at the mercy of public opinion. One act of indiscretion may ruin years of good work. An assertive chef's goal should be to generate an image of sober reliability with a flair for the unexpected. As Ghandi said, "Moderation in all things, even moderation."

When to Party

To restaurant owners and workers, it sometimes appears that alcoholism is an occupational disease of chefs. Not only do new chefs have to cultivate their own image, they are working against some negative preconceived images. Drinking and drug abuse on the job are not habitual in every restaurant, but there are enclaves of users and abusers. Moral and legal issues aside, the amount of alcohol and drugs a chef consumes will be noticed by fellow workers. A judgment will constantly be made about impaired cooking abilities. Chefs who get high during or after work in their own restaurant lessen their respect and authority over the staff. This type of behavior is usually tolerated in mediocre restaurants or those where the owners are preoccupied with abuses of their own.

The annual Christmas party or spring picnic is another matter. These events provide excellent opportunities for chefs to be themselves, to add another, more personal facet to their reputation. This doesn't mean that an annual event is an invitation for a chef to drink excessively and become too familiar with the boss's wife. A faux pas of that magnitude may alienate the owner forever. Even the Christmas party is work on one level. Authority relationships aren't eroded or erased; they are only slightly reduced. Show the owners and fellow workers that you have the same good judgment in recreation that you display at work.

Personalities have a better chance of being appreciated after the noon or dinner rush is completed. A little time spent at the bar or staff table after a shift will give chefs a moment of relaxation with the same people with whom they have worked hard. That's a valuable time because the conflicts of the shift can be ironed out before they become hardened into patterns of dislike. An assertive chef should take the initiative to maintain good working relationships by showing concern for fellow workers.

When to Be Tough

Each kitchen staff has a different overall attitude, depending upon the work ethics of its chef, sous chef and line cooks. The boss's actions will dictate, for the most part, how the rest of the staff handles their duties — responsibly or sloppily. But in any work situation, there are certain workers who are skilled at doing just enough to get by. These individuals need a regular dose of tough talk to convince them that their job performance is definitely linked to their job longevity. They can be fired at any moment for a gross infraction of procedures and need to feel a sense of urgency once in a while.

A tough reprimand should be used in lieu of firing. It is an effective signal that keeps fairly good workers with problems more in tune to their responsibilities. Being tough all day, every day, generates an environment of dislike and distrust—certainly not a favorable one for all workers. If one individual puts the chef in a position of having to be tough regularly, the worker's usefulness must be questioned. Constant tensions are disruptive to a productive, positive crew.

Toughness is characterized by an unmoving, even severe, statement of the owner's or chef's guidelines. It almost always comes into play in the context of food quality and personnel management. The chef must often deliver restaurant policy, and the listener may not be too receptive. State the standard or rules clearly and unequivocally. Workers being corrected or told to do something which they consider unimportant will often try to gloss over the event; they may even pretend that they were never told. If you save your tough speeches for important issues, the staff will retrain more quickly. Use different levels of toughness to convey messages of varying importance to your workers.

When to Throw a Tantrum

This is the ultimate response to trouble. It takes different forms—screaming, slapping, plate flipping and knife throwing, to name a few. I once saw a chef strangling and pushing a cook's head toward the hot fryolator grease; it was a response to an ungarnished hamburger platter! Probably every chef has thrown his hands up in the air while releasing a long tirade of curses. Most of the time, tantrums are the self-indulgent expression of an immature or overworked chef. The only purpose they serve is to shock and alienate the cooks. One main reason that chefs continue to use them is that no one has the power to stop them. The more autocratic a chef is, with perhaps a percentage of the ownership, the more prone this person is to outbursts of temperament. In Europe, for instance, chefs are practically dictators over their staff. Anything they do is law, and, as a result, brutality and tantrums occur often.

There is one situation where a tirade can be an effective tool, but the occasion is limited. Chefs with a firmly entrenched nemesis may try to break the will of their opponent by insulting this person anytime a slip in quality occurs. These are chefs in new positions who lack the power to fire cooks whose attitudes they dislike. Often total power to hire and fire takes months or years to accumulate. In that case, a chef can pressure subordinates to leave by making their working environment miserable. Constant curt, abusive language directed at one person will usually do the trick. However, the chef must be careful that the scheme doesn't backfire. A tantrum is a poor management technique. If the owners are unhappy with other aspects of the chef's performance, they may use radical behavior as an excuse to fire this person, especially if the nemesis and other cooks are teaming up against the chef.

A cook who works for a tantrum-prone chef has already made a decision about how far to be pushed. I once worked on the line of an exclusive Paris restaurant, the whole time playing and replaying imaginary scenes where I alternately yelled at, slapped or walked out on the chef. I was plotting revenge on behalf of a sixteen-year-old apprentice whom I'd seen slapped and sent home crying. Oddly, my plates were perfect. I didn't allow any opportunity for the chef to abuse me. The point is that a chef who throws a tantrum has to be ready for anything. The cooks may become violent or verbally abusive, or simply walk out.

Humorous and Other Slanders

One sure way to make friends is to keep a constant flow of repartee going in the kitchen. The floor staff and line cooks love sardonic wit if it is served up at the proper time. Unfortunately, too much of a good thing can be construed as maliciousness. Individuals who are the butt of jokes will harbor resentment, and a quiet backlash of unpopularity will occur. No matter how hilarious it seems at the time, a joke at the expense of the owners, peers or subordinates is a bad idea. The obvious tendency will be for others to counter with jokes of their own. Some will be funny, but others will be backbiting, malicious attacks on the sardonic chef's character, work and personality. Humorous slander at the expense of others is in a sense a misuse of power.

Nasty comments by the chef about a cook's work, speed or quality have a bad effect when they are delivered face to face and produce disastrous consequences when voiced in the person's absence. No matter how innocent the comment may seem to the chef, it will be very serious to the criticized worker. Any staff member would be highly upset to discover that the chef had been talking about them behind their back. Slander is a petty action. The image it creates is one of an insecure or possibly flippant person.

When to Pick Up the Tab

As a gesture of good will, buying a round of drinks for customers at a table or signing their check is excellent. In most instances, however, it's an extravagant gesture. After all, the customers did come to the restaurant expecting to pay for their food and beverages. Any problems with service or food are usually straightened out by an owner or manager, so the chef's payment of customers' bills must have other motives.

A chef should definitely buy a drink for any business colleague, such as a purveyor's representative, or another chef. Ask the waitron to offer a drink on your behalf. Regular customers at the bar or tables are usually offered plenty of free items by their usual server; it doesn't seem necessary for the chef to offer them too. However, if there is an occasion when the chef sits down with regulars, it is a nice gesture to buy them a drink.

It is not a rule that chefs confer free drinks and food on customers. In fact, most chefs don't have the permission from the owners, so the issue is moot. Every owner restricts the circumstances in which a chef or any staff member may comp checks. As a chef, I feel awkward if I can't sign the check for myself, family and friends. On the other hand, I feel that dining parties should be kept to a maximum of once a week for close family and once a month for extended family and friends. Lunch tabs are easier to sign than dinner tabs; therefore, it must be the dollar amount which signifies a limit. Use your own discretion, which has been informed by your understanding of the owner's opinions. Ask about the ground rules up front or risk a reprimand after signing a big check.

It is common for a chef to offer a free lunch to sales representatives and delivery men in the course of the workday. They rarely have time for more than a quick sandwich or bowl of soup, anyway. But other instances when a chef should sign the check almost never occur. Remember, you are giving away the boss's money. There should be a valid business reason for it, something more important than your personal image.

Love and the Head Chef

Some companies impose rules to prevent their employees from dating or marrying. The rationale is that intercompany relationships disrupt production. Restaurants are much less rigid in their structure, however; intercompany affairs flourish there. Certainly the chef can expect to be romantically involved from time to time, and the relationship doesn't have to harm job performance. The end results will be as varied as the personalities of the chefs involved, from total depression to marriage. (My wife and I met as co-workers in a restaurant where she was a waitress and I was the chef.)

Most restaurant couples seem to do well by adopting official poses at work; they pretend to be uninvolved. If the individuals are mature, their job performance can weather most domestic difficulties short of separation or divorce. Often at the end of a relationship the lingering hatred is so great that one party or the other must move on. The worker in the position of higher responsibility will usually be the one to stay. The other person may even be fired. Be careful if you are the chef involved with the owner or a manager; your job security may depend upon the whim of a dissatisfied lover. That's not a very businesslike relationship, nor are there very predictable solutions to the problem.

A chef's public or restaurant image is rarely affected by an occasional relationship with a fellow employee. Obsessive romanticizing is another matter. Don't use the restaurant as a private game reserve. Your conquests may be numerous, but your job performance will be distorted by the staff's varied opinions of your lifestyle. Such personal observations complicate a chef's authority.

Highlights

Without a solid relationship with bosses, peers, subordinates and customers, chefs will not be able to reach their highest potential.

Since image is defined as a concept held by others, a chef's image is mostly created by the major elements of his or her relationships with owners, peers, subordinates and customers.

Profitability, food quality, personnel management, or any other of the chef's duties should be discussed openly before bad impressions can harden into permanent opinions.

Silence from any quarter—owners, peers, subordinates or customers—signals a bad image.

A chef's image is directly dependent upon job performance, not personality quirks.

Assertive chefs will make themselves available to customers and listen carefully to their special requests and opinions.

Maintain an excellent working relationship with the owners through fine job performance, responsiveness, respect and reliability.

Gauge your peers' reaction to your authority; compare their judgment to the owner's voiced directions; and obtain confirmation about any overlapping or confusing responsibilities.

The best way to maintain good relations with the staff is to be businesslike in your demeanor.

The restaurant business is part of the service industry. This means that the chef has a responsibility to serve in any way possible, including complying with customers' bizarre requests.

An assertive chef's goal should be to generate an image of sober reliability with a flair for the unexpected.

An assertive chef should take the initiative to maintain good working relationships by showing concern for fellow workers.

A tough reprimand should be used in lieu of firing.

If you save your tough speeches for important issues, the staff will retrain more quickly.

A tantrum is a poor management technique.

Nasty comments by the chef about a cook's work, speed or quality have a bad effect when they are delivered face to face and produce disastrous consequences when voiced in the person's absence.

As a gesture of good will, buying a round of drinks for customers at a table or signing their check is excellent.

A chef should definitely buy a drink for any business colleague, such as a purveyor's representative, or another chef.

Be careful if you are the chef romantically involved with the owner or a manager; your job security may depend upon the whim of a dissatisfied lover.

Chapter 21

HOW A CHEF ADVANCES

Introduction

Why is it that some cooks seem to have a knack for getting themselves promoted to head chef, while others are constantly relegated to sous chef positions? Excellent food mechanics with fine training records and job references are often stuck in the ranks for years, cursing Culinary Institute of America graduates who quickly rise to the top. Certainly personality and connections account for some of the early successes of young chefs. But there are definite steps which a cook or head chef can take to help make success more of a science than a mystery.

Personal Goals

Start by defining the qualities your life would have if it were ideal. To paraphrase a line of an old Rodgers and Hammerstein song, "You've got to have a dream. If you don't have a dream, How you gonna have a dream come true?" Personal goals are stronger than career goals for many people, but not all. If your career is all-important, your personal life may revolve around it, at least for now. Very few individuals remain infatuated with the working life, however. Most begin to expand their needs to include their personal life as time makes the restaurant business less glamorous for them.

While the list may vary, the following are important personal matters which all workers should sort out for themselves:

1. Town or location of home.
2. Living quarters.
3. Ability to live on the economy.
4. Total work time versus leisure time.
5. Lifestyle desired (economic level).
6. Opportunities to pursue outside interests.
7. Social-romantic opportunities.
8. Family considerations.

No matter how attractive a job offer appears, if the new position will conflict with several personal goals, your quality of life will go down. Most positions involve a trade-off. Head chefs normally do not get exactly what they want. Presumably, career compensations balance the scale. But a job which conflicts with a chef's general lifestyle cannot last. No matter how attractive the money seems, it won't be enough to completely submerge your personality for long. When considering positions which call for great personal sacrifice, factor the short-term employment opportunity into your decision. What will your job opportunities be one or two years from now, when you've got to get out?

Career Goals

The big goal is money in some form. As stated earlier, not many chefs work solely for glory. And that's good because there isn't much of a market for dilettantes—at least not on the head chef level. There are other career considerations which can be important enough to override salary and fame as the prime motives for employment, however. From time to time as a career progresses, chefs need to change their cuisine focus completely in order to round out their experience and become more valuable professionals. That's when educational and training possibilities assume greater significance.

In the long term, career goals like those mentioned above are often countered by the daily routine of a job. Those short-term goals also enter into a head chef's decision-making process. Consider the following career goals. They contain a variety of essential issues.

1. Salary—gross and net.
2. Benefits.
3. Bonuses.
4. Potential ownership.
5. Work Hours—daily and weekly.
6. Style of cuisine.
7. Type of service.
8. Kitchen environment and equipment.
9. Education—training possibilities.
10. Potential for advancement.
11. Fame—recognition factor.
12. The success record of the owners.

A career without goals or plans proceeds in spurts, first in one direction and then in another, but almost always reaches a dead end. Perhaps at the beginning of a chef's career, in the first or second head chef position, long-range goals don't seem too important. All that seems to matter is getting the first chefdom. If you are that assertive about your career, channel your energy into a more productive result by pursuing exactly what you want. Don't wait for circumstances or luck to make you a head chef. Create your own luck by being actively involved in the search for the right job. Then when the perfect position opens up, you'll be in the right place at the right time to grab it.

One problem perpetual sous chefs have is their scattered, almost wasted, experience. They have an endless string of jobs in good or excellent restaurants, but always at the same level. They never move up, either because the head chef is firmly implanted and they lack the incentive to take over, or because they are constantly looking elsewhere instead of correctly apprising a situation where a chef will be needed soon. Lack of political sophistication may be the reason overqualified sous chefs are working for less qualified cooks. Don't ignore the importance of a well-thought-out plan of action. Clear goals provide the direction and thrust you need to pursue the position which will best utilize and reward your talents.

Job Experience Levels

Nothing can be more devastating than to leave a good position for a new job at a higher salary and increased responsibility, only to be fired because your skills aren't up to the level expected by the new boss. Suddenly, you are out on the street with no job; for a chef, that is practically the ⸀ me as starting over. It is always easier to impress a prospective boss with your qualifications if you're an employed head chef. The job is a credential.

Don't be greedy by taking more than you are due in terms of either money or responsibility. If you aren't up to the challenge or worth the money, this will become evident all too quickly. Judge a prospective job carefully. Ascertain its complexities, demands and style. The following classification of food retailers presents the skills and qualifications necessary for a successful chef in each type of operation.

Fast Food Restaurant

Since the food is simple and done by formula, this type of restaurant requires very little culinary skill. There probably won't even be a head chef. The top kitchen employee will be the kitchen manager, who works in a team with the cooks and manages too. The experience necessary is a previous fast food kitchen job with one to six months' experience, depending upon your aptitude.

Coffee Shop

Most coffee shop owners are involved in the management of all aspects of the business, including menu planning and food purchasing. They will not want a cook with those skills and salary demands. The chef of a coffee shop is the top cook because this person is the fastest food mechanic employed. No management skills are required, simply strict adherence to recipe and presentation standards.

Pub

Under the control of some owner-chef combinations, a pub-restaurant can become a dining phenomenon by attracting much more than its normal share of the public attention. In those cases, the head chef will have the responsibilities of scheduling, quality control, menu planning, purchasing and production. All the elements of a full-blown restaurant are in place, but are operating at a lower level of sophistication, if not volume. Pub food is characterized by simple preparation, style and presentation. Most pubs have fewer than seventy seats, with an average of around fifty. Fast cooking skills are a prime prerequisite, along with an ability to produce tasty, home-style food.

Bistro

A small restaurant with an unusual or foreign menu, the bistro attracts a sophisticated crowd for light dining and snacks. The head chef position may or may not be a substantial one; it depends upon the owner's involvement. As with the coffee shop, a bistro's kitchen staff is generally a crew of cooks, one of whom emerges as the fastest, most responsible worker. That cook will assume the role of quasi-chef but may have very little responsibility outside of preparation and service of the menu. A good work ethic and six months' experience with kitchen tools will give a cook sufficient background to be the best in any bistro.

Full-Menu, Table Service, Medium-Scale Restaurants

Low Volume. There are never more than one hundred covers per one day or evening shift. The culinary demands of a medium-scale restaurant include sauces, soups, roasting, menu planning and proficiency in all phases of preparation and presentation. Often the head chef of a low-volume restaurant is given two responsibilities at the beginning of the job. The first is the basic chef's duties—running the kitchen crew, purchasing, etc. The second is to build sales volume quickly. For some reason unknown to the owner and all the previous chefs, the restaurant's food sales never increased. After hiring several seasoned professionals, the owner may be ready to give a young person his or her first chefdom. This can be an excellent opportunity for someone with a solid cooking background and a flair for marketing (see Chapter 2). On the other hand, the fact that the restaurant is not busy doesn't mean that the job is going to be easy. The reasons the volume is low may be insurmountable.

Medium Volume. There are never more than two hundred covers per one day or evening shift. While it may seem that a more successful restaurant can afford to hire qualified cooks, thereby lessening the chef's main problem, food quality, the high volume means a larger staff, and that spells trouble. The head chef must be highly qualified in line preparation; speed with quality is an important job qualification. The chef must also be prepared to handle management problems such as scheduling crises, equipment breakdowns, purchasing and food storage. Except in unusual circumstances, one year of kitchen experience as a day chef, night chef or sous chef will be sufficient. At times, the noncooking responsibilities will be so heavy that the chef will need to cook and handle food preparation almost by remote control.

High Volume. There are three hundred or more covers three or four times per week. The head chefs of these restaurants may do little or no actual cooking. This depends on their desire and background. Menu planning is their prime responsibility; it's a form of sales promotion and customer attraction. A primary job element is maintaining profit margins. The head chef of a large operation must work within a definite food pc; that involves experience with vendors and food handling.

The culinary skills of a head chef for a medium-scale restaurant should be varied rather than concentrated in one style of upscale or downscale cuisine. The chef should be an efficient generalist, a populist who understands what the public is buying and why. A chef with that experience or a knack for creating popularity will have the main skill for the job.

Full-Menu, Table Service, Upscale Restaurants

Low Volume. The head chef of an upscale restaurant needs years of upscale experience. There can be no last-minute cramming through cookbooks; attention to detail and perfect preparation are skills learned through experience. While it is possible for a cook to master the menu of one upscale restaurant in as little as three months, the head chef must also supply culinary direction for daily specials, holidays and menu changes.

Upscale menus demand such a well-trained chef that the owner is often willing to assume the roles of purchaser and kitchen manager. But many head chefs insist on purchasing and managing their own kitchen. Low-volume restaurants are staffed with a few hard-working professionals. The head chef can expect one of the job prerequisites to be a willingness to work long hours.

Medium Volume. The same attention to culinary perfection is necessary, but with the added complication of a faster-paced environment. Complete mastery of the cuisine style is essential before attempting to assume this head chef position.

High Volume. Very few large restaurants serve truly upscale cuisine. The decor and prices can certainly reach impressive heights, but the food itself loses clarity in the transition to a large operation. The head chef of this type of kitchen needs prestige and culinary authority. This person must be able to attract a following of sous chefs who could be head chefs practically anywhere else. As in any food factory, the problems are quality and speed. The head chef must be able to supply constant supervision on the kitchen line.

Money and profit margins are the second group of traditional responsibilities of the chef. But in a busy upscale restaurant, the chef will need a subordinate to handle the purchasing, scheduling, labor disputes and food handling. The head chef will be absorbed in public relations, a new duty which comes with a prominent club.

Hotel

The head chef of a large hotel has banquets and restaurants of all sizes to serve. The qualifications include the culinary and management skills necessary for upscale to coffee shop-type of restaurants. In addition, hotel chefs must have banquet experience—the simultaneous service of hundreds of identical plates. The chef's job at a hotel varies in specific duties, but usually it is a cooking position, with purchasing, labor management and cost control delegated to stewards and submanagers. Good experience with presentation art such as ice or sugar sculptures, food carving and even linen folding is necessary.

The Job Search

Two factors complicate a head chef's search for a new or better job. One is the style of cuisine and operation that the chef is qualified to produce. The other is the basic salary that the chef demands. At any given time, there may be several restaurants looking for head chefs, but if the money isn't good enough or the cuisine is not part of the individual's experience, an extensive job search will be necessary. The first component a candidate needs is a resume.

Resume

A head chef must demonstrate two types of experience—culinary and executive. The resume is the best document to present the business parts of a chef's background. But there is other important information which interviewers expect to see on a resume, so keep all portions brief. The following is a list of the information which a chef's resume should contain:

1. Name, address, phone number.
2. Job desired or career goals.
3. Work history: a chronology of positions and duties.
4. Special skills.
5. Educational background.

A resume should be only one page long. Other important information, such as references, can be presented during the interview. Here the purpose is to give a clear, brief description of your experience and background. The main qualities of a resume should be honesty and clarity (see Fig. 21-1).

The resume has drawing power. If there are no negative factors, it may win the prospective chef an interview. But don't expect it to clinch the job. For an interview or resume by mail offering, the chef should have backup documentation of experience. Menus are excellent resume aids, particularly if they were designed by the job candidate. A list of the chef's best specials is also effective. Perhaps photographs or newspaper clippings are available. They make excellent visual material to substantiate the chef's experience. Consider the after-resume documentation as a sales presentation. Order the visual aids to support the resume's data in chronological order, and be prepared to sell yourself verbally while the interviewer is reading. But first, the right job opening has to be found. It may come suddenly, by coincidence, or after an extensive search of the job market.

Want Ads

The first step in any job search is to check the want ads. The number of ads appealing to head chefs will indicate whether the job market is tight or plentiful. Part of the job-hunting process is to be in the right place at the right time. For that reason, *always* check the want ads; don't pass up one day. Be sure to include all the newspapers and other periodicals in the

TOM MINER

502 East 81st Street #5F   212-555-1234
New York, New York 10021

Career Goals:

   To assume a position as an Executive Chef with responsibility for the culinary
quality and profit margins of a group of restaurants. No restrictions on style of
presentation or cuisine. Salary commensurate with an excellent starting rate plus
room for growth.

Work History:

Mumbles Restaurant, 1491 Avenue Z, New York, NY 10022
Executive Chef   June 1984 to Present

   Trained and monitored the head chefs of a high-volume restaurant group serving
Eclectic-American cuisine. Duties included menu and specials planning, purchasing,
inventory handling, quality control, personnel hiring and firing, line work in all
stations, and kitchen design for new locations.
   Responsible for a dramatic rise in total sales and a stunning increase in overall
profits.

L'Alouette Restaurant, 241 Oak Street, Fort Collins, CO 80524
Head Chef   October 1983–June 1984
   French Classic and Nouvelle cuisines. Created a new night menu; did all specials;
worked the line at night. Preparation including sauces, soups, roasting, and garde
manger. Purchasing and inventory control.

Le Gallant Verre, 11 Rue de Verneuil, Paris, France
Sous Chef   April 1982-October 1983
   Worked under Chef-Owner Pascal Daguet in one of the finest French Nouvelle
restaurants in Paris. Duties included saucier and garde manger during service.
Preparation of all coulis, fonds, sauces, meats, fowl, and fish during the daily
preparation period.

Special Skills:

   Author of "The Business Chef," a handbook for chefs.
   Fluent in French.
   Professional bookkeeper-accountant background.
   Fluent in several computer languages.
   Handyman skills.

Education:

   Columbia University   Writing   1985-Present
   Golden Gate State College   Accounting   1969-1970
   Iowa State University   Accounting   1967-1969

References: Available upon request.

Figure 21-1. Resume.

306

area which appeals to you. Respond to any ads describing a head chef's position. Especially at the beginning of a job search, don't disqualify a job on the basis of the ad. There may be other aspects of the job which the owner couldn't describe in the limited space but which would make the job more appealing than it seems. The want ads are a public bulletin board used by most employers. They are an excellent source for all but the most exclusive jobs.

Employment Services

Head chefs, executive chefs and other top restaurant managers are often sought through employment agencies. Owners are attracted to this method by its private qualities. Alternatively, like job candidates, owners may realize that they will have to search everywhere before finding the correct match.

An interview with an employment service representative is just as crucial as the meeting with a prospective boss. The agent has the power to promote you if he or she sees potential for a sale. Help the agent to see your salable qualities. Spend some time before the meeting to plan a list of the points you would like to make about yourself. Be certain to convey all the pertinent information during your interview with the agent, but don't push.

One of the qualities you will need to convey is amiability. The employment agent may not be concerned about whether you are an enjoyable person to work with or an ogre, but will be favorably impressed if you handle the interview like a winner—someone who can expect to do well with an owner.

An agent's main purpose is to fill job openings. Help this person to see you in as many slots as possible by clarifying your experience in various areas. If your purpose is to specialize in a particular style of cuisine, don't be too concerned with spreading the focus of your background. Instead, show a long record of employment in quality restaurants. It is always a good idea to come prepared with the names of restaurants which would suit your purposes and experience perfectly. This gives the agent an added understanding of your goals and may inspire a few ideas for your placement.

Networking

After the groundwork has been laid, candidates can extend their sources by talking confidentially to friends, fellow chefs, purveyors, area business owners and possibly food writers. Often the best jobs are found through a friend of a friend. If you are only reading want ads and waiting for an agent's call, the best opportunities are passing you by.

In order to make yourself completely available, approach networking as the public relations aspect of your job search. Plan to spend an evening or two making the rounds to restaurants where fellow chefs are working. Make telephone calls to any sources not reachable in person, and speak to the contacts you have at work. The best way to ensure an effective network is to contact everyone in one week, like a campaign. Later, you should remind these people occasionally, without being intrusive. Finding the right position is grueling work. It demands much more perseverance and labor than the job itself.

The First Interview

As a job candidate in an interview situation, your plan is always simple — keep talking about your qualifications until the interviewer begins to describe the job; then listen. At that point, the person has made a decision about you. If you have passed the first interview successfully, you may say something to destroy a good impression. If you've lost the bid, the best thing to do is move on.

The resume, menus and visual aids are important to an interview's success, but other factors will also be considered by the interviewer. For instance, overdressed or underdressed candidates tend to seem wrong. There may be nothing specific that the interviewer dislikes, but he or she will look further. Dress as if you were a customer at the restaurant. You will immediately blend in and make everyone feel at ease.

A candidate's demeanor is, of course, a prime consideration during the interview. Be yourself unless you are normally an argumentative dilettante; then be as quiet as possible. The interviewer wants to know whether a working relationship can be forged. It is helpful to consider the interview as the beginning of your owner-chef or boss-chef association. Exhibit all the attributes of a good employee—promptness, loyalty, intelligence, good humor and flexibility. If the position would benefit from a chef with a flair for the dramatic or perhaps an eclectic personality, show that side of your character.

The worst thing you can do at an interview is to talk too long about your personal life or last job. Boring behavior will drop you out of the running immediately. Many newspaper clippings, pages of recipes, stacks of photographs—too much of a good thing is harmful. Remember that the main purpose is to get the job. That is best accomplished by showing that you are uniquely qualified for the position. As soon as possible, you should try to become the interviewer's collaborator by helping to solve the problems caused by the available position.

Follow-Up Interviews

With the first hurdle behind you, the interviewer has shown appreciation for your style and qualifications. In the second interview, usually with a more important person, try to change as little as possible. Wear the same type of clothing, if not the identical clothes, and follow the presentation style used during the first interview. consider all the important methods for an initial interview as valid for any subsequent interview.

The Cooking Interview

Some owners may ask you to go into the kitchen and whip up a specialty or two. How do you proceed?

First, ask for a copy of the menu; this will give you a quick idea of what raw goods are available. The best dish is one which is chosen in conjunction with the owner or interviewer. Ask what the person has in mind. If the owner seems reluctant to make a selection, he or she may feel that this decision is your job and part of the test. In this case, simply ask the owner to confirm your selection of raw goods. Suggest the most popular types of foods first—chicken, shrimp, pasta. One of them will certainly be on hand. It would be a demonstration of your confidence to say, "Do you mind if I prepare a chicken dish?"

Would the owner prefer a dish from the menu or an original one? If you are expected to duplicate a dish on the menu, it should be one with which the owner is dissatisfied. The only reason this person would want you to prepare one of the more successful recipes is to test your mechanical skills. In that case, expect someone to brief you on the basic recipe and presentation. Without this information, duplication is impossible. For some reason, you may have been pushed into a no-win situation. How can you better a perfect recipe? More than likely, this type of cooking test is a trap set by one of the decision maker's counselors. Ask the owner which menu dish he or she would like to change or improve; then prepare that dish to perfection.

The Salary/Acceptance Debate

The discussion of salary begins at the first interview and is generally the last agreement made. The chef candidate wants as high a salary as possible but is unsure about the owner's payment history. If the previous chef was earning $50,000, for instance, the new chef can expect to start at $40,000 at least. The owner has the opposite perspective, wanting to hire a new chef at the lowest possible salary. Both parties should be aware of and avoid two classic pitfalls.

First, chefs whose starting salary is too high to be justified will find themselves in a very precarious position. Everything they do will be subject to close scrutiny. The owner who is paying a premium has every right to expect perfection. One slipup or even normal competence will cause the owner to rethink the situation. A chef who demands too high a salary is usually fired on a whim. To avoid this situation, do a little homework to know what chefs in the immediate area are earning, especially at the same scale and style of restaurants.

The second classic mistake is made by the owner. As a chef, watch for a negotiator-opponent who tends to pay too little. A job which does not offer the market rate probably never will. After years of inching up at a slow rate of $2000 per year, the pay may finally become reasonable. Special circumstances would make an individual chef take such a position. For most salaried workers, the pay must be commensurate with the duties, or they move on. Many owners find themselves constantly retraining chefs whom they don't trust and won't pay a decent wage. That is their mistake. Have the good sense to turn down offers for underpaid positions, or you'll be looking for work again in six months.

In addition to salary, power lines are drawn at the all-important hiring meeting. The owner will be in a hurry to put you to work once the salary issue has been resolved, but there are essential elements of the job which need to be clarified before the meeting is concluded. For instance, the chef normally hires and fires all kitchen personnel. Discuss your capabilities in this area. It isn't necessary to achieve iron control from day one. But if the owner has too little confidence in your abilities, the good changes and direction you do institute will be subverted by an insubordinate staff. It is easy to find a workable solution to this potential problem by discussing it in advance, before finally accepting the position.

After clarifying the subordinates' roles, define who the chef's superiors and peers are. Nothing is more aggravating than to start a new job where every day brings another boss into the kitchen. Initially, there will be a need for menu and recipe criticism. But in order to operate effectively, a chef will need to know whose requests are law and whose are opinion. Perhaps a job with seven or eight semiactive (they come in for dinner) owners is unattractive to you. In some cases, an amateur relative of the owner may be assuming quasi-control of the kitchen production. These are extreme examples, but real circumstances nonetheless. Clarify who will be your boss or bosses before taking the job.

The hiring/acceptance meeting is a positive affair. Take the opportunity to express all the enthusiasm you feel for the new position. Expressing confidence and determination in your acceptance speech will clarify your intentions to the owner. Reticence at this time would make the owner uneasy. Be yourself, but show some drive and enthusiasm.

Four Career Strategies

Not every chef has a definite career plan or a desired final goal. Many chefs get into the business by chance and chug along through a series of jobs until the glorious or sad end. Assertive chefs do well to set goals and plan moves. Their careers will advance more rapidly to a successful stage. Consider the following four approaches; then choose the applicable system for yourself, or mix and match them.

The Company Plan

For ninety-five percent of their chef positions, companies need dependable game players. Quite often a mini-bureaucracy has built up under the power of an effective management team. These managers look for chefs whom they can trust to do things the company way. Following this method, the head chef will often be someone who has risen through the ranks, proving his productivity and gamesmanship along the way.

It has been said of management committees that they never have any brilliant ideas, but they veto many stupid ones. If you are the kind of chef who thrives on brilliant ideas, the lower echelons of a large company will be smothering. There may be room for you at the top, however. It all depends upon the political climate of the inner circle. A company with a history of poor performance may be preparing for a purge and shakeup. A lot of money can be made under those circumstances; just be certain that your political antennae are up at all times. Remember, the key here is to win friends and influence people. It also helps if you are an excellent cook and money manager.

The Hopscotch Method

Even a graduate of a culinary school has a lot to learn before a flair for mastery is defined. The quickest way for a learning chef to become more skilled is to work for a number of excellent chefs in all types of restaurants. In my experience, it takes between one week and three months to gain a complete understanding of a chef and a menu's style.

The hopscotch method is the fastest way to climb the salary and culinary ladders. Even though a chronic drifter may have trouble getting work, the first three years of any professional cook's career is filled with stops and starts. Owners and head chefs realize this. Don't be afraid to go after the best culinary opportunity available. Simply protect yourself by giving the appropriate amount of notice.

Sometimes the only way to gain vital experience is to take a job which entails much more responsibility than you are capable of handling. Your first chef's job may be of this type. Mine certainly was. Don't be afraid to step into the driver's seat; that's where the excitement is. The duties which only the chef may do will be kept away from you until you take the plunge. Important aspects of a chef's job such as ordering, scheduling, waste control, hiring and firing, profit control and specials concepts will be difficult the first time. Poor performance may even cause your dismissal. But the learning process is what prepares a chef for eventual success.

One advantage of the hopscotch method is that it puts a chef into the restaurant world of owners and head chefs. The more people a chef knows, the more likely he or she is to hear of the perfect opening. The method has a definite fault, however, if it is used to excess. Head chefs who drift from one chefdom to another will spoil their reputation as dependable workers. The main purpose of the hopscotch method is to further and quicken advancement, but in the upper strata of chefs' jobs, this process must be slow. Two or three years in a position is the advisable minimum.

The Temporary Chef

Individuals with ulterior motives consider themselves temporary chefs and, as a result, have remarkably different attitudes toward work and money.

One kind of temporary chef is the workaholic. These individuals slave for seventy to eighty hours per week with one goal in mind—to save money. If the money is to be used to start their own restaurant, their attitude is one of acute interest in and attention to all details of the retail food and creative cuisine business. The opportunities for chefs with loftier goals are tremendous. As serious, hard workers, they will be able to move quickly into positions of responsibility, where experience and salaries are better.

One seeming advantage of temporary chefs is their attitude of detachment, their ability to move on if the position gets too stressful. It is nice to know that you can always leave. Unfortunately, that detachment can be a detriment. The best experience is usually gained in the hottest, busiest and most stressful restaurants. They're generally the ones making the big money. If your policy is to glide along on the surface, picking up techniques and systems, you may never learn what you've set out to discover. Temporary chefs can learn quickly if they set short-term goals which will eventually lead to the fulfillment of their ultimate goal.

The Loyal Apprentice

With or without a culinary education, the young worker who is fortunate enough to land a job with a superior chef will have the opportunity to rise to the very top of the profession simply by staying put. It may mean years as a dishwasher and garde manger person, but loyalty does have many rewards, especially in a business where many cooks are constantly on the move. One of the most impressive facts of a resume can be that the candidate has a long employment record at one restaurant.

The ideal scenario in this plan is to get a job under an excellent chef, stay with it for a few years, perhaps graduating to the sous chef position, and then achieve a head chef's position with the recommendation of the former chef.

Quitting

The two factors which should govern the way an executive or head chef quits are reputation and money. The chefs who leave without giving any notice or use the occasion of a big argument to hurt the owner are fools. They ruin any possibility of gaining a decent reference. In addition, they will be unemployed until a suitable position can be found.

Never quit a job until a replacement position has been found. It is better to remain on the job, even with a poor attitude, than to cut and run. For example, if your performance became so bad while you were searching for another job that you were fired, the owner may give you severance pay to mollify the situation.

A chef must give at least two weeks' notice; no emergency is dire enough to warrant less. Employers who insist that you begin immediately, leaving the former boss in trouble, are too demanding. And they will probably be too demanding in other areas as well. Be wary of such bosses.

Often the only way to get all the bonuses and vacation pay due to a well-entrenched head chef is to work with the owner in the best of atmospheres. Offering to help train a replacement or making yourself available for telephone consultation are the kinds of gestures which the owner will appreciate. They will allow you to part amicably.

Regional Prominence

Before attempting to gain prominence, a head chef must have an angle which can be marketed to local newspapers, clubs, television stations, magazines, schools and charity organizations. In order to fit into scheduled articles, shows and events, a chef must have at least one credential to publicize—e.g., being the head chef at one of the area's top restaurants, or having worked in a foreign country, or specializing in an exotic cuisine, or apprenticeship experiences with a nationally prominent chef or restaurant. Anything which sets a chef apart from the crowd will work. Even with one very average credential, such as being the chef of a local restaurant, not necessarily one of the upscale or busy ones, a chef can become a local celebrity by offering services free to clubs and charity organizations. After the first interview, article or event, the chef has gained that additional credential and can move on to more interesting and lucrative engagements.

The audience for locally sponsored events or published articles may be large or small, depending upon the size of the area normally solicited. Numbers aren't important if the item is deemed a success. What is important is exposure to the restaurant crowd—the owners, chefs and customers. Prominence among this group will eventually translate into a higher salary or part ownership.

The other benefit of promotional engagements is that they generate enthusiasm for the chef's cooking. Individuals from the audience will talk about the chef favorably. Some customers are bound to visit the chef's restaurant as a direct result of the increased fame. The chef's standing in the community and with the boss will rise.

National Prominence

For most chefs, public relations on the national level are not only impossible, they are a waste of time. Local customers will be nonplussed by the chef's newly published cookbook, except as critics of the end product—the food. However, large cities whose population supports a number of cosmopolitan, upscale restaurants will have a crowd of customers who appreciate the fame that a chef generates. And there are isolated cases of restaurants in obscure locations which have still managed to enter the national arena because of their uniqueness.

Chefs who wish to work in the upper strata, where the salaries and perks are highest, must prove their exceptional ability by gaining national attention. That means gaining publicity. After cooking and managing their way into a top operation, they must spread the good news through meetings and conventions, lectures and teaching, video, television, print publications of recipes, public appearances, reviews of restaurants and books, and, of course, a book of their own. All this media work is extremely time-consuming and absolutely nothing like a normal chef's life. Some individuals will relish it; others will scurry back to the kitchen without another thought of venturing forth again. Remember, the competition for the public spotlight is fierce, so rejections will be frequent and brutally blunt. Only by offering a unique talent can a chef expect to rise to the national level.

Discovering a unique angle is a sure way to gain the limelight. Investigate the market thoroughly to understand what is being promoted successfully. It stands to reason that if you are the type of chef who will prosper in the media, you will spend time learning about the competition, just as you absorbed the cooking styles of master chefs. With solid chef's credentials behind you and a hot idea at hand, begin to approach agents and publishers about your concept. Listen carefully to the advice they offer, and incorporate it into your plan. If there is a disagreement, meet them halfway. Remember that you're temporarily visiting their arena. Expect them to take charge, especially if it's your first foray.

Consulting

Many a chef dreams of stepping out of a hot kitchen and dirty uniform into the cool realm of upper management. Consulting work seems like a snap to accomplished chefs. All you have to do is *talk* about work, right? Unfortunately, that's the same opinion most restaurant owners have: that consultants don't do anything except repeat a lot of obvious sales and menu concepts.

In order to be a successful consultant, a chef needs credibility and a track record of success, or at least a personal reference. Even with these top resume qualities, consultants find themselves having to do a sales pitch for the wary owner. Consultancy is almost always a sales job.

The work does have creative aspects, such as kitchen and menu design. But there are plenty of boring elements too; marketing, menu analysis and profit control can involve nothing but paperwork and number computations. Following is a complete list of a chef-consultant's range of duties. If you were to check off the services which appear creative and interesting to you, would they total more than five or less?

The Business Chef: Rate Chart

Startups and Openings
Menu Creation in Virtually any Style: French Nouvelle or Classic, California Nouvelle, Italian Northern or Southern, Cajun, American Continental, Steakhouse, Seafood, Pasta, Pizza, Southwestern, Caribbean, Mexican, American Chinese, or Fast Food.

Primary Menu (Includes Marketing Research)	$1000
Each Supplemental Menu	250
Image Definition	300
Marketing Research	300
Financing (Loan Presentations)	750
Budget Estimates	250
Head Chef Recruitment	1000
Kitchen Staff Recruitment	750
Scheduling: Kitchen, Floor Staff, Bar Staff and Management	200
Location Search—Three Possible Locations Delivered For	2000
Kitchen Design	500
Kitchen Remodeling	300
Purchase Kitchen Equipment	1000
Purchase Kitchen Supplies	400
Purveyor and Service Contract Setups	300
"The First Week"	2500

A special opening package which includes purchasing, staffing, menu planning, food production supervision; open consultation on front-of-the-house concerns such as decor, equipment placement, table placement, traffic patterns, table settings, linen, music, logos, uniforms, computer operation, manual check-dupe systems and beverage control.

Troubleshooting to Raise Sales
Menu Redesign
   A reworking of old menus to increase sales and profits. Includes market research, prices, recipes and specials formats.

Primary Menu	$750
Each Supplemental Menu	250
Basic Analysis of Sales	1500

   Includes a written report detailing present sales, problems and solutions.

Implementation of the Recommended Sales Drive		1500
Quality Control	First Week	1000
	Each Additional Week	250

Advertising

Includes media selection and ad development	750/ad
Computerized Mailouts	$200/100 forms

Troubleshooting to Lower Food Costs

Analysis of Food Purchasing and Handling Procedures	$1500

   Includes a written report detailing problems and solutions.

Implementation of Solutions	1500

   New purveyors, menu repricing, staff reeducation, improved records and inventory systems.

Follow-Up Visits	250

Troubleshooting to Lower Labor Costs
Complete Analysis of Staff Skills and Productivity $1500
Includes a complete report detailing the problems and solutions.

Implementation of Solutions   1500
Staff Hiring and Firing   Head Chef   1000
                                                 Entire Staff   1750
Follow-Up Visits   250

The "Why Aren't We Making Any Money?" Analysis $1500
A complete investigation of the restaurant's operation, including a written report which
details all profit and loss centers.

The Weekly Checkup: You Name The Problem. $250

Financial Services
Record System Setup $500
Record Keeping   200/week
Payroll   75/week
Banking   100/week
Sales Analysis   200
Expenses Analysis   200
Accounts Receivable   75/week
Accounts Payable   75/week
Inventory   150/week
Computerized Services or Reports   Setup   1500
Complete Package of Weekly Financial Services   700/week

Food Writer—Author
Articles (Up to Ten Pages) $1500
Cookbooks or Manuals (Depending on Length)   5000–20,000
Seminars   Travel and Hotel Expenses Plus   500/day
Lectures   Travel and Hotel Expenses Plus   200

Working Chef
Executive Chef   2000/week
Head Chef   1500/week
Line Chef   250/shift

Special Services
   A conduit to managers, accountants, lawyers, tax services, food writers, chefs' agents,
advertising concerns, and restaurant suppliers of paper goods, equipment, supplies,
liquor/beverages, extermination, garbage removal, air conditioning, electricians, carpenters,
plumbers, kitchen equipment repair, carpet cleaning, window cleaning, painters, porters,
and smokeeaters.

Consultants are paid well, but the trade-off is that they don't work all the time. There are a few exceptions to that rule, but only in the George Lang Corporation category—those superstars of industry who have risen to the top after decades of surefooted success. A consultant is paid much more per hour than a head chef, but the jobs are sporadic.

The work is different too. A chef may not have the skills to be a good consultant. However, it is certainly worth a try, especially if a head chef can keep a steady job and do consulting on the side. But if you have never even considered being a restaurant manager, why would you think that consulting is for you? The style of work is very similar. Moving out of the kitchen may be a disastrous mistake because chefs stop using one of their most valuable talents—their ability to prepare delectable food.

Highlights

There are definite steps which a cook or head chef can take to help make success more of a science than a mystery.

No matter how attractive a job offer appears, if the new position will conflict with several personal goals, your quality of life will go down.

There are other career considerations which can be important enough to overrride salary and fame as the prime motives for employment.

Clear goals provide the direction and thrust you need to pursue the position which will best utilize and reward your talents.

Nothing can be more devastating than to leave a good position for a new job at a higher salary and increased responsibility, only to be fired because your skills aren't up to the level expected by the new boss.

The resume is the best document to present the business parts of a chef's background.

Menus are excellent resume aids, particularly if they were designed by the job candidate.

An interview with an employment service representative is just as crucial as the meeting with a prospective boss.

As a job candidate in an interview situation, your plan is always simple: Keep talking about your qualifications until the interviewer begins to describe the job; then listen.

Be yourself unless you are normally an argumentative dilettante; then be as quiet as possible.

Exhibit all the attributes of a good employee—promptness, loyalty, intelligence, good humor and flexibility.

The discussion of salary begins at the first interview and is generally the last agreement made.

A chef who demands too high a salary usually is fired on a whim.

In addition to salary, power lines are drawn at the all-important hiring meeting.

For ninety-five percent of their chef positions, large companies need dependable game players.

The main purpose of the hopscotch method is to further and quicken advancement, but in the upper strata of chefs' jobs, this process must be slow.

The best experience is usually gained in the hottest, busiest and most stressful restaurants.

The two factors which should govern the way an executive or head chef quits are reputation and money.

Employers who insist that you begin immediately, leaving the former boss in trouble, are too demanding.

Chefs who wish to work in the upper strata, where the salaries and perks are highest, must prove their exceptional ability by gaining national attention.

In order to be a successful consultant, a chef needs credibility and a track record of success, or at least a personal reference.

Consultancy is almost always a sales job.

Moving out of the kitchen may be a disastrous mistake because chefs stop using one of their most valuable talents—their ability to prepare delectable food.

PART 5

APPENDIXES

Appendix A

COOKING SCHOOLS

Alabama

BONNIE BAILEY COOKING SCHOOL
4212 Caldwell Mill Road
Birmingham, AL 35243

CREATIVE IDEAS FOR LIVING
P.O. Box 2522
Birmingham, AL 35201

MARKET PLACE
2306 Whitesburg Dr.
Huntsville, AL 35801

SOUTHERN LIVING COOKING SCHOOL
P.O. Box 2581
Birmingham, AL 35213

Alaska

A MOVEABLE FEAST
338 Old Steese Highway
Fairbanks, AK 99701

Arizona

LOOK WHOSE COOKIN'
Broadway Southwest, 4000 Fiesta Mall
Mesa, AZ 85202

California

BADIA A COLTIBUONO
2561 Washington Street
San Francisco, CA 94115

CALIFORNIA CULINARY ACADEMY
215 Freemont Street
San Francisco, CA 94105

CANTONESE GOURMET COOKING SCHOOL
1715 Clement Street
San Francisco, CA 94121

CHATEAU DE SAUSSIGNAC
1853 Reliez Valley Road
Lafayette, CA 94549

COOKING WITH SUSAN RHOADES
1164 Upper Happy Valley Road
Lafayette, CA 94549

EPICUREAN
8759 Melrose Avenue
Los Angeles, CA 90069

GREAT CHEFS—ROBERT MONDAVI WINERY
P.O. Box 106
Oakville, CA 94562

INNER GOURMENT COOKING SCHOOL
484 Bellefontaine Street
Pasadena, CA 91105

JUDITH ETS-HOKIN CULINARY
3525 California Street
San Francisco, CA 94118

KANORA KITCHEN CRETE
P.O. Box 6533
San Francisco, CA 94101

LE CORDON ROUGE
1750 Bridgeway
Sausalito, CA 94965

LE KOOKERY COOKING SCHOOL
13624 Ventura Blvd.
Sherman Oaks, CA 91423

LET'S GET COOKIN'
4643 Lakeview Canyon Road
Westlake Village, CA 91361

MA CUISINE
8360 Melrose Avenue
Los Angeles, CA 90069

MENUS COOKING SCHOOL
1064 G, Shell Blvd.
Foster City, CA 94404

MICROWAVE COOKING CENTER
17728 Marcello Place
Encino, CA 91316

MISSION GOURMET COOKING SCHOOL
155 Anza Street
Freemond, CA 94539

MON CHERI COOKING SCHOOL AND CATERERS
461 South Murphy
Sunnyvale, CA 94086

MONTANA MERCANTILE
1324 Montana Avenue
Santa Monica, CA 90403

PHYLLIS ANN MARSHALL COOKING SCHOOL
112463 Irving Avenue #E-1
Costa Mesa, CA 92627

PIRET'S PERFECT PAN SCHOOL OF COOKING
6610 Convoy Court
San Diego, CA 92112

SPECIALTY CUISINE WORKSHOPS
Box 2547
Truckee, CA 95734

TANTE MARIE'S COOKING SCHOOL
271 Francisco Avenue
San Francisco, CA 94109

THE TASTING SPOON
1000 Sunset Blvd. Suite D
Los Angeles, CA 90012

UNIQUE FRENCH CUISINE
7086 Estrella Del Mar Road
Carlsbad, CA 92008

Colorado

BROADMOOR COOKING SCHOOL
P.O. Box 38205
Colorado Springs, CO 80937

LES CHEFS D'ASPEN
405 South Hunter
Aspen, CO 81611

Connecticut

THE ANN HOWARD COOKERY
Brickwalk Lane
Farmington, CT 06032

THE COMPLETE KITCHEN
863 Post Road
Darien, CT 06820

THE HAPPY COOKERS
7 Pent Road
Bloomfield, CT 06002

HAY DAY'S COOKING SCHOOL
907 Post Road East
Westport, CT 06880

THE SILO COOKING SCHOOL
Hunt Hill Farm, RFD 3
New Milford, CT 06776

District of Columbia

KITCHEN BAZAAR
4455 Connecticut Avenue, N.W.
Washington, D.C. 20008

Delaware

CREATIVE COOKING—THE COOKING SCHOOL
1812 Marsh Road—Branner Plaza
Wilmington, DE 19810

Florida

BOBBI & CAROLE'S COOKING SCHOOL
7251 SW 57th Court
Miami, FL 33143

CUISINE CLASSICS COOKING SCHOOL
5029 Oxford Dr.
Sarasota, FL 33581

LIVELY KITCHEN, INC.
7214 Manatee Avenue W.
Bradenton, FL 33529

MARY STARNE'S COOKING SCHOOL
P.O. Box 35
Destin, FL 32541

POT N' PAN TREE COOKING SCHOOL
242 S. Ocean Blvd.
Manalapan, FL 33462

SOMEONE'S IN THE KITCHEN WITH MIMI
6057 Fleetwood Rd
Jacksonville, FL 32217

SUE SUTKER'S CREATIVE COOKERY
3205 Fountain Blvd.
Tampa, FL 33609

Georgia

CHEF!
1 Galleria Pkwy Suite 61
Atlanta, GA 30339

THE CLOISTER WINE AND COOKING SCHOOL
Sea Island, GA 31561

COOK'S CORNER, INC.
3500 Peachtree Road NE
Atlanta, GA 30326

PEGGY FOREMAN'S COOKING SCHOOL
211 The Prado NE
Atlanta, GA 30309

URSULA'S COOKING SCHOOL
1764 Cheshire Br. Rd., NE
Atlanta, GA 30324

Illinois

CHARLIE'S KITCHEN
546 Chestnut Street
Winnetka, IL 60093

CHEZ MADELAINE
211 N. Washington Street
Hinsdale, IL 60521

THE COOKING AND HOSPITALITY INSTITUTE OF CHICAGO
858 N. Orleans
Chicago, IL 60611

COOKING IN FRANCE
P.O. Box 153
Western Springs, IL 60558

GOURMET'S OXFORD
P.O. Box 6
Western Springs, IL 60558

LA CUCINA ITALIANA
647 Sheridan Square
Evanston, IL 60202

LA VENTURE
5100 W. Jarlath
Skokie, IL 60077

ORIENTAL FOOD MARKET AND COOKING SCHOOL
2801 W. Howard Street
Chicago, IL 60645

PROPER PAN
4620 N. University St.
Peoria, IL 61614

QUINCY STEAMBOAT COMPANY
833 Kentucky
Quincy, IL 62301

WHAT'S COOKING
P.O. Box 323
Hinsdale, IL 60522

Indiana

COUNTRY KITCHEN SCHOOL
3225 Wells Street
Fort Wayne, IN 46808

THE EIGHT MICE COOKING SCHOOL
Market Square
Lafayette, IN 47904

Louisiana

BETTY LYONS—FOOD AND TABLE CONSULTANT
6323 West End Blvd.
New Orleans, LA 70124

COOKING, INC.
33 Tradewind Court West
Mandeville, LA 70448

LEE BARNES COOKING SCHOOL AND GOURMET SHOP
8400 Oak Street
New Orleans, LA 70118

TOUT DE SUITE A LA MICROWAVE INC.
P.O. Box 30121
Lafayette, LA 70503

WOK & WHISK INC.
6301 Perkins Road
Baton Rouge, LA 70808

Maine

CREATIVE COOKING
23 Forest Avenue
Portland, ME 04101

Maryland

L'ACADEMIE DE CUISINE
5021 Wilson Land
Bethesda, MD 20814

L'ECOLE/BALTIMORE INTERNATIONAL CULINARY ARTS INSTITUTE
19-21 South Gay Street
Baltimore, MD 21202

Massachusetts

COOKING AT THE FRENCH LIBRARY
P.O. Box 58
Boston, MA 02130

CREATIVE CUISINE—CAMBRIDGE SCHOOL OF CULINARY ARTS
2020 Massachusetts Ave.
Cambridge, MA 02140

PEGGY GLASS
72 Williston Road
Newton, MA 02166

Michigan

MID-WEST COOKING SCHOOL
3204 Rochester Road
Royal Oak, MI 48073

Minnesota

BYERLY'S SCHOOL OF CULINARY ARTS
3777 Park Center Blvd.
St. Louis Park, MN 55416

THRICE
850 Grand Avenue
St. Paul, MN 55105

Mississippi

THE EVERYDAY GOURMET INC
2905 Old Canton Road
Jackson, MS 39216

Missouri

DIERBERGS SCHOOL OF COOKING
1422 Elbridge Payne Road, #200
Chesterfield, MO 63017

HALLS PLAZA COOKING SCHOOL
200 East 25th Street
Kansas City, MO 64108

THE PAMPERED PANTRY
8139 Maryland Avenue
St. Louis, MO 63105

Nebraska

LINCOLN COOKING COMPANY
1400 So. 58th Street
Lincoln, NE 68506

Nevada

TRUFFLES
83 W. Plumb Lane
Reno, NV 89509

New Jersey

ANNIE'S KITCHEN
369 Mountain Blvd.
Watchung, NJ 07060

CAROLE WALTER/FOOD AND BAKING PROFESSIONAL
8 Murphy Court
West Orange, NJ 07052

COOKING AT THE KITCHEN SHOP
433 Cedar Lane
Teaneck, NJ 07666

COOKTIQUE
9 Railroad Ave.
Tenafly, NJ 07670

THE COOKING STUDIO
778 Morris Turnpike
Short Hill, NJ 07078

THE UNCOMPLICATED GOURMET, INC.
14 Spice Drive, Washington Twp.
Westwood, NJ 07675

New York

A LA BONNE COCOTTE
23 8th Avenue
New York, NY 10014

ANNE MARIE'S COOKING SCHOOL
164 Lexington Ave.
New York, NY 10016

ANNE SEKELY SCHOOL FOR COOKING
229 E. 79th Street
New York, NY 10021

CAROL'S CUISINE, INC.
1571 Richmond Road
Staten Island, NY 10304

THE CHOCOLATE GALLERY
c/o Ultra Costmetics
135 W. 50th St.
New York, NY 10020

COOKING WITH CLASS INC.
226 E. 54th St.
New York, NY 10022

CORDON ROSE
110 Bleecker Street
New York, NY 10012

CULINARY CENTER OF NEW YORK
100 Greenwich Ave.
New York, NY 10011

CULINARY INSTITUTE OF AMERICA
Route 9
Hyde Park, NY 12538

DE GUSTIBUS AT MACY'S
1056 Fifth Avenue
New York, NY 10028

EDITH THEMAL COOKING SCHOOL
111-15 75 Ave.
Forest Hills, NY

EPICUREAN GALLERY LTD.
443 E. 75th St.
New York, NY 10021

THE FRENCH CULINARY INSTITUTE
462 Broadway
New York, NY 10013

INTERNATIONAL PASTRY ARTS CENTER
357 Adams Street
Bedford Hills, NY 10507

KAREN LEE'S CHINESE COOKING CLASSES AND CATERING
142 West End Ave. #30 V.
New York, NY 10023

THE KINGS CHOCOLATE HOUSE
112-09 Rockaway Blvd.
Ozone Park, NY 11420

KITCHEN PRIVILEGES CULINARY CENTER
5 Bond Street
Great Neck, NY 11021

LEARNING WITH PROFESSIONALS
325 E. 57th Street
New York, NY 10022

MARY BETH CLARK COOKING SCHOOL
340 E. 64th St.
New York, NY 10021

NEW YORK COOKING CENTER
27 West 34th Street
New York, NY 10001

NEW YORK FOOD AND HOTEL MANAGEMENT SCHOOL
154 W. 14th Street
New York, NY 10003

NEW YORK INSTITUTE of TECHNOLOGY
Old Westbury, NY 11568

NEW YORK RESTAURANT SCHOOL
27 W. 34th St.
New York, NY 10016

PETER KUMP'S NEW YORK COOKING SCHOOL
307 E. 92nd St.
New York, NY 10128

SUNRISE CUISINE
65 Sunrise Terrace
Staten Island, NY 10304

THE WIRE WHISK COOKING CENTER
155 Main Street
Northport, NY 11768

North Carolina

COOKS CORNER LTD.
401 State Street
Greensboro, NC 27405

THE KITCHEN CUPBOARD
654 Arlington Blvd.
Greenville, NC 27834

THE SAUCEPAN
3 Ann Street
Wilmington, NC 28401

THE STOCKED POT & COMPANY
114 Reynolda Village
Winston Salem, NC 27106

Ohio

AMERICAN CHEF INSTITUTE
2444 Burgandy Lane
P.O. Box 32352
Columbus, OH 43232

LA BELLE POMME
P.O. Box 16538
Columbus, OH 43216

LAZARUS CREATIVE KITCHEN
7th & Race Street
Cincinnati, OH 45202

ZONA SPRAY COOKING SCHOOL
140 N. Main Street
Hudson, OH 44236

Oklahoma

CREATIVE COOKERY
6509 N. May Ave.
Oklahoma City, OK 73116

GOURMET GADGETRE LTD.
1105 Ferris Avenue
Lawton, OK 73507

THE MCCARTNEYS KITCHEN
7001 Northwest Expressway
Oklahoma City, OK 73132

Oregon

CLOUDTREE & SUN
112 N. Main Street
Gresham, OR 97030

COOK'S NOOK
2807 Oak Street
Eugene, OR 97405

HOT POTS COOKING SCHOOL
P.O. Box 7
Lincoln City, OR 97367

Pennsylvania

CHARLOTTE ANN ALBERTSON COOKING SCHOOL
P.O. Box 27
Wynnewood, PA 19096

COOK'S NOOK COOKING SCHOOL
128 E. Neshanock Ave.
New Wilmington, PA 16142

THE GARDEN
1617 Spruce Street
Philadelphia, PA 19103

JACQUALIN ET CIE
P.O. Box 52, Route 202
Lahaska, PA 18931

KAY'S SCHOOL OF COOKERY
552 North Neville Street
Pittsburgh, PA 15213

KITCHEN KREATIONS
5250 Simpson Ferry Road
Mechanicsburg, PA 17055

THE KITCHEN SHOPPE COOKING SCHOOL
101 Shady Lane
Carlisle, PA 17013

LA TOQUE INTERNATIONAL, LTD.
P.O. Box 146
Gladwyne, PA 19035

TO MARKET, TO MARKET
321 S. 6th Street
Philadelphia, PA 19106

Rhode Island

JOHNSON & WALES COLLEGE, CULINARY ARTS DIVISION
One Washington Avenue
Providence, RI 02905

South Carolina

IN GOOD TASTE
1124 Sam Rittenburg
Charleston, SC 29412

Tennessee

CONTE-PHILIPS
48 White Bridge Road
Nashville, TN 37205

LA MAISON MERIDIEN
1252 Peabody Ave.
Memphis, TN 38104

Texas

THE COOKING SCHOOL
6003-A Berkshire Lane
Dallas, TX 75225

COOKING WITH AMBER
6211 West Northwest Highway
Suite C-120
Dallas, TX 75225

THE FRENCH APRON, INC.
P.O. Box 9123
Fort Worth, TX 76107

LEPANIER, INC.
7275 Brompton Road
Houston, TX 77025

THE LITTLE HOUSE
204 W. Church
Victoria, TX 77901

MAISON BLEU GOURMET SHOP/COOKING
400 South Alamo
San Antonio, TX 78205

PEEPLES CHOICE/COOKIN' THYME
150 West Bay Area Blvd.
Webster, TX 77598

THE STOCKPOT ETC. INC.
P.O. Box 527
Longview, TX 75606

Virginia

DOLORES KOSTELNI COOKING SCHOOL
Rt. 4 Box 251 Turtle Brooke
Lexington, VA 24450

GIANT'S SCHOOL OF COOKING
1187 Azalea Garden Road
Norfolk, VA 23502

POTLUCK
314-316 William Street
Fredericksburg, VA 22401

Washington

ARCADE SCHOOL: FREDERICK & NELSON
5th and Pine Streets
Seattle, WA 98111

BON VIVANT SCHOOL OF COOKING
4925 Northeast 86th Street
Seattle, WA 98115

FINAL TOUCH COOKING SCHOOL
3 North Wenatchee Avenue
Wenatchee, WA 98801

KITCHEN KITCHEN
242 Bellevue Sq.
Bellevue, WA 98004

MAGNOLIA KITCHEN SHOPPE & COOKING SCHOOL
2416 32nd West
Seattle, WA 98199

SUR LA TABLE
84 Pine Street
Seattle, WA 98101

Wisconsin

COOK'S HABITAT
101 W. Wisconsin Avenue
Milwaukee, WI 53201

THE EPICURE COOKING SCHOOL
6119 Odana Road
Madison, WI 53719

MODERN GOURMET OF MILWAUKEE
P.O. Box 17552
Milwaukee, WI 53217

Appendix B

KITCHEN EQUIPMENT

Aluminum Au Gratin Dishes
Aluminum Roasting Pans
Aluminum Sauce Pots
Aluminum Saute Pans
Aluminum Scoops
Bain Marie Pots
Baking Shells
Baskets, Fry
Baster
Blender
Boning Knife
Bouillion Strainer
Bowls, Mixing
Brazier
Broiler
Butcher Knives
Butcher Saw
Cake Pans
Can openers
Carts
Casserole Dishes
Cast Iron Skillets
Ceramic Baking Dishes
Cheese Graters
Cleaver, Heavy
Cleaver, Stainless
Coffee Makers
Copper Pans
Cork Screw
Cutters, Special
Cutting Boards
Delivery or Storage Cabinet
Dupe Holder
Food Processor
Forks
Freezer

French Whips
Fryolators
Funnel
Garlic Press
Griddle
Grill
Holding Warmers
Hotel Pans
Inner Wire Baskets
Knife Rack
Ladles
Mandolin
Measures
Measuring Cups
Microwaves
Mixer
Mixing Paddle
Ovens
Pasta Strainer
Pastry Blender
Peelers
Pepper Mill
Pie Marker
Pie Pans
Pie Server
Portable Plate Warmer
Portion Scale
Pot Racks
Poultry Shears
Proofing Cabinet
Pullman Pan
Ramekins
Refrigeration—Lo-boy Bain Marie,
    Reachin, Walk-In
Robot Coupe
Rolling Pin

Salamander
Sauce Pots
Sheet Pans
Shelving
Sizzling Platters
Skewers
Skimmers
Slotted Spoons
Solid Spoons
Spatulas
Steamer

Steam Table
Steel
Stock Pots
Stove
Teflon Pans
Thermometer
Timer
Toasters
Tongs
Warming Lights
Wooden Spoons

Appendix C

GLOSSARY OF TERMS

AESTHETICS   Those attributes of food preparation and decoration which pertain to sensual perception, as opposed to the business or profit aspects.

AMBIANCE   The mood of a restaurant's front-of-the-house operation.

BACK OF THE HOUSE   The behind-the-scenes workers and operations of a restaurant such as management, kitchen personnel, and the office and kitchen.

BREADING   The process used to coat vegetables, meats and cheeses with various layers of flavorful ingredients, one of which is bread crumbs.

CHEFDOM   A head chef's domain or jurisdiction.

COMP, COMPED   To sign a check for a customer rather than having the person pay; usually a gesture of goodwill.

COMPANY PLAN   A cook's method for rising through the ranks of a large company in order to become the head chef.

CONCEPT RESTAURANT   A business approach in which the ambiance and menu are tied together with a theme, decor and unique style.

CONTRIBUTION MARGIN   Margin infers profit. In this case, it is a specific term and calculation used to determine a menu item's dollar contribution to the total revenue picture.
Menu Price − Cost of the Item = Contribution Margin.

COST MARGIN   The portion of a sales figure which is the expense.

COST OF GOODS SOLD   Calculated in dollars or percentages, this expense figure pinpoints the cost of the food used to produce one dish or the entire menu.

CULINARIAN   A professional who prepares or presents food.

CULINARY HISTORY   A region's culinary background, especially the history of the foods, dishes and recipes which the people of the region favor.

DILETTANTE   A chef or cook who dabbles at cooking but never sweats.

DISH   The final production of a recipe.

DRAWING POWER   A restaurant's ability to attract customers.

DUPES   The pieces of paper used by the floor staff to request food from the kitchen.

ECLECTIC   A spontaneous blend which shows no common source or purpose.

EXECUTIVE CHEF   A chef whose responsibilities include the management of several sous chefs or head chefs.

FALSE CULINARY ILLUSIONS   A chef's inflated opinion of the restaurant's style and scale of presentation. Also, a cook's condescending opinion that his or her skills are wasted in the present position.

FIELD OF COMPETITION   The restaurants and food sellers who compete for the purchase dollars of a specific area or clientele.

FIXED EXPENSES   Weekly, monthly or annual costs which do not fluctuate, such as rent.

FLOOR   The areas of the restaurant where the customers are allowed.

FOOD PC   The percentage of costs or expenses which is directly attributed to food purchases.

FOOD STYLISTS   Culinarians who arrange the color and presentation of food in order to maximize its visual qualities.

FREEBIES   Items given away for free.

FRONT OF THE HOUSE   The personnel and operations which function in the dining rooms and bars, where the customers are being served.

GARDE MANGER   The cold station of a kitchen, including the items prepared there and the cook who works there.

GUESSTIMATION   An estimate based on little or no data, except for the experience and instincts of the estimator.

HANDLING TECHNIQUES   The methods used to care for food from the moment the goods arrive until the time when they are served to the customers.

HANDS-ON   Manual participation in a chore or process.

HEAD CHEF   The kitchen boss responsible for culinary quality and profit margins.

HOPSCOTCH METHOD   A career advancement plan which necessitates moving from one job to another more beneficial one.

HOUSE   A restaurant.

IMAGE   The reputation a chef has cultivated and received by association.

JOB MARKET   The available career opportunities at any given time and place.

LABOR PC   A percentage or expense which is based on the payroll, especially for the kitchen personnel.

LEADER ITEM   A menu item which is sold at an unusually low price.

LINE   The kitchen area where food is prepared in its final stages and presented to the floor staff. Also, the hot top or shelf where the food is placed for pickup by the floor staff.

LINE COOK   A cook working on the final stages of food preparation.

MASTER PREPARATION LIST   A compilation of every duty necessary for the complete preparation of a menu for line production.

MENU ANALYSIS   A data-based study of a menu's profit and loss centers, together with an examination of customer acceptance of specific dishes.

MENU DESIGN   The process of deciding which dishes, categories of food and style of cuisine best suit a particular restaurant.

NEMESIS   A subordinate, usually the sous chef, who has disruptively powerful ties to the owner.

NETWORKING   The connection of collegues, friends and acquaintances into a system for the dissemination or gathering of information.

NICHE   A spot within a market. Pertains to the culinary styles and price ranges used extensively by the competition and the remaining viable options.

OPERATING EXPENSES   The category of costs which includes all backup services, fixed expenses, supplies and utilities. Any expense other than labor or food.

OWNER-MANAGER   The person with the authority to hire and fire the chef; also the head decision maker.

PARS   Amounts necessary to fill a quota in the inventory stocks or prepared foods.

PC   An abbreviation for "percentage," usually a food- or labor-based figure which pinpoints the profitability of a kitchen operation.

PERCENTAGE   See PC.

PERISHABLE GOODS   Foodstuffs which are subject to deterioration by time and the elements.

PLANNED OBSOLESCENCE   An employment strategy which keeps payroll costs low by planning for a high turnover of workers who receive below-market salaries.

POINTS   Percentage points; usually refers to a share of the business, such as the amount of ownership given to a worthy chef.

POPULARITY INDEX   A ranking in percentages which is calculated by dividing the number sold of a specific item by the total number of items sold.

PREPARATION COOK   A kitchen worker whose duties involve the preparation of food for use on the line.

PREPARATION   The work done to ready the food for the final stage of cooking.

PRESENTATION   The arrangement and decoration of the finished plates.

PRIME LOCATION   A restaurant location which has all the qualities to make it an excellent competitive choice.

PROFIT MARGIN   The percentage of the sales dollar left after all of the expenses have been paid, or the percentage of the sale price of a particular dish which is profit.

PURVEYOR   A seller of goods, especially food.

QUALITY CONTROL   The actions taken to ensure the cook's adherence to recipe guidelines and restaurant standards for the purpose of perfecting food taste and visual excellence.

RAW GOODS   Recipe ingredients.

REGIONAL   A particular area of the United States which has developed a unique cuisine and style.

REMUNERATION   Rewards; in this case, the perks and payments chefs receive.

ROTATION   The process of moving new goods to the back and old goods to the front of the shelf to aid the kitchen staff's use of the oldest goods first.

RUSH   The peak business hours or period.

SCALE—HIGH, MEDIUM, LOW   The grade of service and the price of the menu items, both of which are indicators of the style of food and its presentation.

SERVICE INDUSTRY   The group of businesses which supply anything useful, such as installation, maintenance, or other labor-based exchanges.

SHELF LIFE   The amount of time a raw good will remain in usable condition.

SOUS CHEF   Literally, the "under chef." This chef is generally the second in command of a kitchen crew.

SPECIALS   Food offerings which are not on the menu or price incentives for customers.

SPECIALTY ITEMS   Raw goods not used in the regular preparation of menu items. They are often expensive imports.

SPECS   The specific ingredients and cooking procedures for a particular dish's preparation.

STATION   A work area, especially in the kitchen.

TAB   A customer's bill.

TEMPORARY CHEF   A chef who plans to enter another career field.

TRACK RECORD   The history of a chef's past successes and failures.

TRAILING   The training shift or period of work when a new employee is working under another permanent employee.

TRENDS   Culinary styles which represent a departure from existing styles. Also, unique cuisines which are enjoying a period of increased critical acclaim and/or customer acceptance.

TURNOVER   The number of customers one chair will seat during a service. For example, if a restaurant with one hundred chairs sells three hundred dinners in one evening, the turnover rate is three.

UNIT (REFER)   A large refrigeration box such as a walk-in or reach-in.

VOLUME—HIGH, MEDIUM, LOW   The quantity of sales in dollars. This term is used to describe the number of customers.

INDEX

INDEX